COLLINS

PORTUGUESE

PHRASE BOOK

HarperCollins Publishers

first published in this edition 1995

© HarperCollins Publishers 1995

ISBN 0 00 470868-7

A catalogue record for this book is available from the British Library

Typeset by Morton Word Processing Ltd, Scarborough
Printed in Great Britain by
HarperCollins Manufacturing, Glasgow

Introduction

Your **Collins Phrase Book** is designed to give you instant access to all
the words and phrases you will want while travelling abroad on business
or for pleasure.

Unlike other phrase books it is arranged in A-Z order to take you straight
to the word you want without having to search through different topics.
And its simple, easy-to-use pronunciation guide to every word and phrase
will ensure you communicate with confidence.

At the bottom of each page there is a list of ABSOLUTE ESSENTIALS – the key
phrases and expressions you will need in any situation. And between the
two sides of your **Phrase Book** you will find further explanations of
pronunciation, charts showing how to convert from metric to imperial
measures and easy reference lists of *Car Parts, Colours, Countries, Drinks,
Fish and Seafood, Fruit and Nuts, Meats, Shops,* and *Vegetables.* These pages
have a grey border to help you find them easily and to show you where
one side of the **Phrase Book** ends and the other begins.

And finally, in the comprehensive glossary at the end of your **Phrase
Book** you will find over 4,000 foreign-language words and phrases clearly
translated. So in one complete package you have all the benefits of a
dictionary with the simplicity of a phrase book. We hope you will enjoy
using it.

Abbreviations used in the text

adj	adjective
adv	adverb
Anat	anatomical
cm	centimetre(s)
conj	conjunction
equiv	equivalent
etc	etcetera
f	feminine noun
fpl	feminine plural noun
g	gram(s)
kg	kilogram(s)
km	kilometre(s)
l	litre(s)
m	masculine noun; metre(s)
m/f	masculine or feminine noun
mpl	masculine plural noun
n	noun
pl	plural noun
prep	preposition
®	registered trade mark
sing	singular
vb	verb

ENGLISH–PORTUGUESE

a	um	"oom"
	uma	"oomuh"
▷ **a man**	um homem	"oom omayng"
▷ **a woman**	uma mulher	"oomuh moolyehr"
abbey	a abadia	"abuh-deeuh"
about	cerca de	"sehrkuh duh"
	por volta de	"poor voltuh duh"
▷ **about ten o'clock**	por volta das dez	"poor voltuh dush desh"
above	por cima de	"poor seemuh duh"
accident	o acidente	"aseedent"
▷ **I've had an accident**	tive um acidente	"teev oom aseedent"
▷ **there's been an accident**	houve um acidente	"ohv oom aseedent"
accommodation	o alojamento	"alojuhmentoo"
▷ **I need 3 nights' accommodation**	preciso de alojamento para três noites	"preseezoo duhloojamentoo paruh tresh noytsh"
ache[1] *n*	a dor	"dor"
to **ache**[2] *vb*	doer	"dooehr"
▷ **my head aches**	dói-me a cabeça	"doymuh uh kabaysuh"
▷ **I've got a stomach ache**	dói-me o estômago	"doymuh oo shtohmagoo"
acre (*metric equiv = 0.40 hectares*)	o acre	"ahkre"
activities:		
▷ **do you have activities for children?**	têm actividades para crianças?	"tayng ateevee-dahdsh paruh kreeansush"
▷ **what indoor/outdoor activities are there?**	que tipo de actividades há dentro de casa/ao ar livre	"kuh teepoo duh ateevee-dahdsh a dentroo duh kahzuh/ow ar leevr"
adaptor (*electrical*)	o adaptador	"adap-tuhdor"
address	a morada	"moo-rahduh"

English	Portuguese	Pronunciation
▷ my address is ...	a minha morada é ...	"uh **meen**yuh moo-**rah**duh e"
▷ take me to this address	leve-me a esta morada	"**lev**muh uh **esh**-tuh moo-**rah**duh"
▷ will you write down the address please?	pode escrever a morada, por favor?	"**pod** shkre**vehr** uh moo-**rah**duh, poor fa**vor**"
adhesive tape	a fita adesiva	"**fee**tuh aduh-**zee**vuh"
▷ I need some adhesive tape	preciso de fita adesiva	"pre**see**zoo duh **fee**tuh aduh-**zee**vuh"
admission charge	o bilhete de entrada	"beel-**yet** dayn-**trah**duh"
adult	o adulto	"a**dool**too"
	a adulta	"a**dool**tuh"
advance:		
▷ in advance	antecipadamente	"antuh-seepah-duh**ment**"
▷ do I pay in advance?	pago antecipadamente?	"**pah**goo antuh-seepah-duh**ment**"
▷ do I need to book in advance?	preciso de reservar antecipadamente?	"pre**see**zoo duh ruhzer**var** antuh-seepah-duh**ment**"
aerobics	a aeróbica	"uheh-**roh**beekuh"
African	africano	"afree-**kah**noo"
	africana	"afree-**kah**nuh"
after	depois	"duh**poysh**"
afternoon	a tarde	"tard"
aftershave	o aftershave	"aftershave"
again	outra vez	"**oh**truh vesh"
▷ can you try again?	pode tentar outra vez?	"**pod** ten**tar** **oh**truh vesh"
agent	o agente	"a**jent**"
ago:		
▷ long ago	há muito tempo	"a **mween**too tempoo"
▷ a week ago	há uma semana	"a **oo**muh se**mah**nuh"

AIDS	a sida	"**see**duh"
air conditioning	o ar condicionado	"ar kondees-yoo**nah**doo"
▷ the air conditioning is not working	o ar condicionado não funciona	"oo ar kondee-syoo**nah**doo **nowng** foongsee-**oh**nuh"
air hostess	a assistente de bordo	"aseesh**tent** duh **bor**doo"
airline	a companhia aérea	"kompan-**yee**uh auh-**ehr**yuh"
air mail	o correio aéreo	"koo-**rray**oo auh-**ehr**yoo"
air mattress	o colchão pneumático	"kol**showng** pnayoo-**ma**tiko"
airport	o aeroporto	"uh-ehroo-**por**too"
▷ to the airport, please	para o aeroporto, por favor	"**pa**ruh oo uh-ehroo-**por**too poor fa**vor**"
aisle	a coxia	"koo**shee**uh"
▷ I'd like an aisle seat	queria um lugar junto à coxia	"**kree**uh oom loo**gar** joontoo a koo**shee**uh"
alarm call	a chamada para despertar	"sha**mah**duh **pa**ruh dshper**tar**"
▷ an alarm call at 7 am please	uma chamada para despertar às 7 da manhã, por favor	"**oom**uh sha**mah**duh **pa**ruh dshper**tar** ash **seht** duh man**yang** poor fa**vor**"
alarm clock	o despertador	"dshperta**dor**"
alcohol	o álcool	"**alk**wol"
alcoholic	alcoólico	"alk**wol**-ikoo"
	alcoólica	"alk**wol**-ikuh"
all	todo	"**toh**doo"
	toda	"**toh**duh"
	todos	"**toh**doosh"
	todas	"**toh**dush"

ABSOLUTE ESSENTIALS

I don't understand	não compreendo	"nowng kompree**een**doo"
I don't speak Portuguese	não falo português	"nowng **fah**loo poortoo**gaysh**"
do you speak English?	fala inglês?	"**fah**luh eeng**lesh**"
could you help me?	podia ajudar-me?	"poo**dee**uh ajoo**dar**muh"

allergic	alérgico	"a**lehr**-jikoo"
	alérgica	"a**lehr**-jikuh"
▷ **I'm allergic to penicillin**	sou alérgico(a) à penicilina	"soh a**lehr**-jikoo(uh) a puneesee-**lee**nuh"
allowance:		
▷ **I have the usual allowances of alcohol/ tobacco**	trago as quantidades de álcool/tabaco autorizadas	"**trah**go ush kwantee**dah**dush **dal**kwol/too**bah**koo owtooree**zah**dush"
all right (*agreed*)	está bem?	"shta bayng"
▷ **are you all right?**	você está bem?	"vo**seh** shta bayng"
almond	a amêndoa	"a**mayn**-dwuh"
almost	quase	"kwahz"
also	também	"tam**bayng**"
always	sempre	"**sem**pruh"
am:		
▷ **I am**	sou	"so"
ambulance	a ambulância	"amboo-**lans**yuh"
▷ **call an ambulance**	chame uma ambulância	"shahm **oom**uh amboo-**lans**yuh"
America	a América	"a**mer**ikuh"
American	americano	"amuhree-**kah**noo"
	americana	"amuhree-**kah**nuh"
amusement park	o parque de diversões	"**park** duh deever-**soynsh**"
anaesthetic	o anestético	"anush-**tet**ikoo"
anchovy	a anchova	"an**sho**vuh"
and	e	"ee"
anorak	a anorak	"anoo**rak**"

ABSOLUTE ESSENTIALS		
I would like ...	queria ...	"**kree**uh"
I need ...	preciso de ...	"pre**see**zoo duh"
where is ...?	onde fica ...?	"ond **fee**kuh"
I'm looking for ...	procuro ...	"pro**koo**roo"

another	um outro	"oom **oh**troo"
	uma outra	"**oom**uh **oh**truh"
▷ **another beer?**	outra cerveja?	"**oh**truh ser**vay**juh"
antibiotic	o antibiótico	"anteebee-**o**tikoo"
antifreeze	o anticongelante	"antee-konje**lant**"
antihistamine	a anti-histamina	"antee-**eesh**tameenuh"
antiseptic	o antiséptico	"antee-**sep**tikoo"
any:		
▷ **I haven't any**	não tenho nenhumas	"**nowng ten**yoo nen-**yoom**ush"
▷ **have you any apples?**	tem maçãs?	"tayng ma**sansh**"
apartment	o apartamento	"apartuh-**men**too"
▷ **we've booked an apartment in the name of ...**	reservámos um apartamento em nome de ...	"ruhzer-**va**moozoom apartuh-**men**too ayng nom duh"
aperitif	o aperitivo	"apuhree-**tee**voo"
▷ **we'd like an aperitif**	queríamos um aperitivo	"**kree**uh-mooz oom apuhree-**tee**voo"
apple	a maçã	"ma**sang**"
appointment (*friends*)	o encontro	"ayng-**kon**troo"
(*doctor, etc*)	a marcação	"markuh-**sowng**"
▷ **I'd like to make an appointment**	queria fazer uma marcação	"**kree**uh fa**zehr** oomuh markuh-**sowng**"
▷ **can I please have an appointment?**	posso fazer uma marcação, por favor?	"**pos**oo fa**zehr** oomuh markuh-**sowng**, poor fa**vor**"
▷ **I have an appointment with ...**	tenho um encontro/ uma marcação com ...	"**ten**yoo oom ayng-**kon**troo/**oom**uh markuh-**sowng** kong"
apricot	o damasco	"da**mash**-koo"
April	Abril	"uh**breel**"

are:

▷ **you are**	és	"esh"
(*plural*)	sois	"soysh"
(*polite form*)	você é	"vo**seh** é"
▷ **we are**	somos	"**so**moosh"
▷ **they are**	sâo	"**sowng**"

arm	o braço	"**brah**soo"
armbands (*for swimming*)	as braçadeiras	"brasuh-**day**rush"
arrival	a chegada	"sh**gah**duh"
arrivals (*at airport*)	chegadas	"sh**gah**dush"
to **arrive**	chegar	"sh**gar**"
▷ **what time does the bus/train arrive?**	a que horas chega o autocarro/comboio?	"uh kuh **o**rush **shuh**guh oo owto-**ka**rroo/kong-**boh**yoo"
▷ **we arrived early/late**	chegámos cedo/tarde	"sh**ga**moosh **say**doo/tard"
art gallery	a galeria de arte	"galuh-**ree**uh dart"
	o museu de arte	"moo**zay**oo dart"
artichoke	a alcachofra	"alkuh-**shof**ruh"
ascent:		
▷ **when is the last ascent?**	quando é a última vez que sobe?	"**kwand**oo e uh **ool**timuh **vaysh** kuh **sob**"
ashore:		
▷ **can we go ashore now?**	podemos ir a terra agora?	"poo-**dem**oosh eer uh **te**rruh a**gor**uh"
ashtray	o cinzeiro	"seen-**zay**roo"
asparagus	o espargo	"sh**par**goo"
aspirin	a aspirina	"ashpee-**ree**nuh"
asthma	a asma	"**aj**muh"
▷ **I suffer from asthma**	sofro de asma	"**soh**froo d**aj**muh"

ABSOLUTE ESSENTIALS

yes (please)	sim (por favor)	"**seeng** (por fa**vor**)"
no (thank you)	não (obrigado/a)	"**nowng** (ohbree**gah**doo/uh)"
hello	olá	"oh**la**"
goodbye	adeus	"a**day**oosh"

at	em	"ayng"
▷ **at home**	em casa	"ayng **kah**zuh"
Athens	Atenas	"a**te**nush"
aubergine	a beringela	"bereen-**je**luh"
August	Agosto	"a**gosh**too"
Australia	a Austrália	"owsh**trah**leeuh"
Australian	australiano	"owshtralee-**ah**noo"
	australiana	"owshtralee-**ah**nuh"
Austria	a Áustria	"**owsh**-treeuh"
Austrian	austríaco	"owsh-**tree**uhkoo"
	austríaca	"owsh- **tree**uhkuh"
automatic	automático	"owtoo-**ma**tikoo"
	automática	"owtoo-**ma**tikuh"
▷ **is it an automatic (car)?**	é (um carro) automático?	"e (oom **ka**rroo) owtoo-**ma**tikoo"
autumn	o outono	"oh**toh**-noo"
avalanche	a avalanche	"avuh-**lansh**"
▷ **is there a danger of avalanches?**	há perigo de avalanche?	"a puh**ree**goo duh avuh-**lansh**"
avocado	o abacate	"aba**kat**"
baby	o bebé	"be**be**"
baby food	a comida de bebé	"koo**mee**duh duh be**be**"
baby seat (*in car*)	a cadeira de bebé	"ka**day**-ruh duh be**be**"
baby-sitter	a babysitter	"babysitter"
baby-sitting:		
▷ **is there a baby-sitting service?**	há serviço de babysitter?	"a ser**vee**soo duh babysitter"
back[1] *n* (*of body*)	as costas	"**kosh**tush"

ABSOLUTE ESSENTIALS

I don't understand	não compreendo	"nowng kompree**een**doo"
I don't speak Portuguese	não falo português	"nowng **fah**loo poortoo**gaysh**"
do you speak English?	fala inglês?	"**fah**luh een**glesh**"
could you help me?	podia ajudar-me?	"poo**dee**uh ajoo**dar**muh"

▷ **I've got a bad back**	tenho problemas de costas	"**ten**yoo proo**blem**ush duh **kosh**tush"
▷ **I've hurt my back**	magoei-me nas costas	"muhgoo-**ay**muh nush **kosh**tush"

back² adv:

▷ **we must be back at the hotel before six o'clock**	temos de regressar ao hotel antes das seis horas	"**teh**moosh duh ruhgre-**sar** ow oh**tel** antsh dush sayz **o**rush"
backpack	a mochila	"moo**shee**luh"
bacon	o toucinho	"toh-**seen**yoo"
bad (*food*)	estragado	"shtra-**gah**doo"
	estragada	"shtra-**gah**duh"
(*weather, news*)	mau	"mow"
	má	"ma"
badminton	o badminton	"**bahd**minton"
bag	o saco	"**sah**koo"
(*suitcase*)	a mala	"**mah**luh"
baggage	a bagagem	"ba**gah**-jayung"
baggage allowance:		
▷ **what is the baggage allowance?**	qual é a bagagem permitida?	"kwal e uh ba**gah**-jayung permee-**tee**duh"
baggage reclaim	a recolha de bagagem	"re**kohl**yuh duh ba**gah**-jayung"
baker's	a padaria	"paduh-**ree**uh"
balcony	a varanda	"vuh**ran**duh"
▷ **do you have a room with a balcony?**	tem um quarto com varanda?	"tayng oom **kwar**too kong vuh**ran**duh"
ball	a bola	"**bol**uh"
ball game	o jogo de futebol	"**joh**goo duh **foot**bal"
banana	a banana	"ba**nah**nuh"
band (*musical*)	a banda musical	"**ban**duh moozee**kal**"

bandage	a ligadura	"leeguh-**doo**ruh"
bank	o banco	"**ban**koo"
▷ **is there a bank nearby?**	há um banco aqui perto?	"a oom **ban**koo akee **per**too"
bar	o bar	"bar"
barber	o barbeiro	"bar**bay**roo"
basket	o cesto	"**sesh**too"
Basle	a Basileia	"buhzee-**lay**uh"
bath	o banho	"**bahn**yoo"
▷ **to take a bath**	tomar banho	"too**mar bahn**yoo"
bathing cap	a touca de banho	"**toh**kuh duh **bahn**yoo"
bathroom	a casa de banho	"**kah**zuh duh **bahn**yoo"
battery (*for car*)	a bateria	"batuh-**ree**uh"
(*for appliance*)	a pilha	"**peel**yuh"
to **be**	ser	"sehr"
	estar	"shtar"

I am	sou	"so"
you are (*informal singular*)	és	"esh"
(*formal singular*)	você é	"voseh e"
he/she/it is	ele/ela é	"el/eluh e"
we are	somos	"**so**moosh"
you are (*informal plural*)	sois	"soysh"
(*formal plural*)	vocês são	"vosehsh **sowng**"
they are	eles/elas são	"elsh/elush **sowng**"

beach	a praia	"**prah**yuh"
beach ball	a bola de praia	"**bo**luh duh **prah**yuh"
beach umbrella	o guarda-sol	"**gwar**duh **sol**"

ABSOLUTE ESSENTIALS

do you have ...?	tem ...?	"tayng"
is there ...?	há ...?	"ah"
are there ...?	há ...?	"ah"
how much is ...?	quanto custa ...?	"**kwan**too **koosh**tuh"

bean	o feijão	"fay**jowng**"
beautiful	belo	"**bel**oo"
	bela	"**bel**uh"
bed	a cama	"**kah**muh"
bedding	a roupa de cama	"**roh**puh duh **kah**muh"
▷ is there any spare bedding?	há alguma roupa de cama extra?	"a al**goo**muh **roh**puh duh **kah**muh **esh**truh"
bedroom	o quarto	"**kwar**too"
beef	a carne de vaca	"karn duh **vah**kuh"
beefburger	o beefburger	"beef**boor**ger"
beer	a cerveja	"ser**vay**juh"
▷ a draught beer, please	um fino, por favor	"oom **fee**noo, poor fa**vor**"
beetroot	a beterraba	"betuhr-**rah**buh"
before	antes de	"**antsh** duh"
to **begin**	começar	"koomuh**sar**"
behind	atrás de	"a**trash** duh"
below	por baixo de	"poor **by**-shoo duh"
belt	o cinto	"**seen**too"
Berlin	Berlim	"ber**leeng**"
beside	ao lado de	"ow **lah**doo duh"
best	o/a melhor	"mul-**yor**"
▷ the best	o/a melhor	"oo/uh mul-**yor**"
better (than)	melhor (do que)	"mul-**yor** (doo kuh)"
between	entre	"**en**truh"
bicycle	a bicicleta	"beesee-**kle**tuh"
big	grande	"grand"

bigger	maior	"mah**yor**"
▷ **do you have a bigger one?**	tem um/uma maior?	"tayng oom/**oom**uh mah**yor**"
bikini	o biquini	"bee**kee**nee"
bill	a conta	"**kon**tuh"
▷ **put it on my bill**	ponha na minha conta	"**pon**yuh nuh **meen**yuh **kon**tuh"
▷ **the bill, please**	a conta, por favor	"uh **kon**tuh poor fa**vor**"
▷ **can I have an itemized bill?**	pode-me dar uma factura com os artigos discriminados?	"**pod**muh dar **oom**uh fak**too**ruh kong ooz ar**tee**goosh deeshkree-**meenah**doosh"
bin	o caixote do lixo	"ky**shot** doo **lee**shoo"
binoculars	os binóculos	"bee**nok**-ooloosh"
bird	o pássaro	"**pas**uhroo"
birthday	o aniversário	"aneever-**sary**oo"
▷ **Happy Birthday!**	feliz aniversário!	"fuh**leesh** aneever-**sary**oo"
birthday card	o postal de aniversário	"poosh**tal** daneever-**sary**oo"
bit	o bocado	"boo**kah**doo"
▷ **a bit of**	um bocado (de)	"oom boo**kah**doo (duh)"
to bite (insect)	picar	"pee**kar**"
(dog, food)	morder	"moor**dehr**"
bitten	mordido	"mor**dee**doo"
	mordida	"mor**dee**duh"
(by insect)	picado	"pee**kah**doo"
	picada	"pee**kah**duh"
bitter	amargo	"a**mar**goo"
	amarga	"a**mar**guh"

ABSOLUTE ESSENTIALS

I don't understand	não compreendo	"nowng kompree**een**doo"
I don't speak Portuguese	não falo português	"nowng **fah**loo poortoo**gaysh**"
do you speak English?	fala inglês?	"**fah**luh een**glesh**"
could you help me?	podia ajudar-me?	"poo**dee**uh ajoo**dar**muh"

black	preto	"**pray**too"
	preta	"**pray**tuh"
blackcurrant	a groselha	"gro**zel**yuh"
blanket	o cobertor	"koober**tor**"
bleach	a lixívia	"lee**sheev**-yuh"
blister	o calo	"**kal**oo"
blocked	bloqueado	"blook**yah**doo"
	bloqueada	"blook**yah**duh"
blood group	o grupo sanguíneo	"**groo**poo san**geen**yoo"
▷ my blood group is ...	o meu grupo sanguíneo é ...	"oo **may**oo **groo**poo san**geen**yoo e"
blouse	a blusa	"**bloo**zuh"
blow-dry	secar (o cabelo)	"se**kar** (oo ka**bay**loo)"
▷ a cut and blow-dry, please	cortar e secar, por favor	"koor**tar** ee se**kar** poor fa**vor**"
blue	azul	"a**zool**"
boarding card	o cartão de embarque	"kar**towng** daym**bark**"
boarding house	a pensão	"payn**sowng**"
boat	o barco	"**bark**oo"
boat trip	a viagem de barco	"vee**ah**-jayng duh **bark**oo"
▷ are there any boat trips on the river/lake?	há passeios de barco no rio/lago?	"a pa**say**oosh duh **bark**oo noo **ree**oo/**lah**goo"
boiled	cozido	"coo**zee**doo"
	cozida	"coo**zee**duh"
Bonn	Bona	"**boh**nuh"
book[1] *n*	o livro	"**lee**vro"
▷ book of tickets	a caderneta de bilhetes	"kader-**neh**tuh duh bee**lyetsh**"

to **book²** *vb*	reservar	"ruhzer**var**"
▷ **the table is booked for eight o'clock this evening**	a mesa está reservada para as oito horas da noite	"uh **may**zuh shta ruhzehr-**vah**duh prazoytoo orush duh noyt"
▷ **can you book me into a hotel?**	pode reservar-me um hotel?	"pod ruhzehr-**var**muh oom oh**tel**"
▷ **should I book in advance?**	é preciso reservar antecipadamente?	"e pre**see**zoo ruhzer**var** antuh-seepah-duh**ment**"
booking	a reserva	"ruh**zehr**vuh"
▷ **can I change my booking?**	posso alterar a minha reserva?	"**pos**oo alte**rar** uh **meen**yuh ruh**zehr**vuh"
▷ **I confirmed my booking by letter**	confirmei a minha reserva por carta	"komfeer**may** uh **meen**yuh ruh**zehr**vuh poor **kar**tuh"
booking fee:		
▷ **is there a booking fee?**	paga-se pela reserva?	"**pag**uhsuh **pay**luh ruh**zehr**vuh"
booking office	a bilheteira	"beelyuh-**tay**ruh"
bookshop	a livraria	"leevruh-**ree**uh"
boot (*in a car*)	a mala do carro	"**mal**uh doo **kar**roo"
boots	as botas	"**bot**ush"
border	a fronteira	"fron**tay**ruh"
botanic gardens	o jardim botânico	"jar**deeng** bo**tah**nikoo"
both	ambos	"**amb**oosh"
	ambas	"**amb**ush"
bottle	a garrafa	"gar**rah**fuh"
▷ **a bottle of mineral water**	uma garrafa de água mineral	"**oom**uh gar**rah**fuh **dahg**wuh meenuh**ral**"
▷ **a bottle of gas**	uma garrafa de gás	"**oom**uh gar**rah**fuh duh **gash**"
bottle opener	o abre-garrafas	"abruh-gar**rah**fush"

ABSOLUTE ESSENTIALS

do you have ...?	tem ...?	"tayng"
is there ...?	há ...?	"ah"
are there ...?	há ...?	"ah"
how much is ...?	quanto custa ...?	"**kwan**too **koosh**tuh"

box 14

box	a caixa	"**ky**shuh"
box office	a bilheteira	"beelyuh-**tay**ruh"
boy	o rapaz	"ra**pash**"
boyfriend	o namorado	"namoo**rah**doo"
bra	o soutien	"soot**yang**"
bracelet	a pulseira	"pool**say**ruh"
brake fluid	o óleo dos travões	"**ol**yoo doosh tra**voynsh**"
brakes	os travões	"tra**voynsh**"
brandy	o brandy	"**bran**dee"
▷ **I'll have a brandy**	quero um brandy	"**keh**roo oom **bran**dee"
bread	o pão	"powng"
▷ **could we have some more bread?**	pode trazer mais pão?	"pod tra**zehr** mysh powng"
breakable	frágil	"**frah**jeel"
breakdown	a avaria	"avuh-**ree**uh"
breakdown van	o pronto-socorro	"prontoo-soo**korr**oo"
▷ **can you send a breakdown van?**	pode mandar um pronto-socorro?	"pod man**dar** oom prontoo-soo**korr**oo"
breakfast	o pequeno-almoço	"puh**kay**noo-al**moh**soo"
▷ **what time is breakfast?**	a que horas é o pequeno-almoço?	"uh kee **or**uz e oo puh**kay**noo-al**moh**soo"
▷ **can we have breakfast in our room?**	podemos tomar o pequeno-almoço no quarto?	"poo**deh**moosh too**mar** oo puh**kay**noo-al**moh**soo noo **kwar**too"
breast (*of woman; chest; of chicken*)	o peito	"**pay**too"
to **breastfeed**	amamentar	"amuh-men**tar**"
to **breathe**:		
▷ **he can't breathe**	ele não pode respirar	"ayl nowng pod rushpee**rar**"

briefcase	a pasta	"**pash**tuh"
to bring	trazer	"tra**zehr**"
Britain	a Grã-Bretanha	"gram-bruh**tahn**yuh"
▷ **have you ever been to Britain?**	já foi à Grã-Bretanha?	"ja foy a gram-bruh**tahn**yuh"
British	britânico	"bree**tah**-nikoo"
	britânica	"bree**tah**-nikuh"
broccoli	os brocolos	"**broh**kooloosh"
brochure	a brochura	"bro**shoo**ruh"
broken	partido	"per**tee**doo"
	partida	"per**tee**duh"
▷ **I have broken the window**	parti a janela	"par**tee** uh ja**nel**uh"
▷ **the lock is broken**	a fechadura está estragada	"uh feshuh-**doo**ruh shta shtru**gah**-duh"
broken down (*machine, car*)	avariado	"avuhree-**ah**doo"
	avariada	"avuhree-**ah**duh"
▷ **my car has broken down**	o meu carro avariou-se	"oo **may**oo **kar**roo avaree-**oh**suh"
broken into:		
▷ **my car has been broken into**	assaltaram-me o carro	"assal**tah**-rowngmuh oo **kar**roo"
brooch	o broche	"brosh"
broom	a vassoura	"va**soh**ruh"
brother	o irmão	"eer**mowng**"
brown	castanho	"kash-**tahn**yoo"
	castanha	"kash-**tahn**yuh"
brush	a escova	"**shkov**uh"
Brussels	Bruxelas	"broo**shel**ush"

ABSOLUTE ESSENTIALS

I don't understand	não compreendo	"nowng kompree**een**doo"
I don't speak Portuguese	não falo português	"nowng **fah**loo poortoo**gaysh**"
do you speak English?	fala inglês?	"**fah**luh een**glesh**"
could you help me?	podia ajudar-me?	"poo**dee**uh ajoo**dar**muh"

Brussels sprouts	as couves de Bruxelas	"kohvsh duh **broo**shelush"
bucket	o balde	"**bal**duh"
buffet	o bufete	"boo**fet**"
buffet car	o vagão restaurante	"va**gowng** rushtoh**rant**"
bulb	a lâmpada	"**lahm**paduh"
bum bag	o cinto com porta-moedas	"**seen**too kong **por**tuh-moo**eh**-dush"
bun	o bolo	"**boh**loo"
bureau de change	a loja de câmbio	"**lo**juh duh **kamb**yoo"
burst	rebentado rebentada	"ruhben-**tah**doo" "ruhben-**tah**duh"
▷ **a burst tyre**	um pneu furado	"oom **pnay**oo foo**rah**doo"
bus	o autocarro	"owto**karr**oo"
▷ **where do I get the bus to town?**	onde se apanha o autocarro para a cidade?	"**on**duh see a**pahn**yuh oo owto**karr**oo pra seedahd"
▷ **does this bus go to ...?**	este autocarro vai para ...?	"aysht owto**karr**oo vy paruh"
▷ **where do I get a bus for the airport?**	onde se apanha o autocarro para o aeroporto?	"**on**duh see a**pahn**yuh oo owto**karr**oo pro uh-ehroo-**por**too"
▷ **which bus do I take for the museum?**	que autocarro apanho para o museu?	"kuh owto**karr**oo a**pahn**yoo paruh o moo**say**oo"
▷ **how frequent are the buses to town?**	com que frequência é que há autocarros para a cidade?	"kong kuh fruh**kwayn**-seea e kuh a owto**karr**oosh paruh uh seedahd"
▷ **what time is the last bus?**	a que horas é o último autocarro?	"uh kuh **o**rush e oo **ool**teemoo owto**karr**oo"
▷ **what time does it leave?**	a que horas parte?	"uh kuh **o**rush part"

▷ **what time does the bus arrive?**	a que horas chega o autocarro?	"uh kuh **o**rush **sheh**guh oo owto**karr**oo"
business	os negócios	"ne**gos**-yoosh"
▷ **I am here on business**	estou aqui em negócios	"shtoh a**kee** ayng ne**gos**-yoosh"
▷ **a business trip**	uma viagem de negócios	"**oo**muh vee**ah**-jayng duh ne**gos**-yoosh"
bus station	a estação de autocarros	"shta**sowng** dowto**karr**oosh"
bus stop	a paragem de autocarro	"pa**rah**-jayng dowto**karr**oo"
bus tour	a excursão de autocarro	"shkoor**sowng** dowto**karr**oo"
busy	ocupado ocupada	"ohkoo-**pah**doo" "ohkoo-**pah**duh"
▷ **the line is busy**	a linha está interrompida	"uh **leen**ya shta eenteh-rrom**pee**duh"
but	mas	"mush"
butcher's	o talho	"**tal**yoo"
butter	a manteiga	"man**tay**guh"
button	o botão	"boo**towng**"
to **buy**	comprar	"kom**prar**"
▷ **where do we buy our tickets?**	onde compramos os bilhetes?	"**ond**uh kom**prah**-moozooj bee**lyetsh**"
▷ **where can I buy some postcards?**	onde posso comprar postais?	"ond **pos**oo kom**prar** poosh**tish**"
by (*close to*) (*via*) (*beside*)	perto de por ao lado de	"**pehr**too duh" "poor" "ow **lah**doo duh"
bypass	a vereda	"vuh-**reh**duh"

ABSOLUTE ESSENTIALS

do you have ...?	tem ...?	"tayng"
is there ...?	há ...?	"ah"
are there ...?	há ...?	"ah"
how much is ...?	quanto custa ...?	"**kwan**too **koosh**tuh"

cabaret	o espectáculo de variedades	"shpe**ta**kooloo duh vareeuh-**dah**dush"
▷ **where can we go to see a cabaret?**	onde é que há um espectáculo de variedades?	"**on**dee e kee a oom shpe**ta**kooloo duh vareeuh-**dah**dush"
cabbage	a couve	"kohv"
cabin (*hut*)	a barraca	"buh**rrah**kuh"
(*on ship*)	o camarote	"kamuh**roht**"
▷ **a first/second class cabin**	um camarote de primeira/segunda classe	"oom kamuh**roht** duh pree**may**ruh/ see**goon**duh klass"
cable car	o teleférico	"tuhluh-**feri**koo"
cactus	o cacto	"**kah**too"
café	o café	"kuh**fe**"
cagoule	o kispo	"**keesh**poo"
cake	o bolo	"**boh**loh"
calculator	a máquina calculadora	"**mah**kinuh kalkooluh-**do**ruh"
call[1] *n* (*on telephone*)	uma chamada	"sha**mah**duh"
▷ **I'd like to make a call**	queria fazer uma chamada	"**kree**uh fa**zehr** oomuh sha**mah**duh"
▷ **a long-distance call**	uma chamada interurbana	"oomuh sha**mah**duh eenteroor-**bah**nuh"
▷ **an international call**	uma chamada internacional	"oomuh sha**mah**duh eenter-nasyoo**nal**"
to call[2] *vb*	chamar	"sha**mar**"
	telefonar	"tuhluh-foo**nar**"
▷ **may I call you tomorrow?**	posso telefonar-lhe amanhã?	"**pos**oo tuhluh-foo**nar**lyuh amuh**nyang**"
▷ **please call me back**	volte a telefonar-me, por favor	"**volt** uh tuhluh-foo**nar**muh, poor fa**vor**"
call box	a cabine telefónica	"**kah**been tuhluh-**foh**nikuh"

calm	calmo	"**kal**moo"
	calma	"**kal**muh"
▷ keep calm!	fique calmo!	"feek **kal**moo"
camcorder	a máquina de filmar	"**mah**kinuh duh feel**mar**"
camera	a máquina fotográfica	"**mak**inuh footoo-**grafi**kuh"
to camp	acampar	"akam**par**"
▷ may we camp here?	podemos acampar aqui?	"poo**day**moosh akam**par** a**kee**"
campbed	a cama de desarmar	"**kah**muh duh dzuhr**mar**"
camp site	o parque de campismo	"park duh kam**peej**-moo"
▷ we're looking for a camp site	procuramos um parque de campismo	"prookoo-**rah**mooz oom park duh kamp**peej**-moo"
can¹ *n*	a lata	"**lah**tuh"
can² *vb (to be able)*	poder	"po**dehr**"

I can	posso	"**pos**oo"
you can *(informal singular)*	podes	"**poh**dush"
(formal singular)	você pode	"voseh **poh**d"
he/she/it can	ele/ela pode	"el/eluh **poh**d"
we can	podemos	"poo**deh**moosh"
you can *(informal plural)*	podeis	"poo**daysh**"
(formal plural)	vocês podem	"vosehsh **poh**dayng"
they can	eles/elas podem	"elsh/**e**lush **poh**dayng"

▷ we can't come	não podemos vir	"nowng poo**deh**-moosh **veer**"
Canada	o Canadá	"kanuh**da**"
Canadian	canadiano	"kana-dee**ah**noo"
	canadiana	"kana-dee**ah**nuh"

ABSOLUTE ESSENTIALS

I don't understand	não compreendo	"nowng kompree**een**doo"
I don't speak Portuguese	não falo português	"nowng **fah**loo poortoo**gaysh**"
do you speak English?	fala inglês?	"**fah**luh een**glesh**"
could you help me?	podia ajudar-me?	"poo**dee**uh ajoo**dar**muh"

canal	o canal	"kuh**nal**"
to **cancel**	cancelar	"kans**lar**"
▷ I want to cancel my booking	quero cancelar a minha reserva	"**ker**oo kans**lar** uh meenya ruh**zehr**vuh"
cancellation:		
▷ are there any cancellations?	houve cancelamentos?	"**ohv** kannsluh-**ment**oosh"
canoe	a canoa	"ka**noh**uh"
canoeing:		
▷ where can we go canoeing?	onde podemos ir praticar canoagem?	"ond poo**deh**-moosh eer pratee**kar** kuhnoo-**ahj**ayng"
can-opener	o abre-latas	"abruh-**lah**tush"
car	o carro	"**kar**roo"
▷ I want to hire a car	quero alugar um carro	"**keh**roo aloo**gar** oom **kar**roo"
▷ my car has been broken into	assaltaram-me o carro	"assal-**tah**rowng-muh oo **kar**roo"
▷ my car has broken down	o meu carro avariou-se	"oo mayoo **kar**roo avuh-ree**oh**-suh"
carafe	o jarro	"**jar**roo"
▷ a carafe of house wine	um jarro de vinho da casa	"oom **jar**roo duh **veen**yoo duh **kah**zuh"
caravan	a caravana	"karuh-**vah**nuh"
▷ can we park our caravan there?	podemos estacionar a caravana ali?	"poo**day**-moosh shtasyoo**nar** uh kara-**vah**nuh a**lee**"
caravan site	o parque de caravanas	"**park** duh kara-**vah**nush"
carburettor	o carburador	"karbooruh**dor**"
card (*greetings*)	o cartão	"kar**towng**"
(*playing*)	a carta	"**kar**tuh"

ABSOLUTE ESSENTIALS

I would like ...	queria ...	"**kree**uh"
I need ...	preciso de ...	"pre**see**zoo duh"
where is ...?	onde fica ...?	"ond **fee**kuh"
I'm looking for ...	procuro ...	"pro**koo**roo"

▷ **birthday card**	o postal de aniversário	"oo poosh**tal** duh aneever-**sar**yoo"
cardigan	o casaco de lã	"ka**zah**koo duh lang"
careful	cuidadoso	"kweeduh-**doh**zoo"
	cuidadosa	"kweeduh-**doh**zuh"
▷ **be careful!**	tenha cuidado!	"tenya kwee**dah**doo"
car ferry	o ferry	"ferry"
car (registration) number	a matrícula do carro	"ma**tree**-kooluh doo **kar**ro"
car park	o parque de estacionamento	"**park** duh shtasyoonuh-**men**too"
▷ **is there a car park near here?**	há um parque de estacionamento perto daqui?	"a oom park dushtasyoonuh-**men**too **per**too duhkee"
carpet	o tapete	"ta**pet**"
carriage (*railway*)	a carruagem	"karr-**wah**jayng"
carrier bag	a saca (de plástico)	"**sah**kuh (duh **plash**tikoo)"
▷ **can I have a carrier bag please?**	pode dar-me uma saca, por favor?	"pod **dar**muh oomuh **sah**kuh, poor fa**vor**"
carrot	a cenoura	"suh**noh**ruh"
to **carry**	transportar	"transhpoor**tar**"
car wash	a lavagem automática	"la**vah**-jayng owtoo-**ma**tikuh"
▷ **how do I use the car wash?**	como se faz uma lavagem automática?	"**koo**moo sfash oomuh la**vah**-jayng owtoo-**ma**tikuh"
case (*suitcase*)	a mala	"**mah**luh"
cash[1] *n*	o dinheiro	"deeny**ay**roo"
▷ **I haven't any cash**	não tenho dinheiro nenhum	"nowng **teny**oo deeny**ay**roo neny**oom**"

ABSOLUTE ESSENTIALS

do you have ...?	tem ...?	"tayng"
is there ...?	há ...?	"ah"
are there ...?	há ...?	"ah"
how much is ...?	quanto custa ...?	"**kwan**too **koosh**tuh"

▷ **can I get cash with my credit card?**	posso obter dinheiro com o meu cartão de crédito?	"**poss**oo ob**tehr** deen**yay**roo kong o mayoo kar**towng** duh **kreh**ditoo"
to **cash**[2] *vb* (*cheque*)	levantar	"luhvan**tar**"
▷ **can I cash a cheque?**	posso levantar um cheque?	"**pos**oo luhvan**tar** oom shek"
cash desk	a caixa	"**ky**shuh"
cash dispenser	a máquina automática	"**ma**kinuh owtoo-**ma**tikuh"
cashier	o caixa	"**ky**shuh"
casino	o casino	"ka**zee**noo"
cassette	a cassete	"ka**set**"
cassette player	o leitor de cassetes	"**lay**tor duh **kah**setsh"
castle	o castelo	"kash**te**loo"
▷ **is the castle open to the public?**	o castelo está aberto ao público?	"oo kash**te**loo shta a**behr**too ow **poob**likoo"
to **catch**	apanhar	"apan**yar**"
▷ **where do we catch the bus to ...?**	onde se apanha o autocarro para ...?	"ond suh**pan**ya oo owto**ka**rro paruh"
cathedral	a catedral	"katuh**dral**"
▷ **excuse me, how do I get to the cathedral?**	desculpe, como é que se vai para a catedral?	"dush**koolp koh**moo e kuh suh vy pra katuh**dral**"
Catholic	católico católica	"ka**to**likoo" "ka**to**likuh"
cauliflower	a couve-flor	"kohv-**flor**"
cave	a caverna	"ka**vehr**nuh"
caviar	o caviar	"kuh**viar**"
CD	o CD	"seh**deh**"
celery	o aipo	"**y**poo"

cemetery	o cemitério	"suhmee-**tehr**yoo"
centimetre	o centímetro	"sentee-metroo"
central	central	"sentral"
central station	a estação central	"shtuh**sowng** sentral"
▷ **where is the central station?**	onde fica a estação central?	"ond **fee**kuh uh shtuh**sowng** sentral"
centre	o centro	"**sen**troo"
▷ **how far are we from the town centre?**	a que distância estamos do centro da cidade?	"uh kuh deesh-**tan**sya **shtah**moosh doo **sen**troo duh seedahd"
cereal (*for breakfast*)	o cereal	"suhreeal"
certain (*sure*)	certo	"**sehr**too"
	certa	"**sehr**tuh"
certificate	o certificado	"serteefee-**kah**doo"
▷ **an insurance certificate**	um certificado de seguros	"oom serteefee-**kah**doo duh suh**goo**roosh"
chain	a corrente	"koor**rent**"
▷ **do I need snow chains?**	preciso de correntes para a neve?	"pre**see**zoo duh koor**rentsh** paruh uh **nev**"
chair	a cadeira	"ka**day**ruh"
chairlift	a cadeira de elevação	"ka**day**ruh duh eeluh-vuh**sowng**"
chalet	a vivenda	"vee**ven**duh"
champagne	o champanhe	"sham**pan**yuh"
change[1] *n* (*money*)	o troco	"**troh**koo"
▷ **do you have change?**	tem troco?	"tayng **troh**koo"
▷ **could you give me change of 100 escudos?**	podia dar-me troco de 100 escudos?	"poo**dee**uh **dar**muh **troh**koo duh **sayng** shkoodoosh"

ABSOLUTE ESSENTIALS

I don't understand	não compreendo	"nowng kompree**een**doo"
I don't speak Portuguese	não falo português	"nowng **fah**loo poortoo**gaysh**"
do you speak English?	fala inglês?	"**fah**luh een**glesh**"
could you help me?	podia ajudar-me?	"poo**dee**uh ajoo**dar**muh"

▷ sorry, I don't have any change	desculpe, não tenho troco	"dush**koolp** nowng tenyoo **troh**koo"
▷ keep the change	fique com o troco	"**fee**kuh kong oo **troh**koo"
to change² *vb* (*money*)	trocar	"troo**kar**"
	cambiar	"kamb**yar**"
(*clothes*)	mudar	"moo**dar**"
▷ where can I change some money?	onde posso cambiar dinheiro?	"**on**duh **pos**oo kamb**yar** deen**yay**roo"
▷ I'd like to change these traveller's cheques	queria trocar estes traveller cheques	"**kree**uh troo**kar aysh**tush traveller sheksh"
▷ I want to change some pounds into escudos	queria cambiar libras por escudos	"**kree**uh kamb**yar lee**brush poor sh**koo**doosh"
▷ where can I change the baby?	onde é que posso mudar o bebé?	"**on**dee e kuh **pos**oo moo**dar** oo be**be**"
▷ where do we change? (*clothes*)	onde é que nos mudamos?	"**on**dee e kuh noosh moo**dah**moosh"
▷ where do I change? (*bus etc*)	onde é que mudo?	"**on**dee e kuh **moo**doo"
▷ is the weather going to change?	o tempo vai mudar?	"oo **tem**poo vy moo**dar**"
▷ can I change my booking?	posso alterar a minha reserva?	"**pos**oo alte**rar** uh **meen**yuh ruh**zehr**vuh"
changing room	a sala de provas	"**sal**uh duh **prov**ush"
Channel tunnel	o túnel do Canal da Mancha	"**too**nel doo ka**nal** duh **man**shuh"
chapel	a capela	"ka**pel**uh"
charge	o custo	"**koosh**too"
▷ is there a charge per kilometre?	há alguma taxa por quilómetro?	"a al**goo**muh **tash**uh poor kee**lo**metroo"
▷ I want to reverse the charges	quero que seja pagável no destino	"**keh**roo kuh **se**juh pa**gah**vel noo dush**tee**noo"
▷ how much do you charge?	quanto dinheiro cobra?	"**kwan**too deen**yay**roo **koh**bruh"

▷ **is there a charge?**	há alguma taxa?	"a al**goo**muh **tah**shuh"
▷ **please charge it to my room**	por favor inclua na despesa do quarto	"poor fa**vor** een**klw**a nuh dsh**peh**zuh doo **kwar**too"
cheap	barato barata	"ba**rah**too" "ba**rah**tuh"
cheaper	mais barato mais barata	"mysh ba**rah**too" "mysh ba**rah**tuh"
▷ **have you anything cheaper?**	tem alguma coisa mais barata?	"tayng al**goo**muh **koy**zuh mysh ba**rah**tuh"
to check	verificar	"vereefee**kar**"
to check in	fazer o check-in	"fa**zehr** oo **check**in"
▷ **I'd like to check in, please**	queria fazer o check-in, por favor	"**kree**uh fa**zehr** oo **check**in poor fa**vor**"
▷ **where do I check in for the flight to London?**	onde faço o check-in para o voo de Londres?	"**on**duh **fah**soo oo **check**in paruh oo **voh**oo duh **lon**drush"
▷ **where do I check in my luggage?**	onde faço o check-in para a bagagem?	"**on**duh **fah**soo oo **check**in paruh uh ba**gah**jayng"
▷ **when do I have to check in?**	onde tenho de fazer o check-in?	"ond **ten**yoo duh fa**zehr** oo **check**in"
check-in desk	o balcão do check-in	"bal**kowng** doo **check**in"
cheerio	adeus	"a**day**oosh"
cheers!	saúde!	"sa**ood**"
cheese	o queijo	"**kay**joo"
cheeseburger	o cheeseburger	"cheese**boor**ger"
cheesecake	a queijada	"kay**jah**duh"
chemist's	a farmácia	"far**mas**yuh"
cheque	o cheque	"shek"
▷ **can I pay by cheque?**	posso pagar com um cheque?	"**pos**oo pa**gar** kong oom shek"

ABSOLUTE ESSENTIALS

do you have ...?	tem ...?	"tayng"
is there ...?	há ...?	"ah"
are there ...?	há ...?	"ah"
how much is ...?	quanto custa ...?	"**kwan**too **koosh**tuh"

▷ I want to cash a cheque, please	queria levantar um cheque, por favor	"**kree**uh luhvan**tar** oom shek poor favor"
cheque book	o livro de cheques	"**lee**vroo duh sheksh"
▷ I've lost my cheque book	perdi o meu livro de cheques	"per**dee** oo mayoo **lee**vroo duh sheksh"
cheque card	o cartão garantia	"kar**towng** garan**tee**uh"
cherry	a cereja	"suh**ray**juh"
chest	o peito	"**pay**too"
▷ I have a pain in my chest	dói-me o peito	"**doy**muh oo **pay**too"
chestnut	a castanha	"kash**tahn**yuh"
chewing gum	a pastilha elástica	"pash**teel**yuh ee**lash**-tikuh"
chicken (food)	a galinha frango	"ga**leen**yuh" "**fran**goo"
chickenpox	a varicela	"varee-**sel**uh"
chicken soup	a canja de galinha	"**kan**juh duh ga**leen**ya"
child	a criança	"kree** an**suh"
child minder	o educador infantil	"eedoo-kuh**dor** eenfan**teel**"
	a educadora infantil	"eedoo-kuh**dor**uh eenfan**teel**"
children	as crianças	"kree**an**sush"
▷ is there a children's pool?	há uma piscina para crianças?	"a **oom**uh peesh-**see**nuh **par**uh kree**an**sush"
▷ is there a paddling pool for the children?	há uma piscina baixa para as crianças?	"a oomuh peesh-**see**nuh **by**shuh par**ash** kree**an**sush"
chilli	o pimentão-de-cheiro	"peemen**towng** duh **shay**roo"
chips	as batatas fritas	"ba**tah**tush **free**tush"

chives	o cebolinho	"suhboo-**leen**yoo"
chocolate	o chocolate	"shookoo**lat**"
▷ **I'd like a bar of chocolate, please**	queria um chocolate, por favor	"**kree**uh oom shookoo**lat** poor fa**vor**"
chocolates	os chocolates	"shookoo**latsh**"
chop:		
▷ **a pork/lamb chop**	uma costeleta de porco/carneiro	"oomuh kooshtuh-**leh**tuh duh **pohr**koo/kar**nay**roo"
Christmas	o Natal	"na**tal**"
▷ **Merry Christmas!**	Feliz Natal!	"fe**leesh** na**tal**"
church	a igreja	"ee**gre**juh"
▷ **where is the nearest church?**	onde fica a igreja mais próxima?	"**on**duh **fee**kuh uh ee**gre**juh mysh **pross**eemuh"
▷ **where is there a Protestant/Catholic church?**	onde é que há uma igreja protestante/católica?	"**on**duh e kee a **oom**uh ee**gre**juh prootush**tant**/ka**to**likuh"
cider	a sidra	"**see**druh"
cigar	o charuto	"sha**roo**too"
cigarette	o cigarro	"see**gar**roo"
▷ **a packet of cigarettes, please**	um maço de cigarros, por favor	"oom **mah**soo duh see**gar**roosh poor fa**vor**"
cigarette papers	as mortalhas	"moor**tal**yush"
cinema	o cinema	"see**nay**muh"
▷ **what's on at the cinema?**	que filmes estão a passar no cinema?	"kuh feelmsh shtowng uh pa**sar** noo see**nay**muh"
circus	o circo	"**seer**koo"
city	a cidade	"see**dahd**"
clean[1] *adj*	limpo	"**leem**poo"
	limpa	"**leem**puh"

ABSOLUTE ESSENTIALS

I don't understand	não compreendo	"nowng kompree**en**doo"
I don't speak Portuguese	não falo português	"nowng **fah**loo poortoo**gaysh**"
do you speak English?	fala inglês?	"**fah**luh een**glesh**"
could you help me?	podia ajudar-me?	"poo**dee**uh ajoo**dar**muh"

▷ the room isn't clean	o quarto não está limpo	"oo **kwar**too nowng shta **leem**poo"
▷ could I have a clean spoon/fork please?	podia trazer-me uma colher limpa/um garfo limpo, por favor?	"poodeeuh tra**zehr**-muh oomuh koo**lyer leem**puh/oom **gar**foo **leem**poo poor fa**vor**"
to **clean²** *vb*	limpar	"leem**par**"
▷ where can I get this skirt cleaned?	onde é que posso mandar limpar esta saia?	"**on**dee e kuh **pos**oo man**dar** leem**par esh**tuh **sy**uh"
cleaner	a mulher da limpeza	"moo**lyehr** duh leem**pay**zuh"
▷ which day does the cleaner come?	em que dia é que a mulher da limpeza vem?	"ayng kuh **dee**uh e kee uh moo**lyehr** duh leem**pay**zuh vayng"
cleansing cream	o creme de limpeza	"krem duh leem**pay**zuh"
cleansing solution (*for contact lenses*)	o líquido de limpeza	"**lee**kidoo duh leem**pay**zuh"
client	o/a cliente	"klee-**ent**"
cliff	o penhasco	"puh-**nyash**koo"
climbing	o alpinismo	"alpee**neej**-moo"
climbing boots	as botas de alpinismo	"**bo**tush dalpee**neej**-moo"
cloakroom	o vestiário	"vushtee-**ar**yoo"
clock	o relógio	"re**loj**-yoo"
close¹ *adj* (*near*)	perto perta	"**pehr**too" "**pehr**tuh"
to **close²** *vb*	fechar	"fe**shar**"
▷ what time do you close?	a que horas fecha?	"uh kuh **o**rush **fay**shuh"
▷ the door will not close	a porta não fecha	"uh **por**tuh nowng **fay**shuh"
closed	fechado(a)	"fu**shah**doo(uh)"

cloth	o tecido	"tuh**see**doo"
clothes	as roupas	"**roh**push"
clothes peg	a mola da roupa	"**mo**luh duh **roh**puh"
cloudy	nublado	"noo**blah**doo"
	nublada	"noo**blah**duh"
clove	o cravinho	"kra**vee**nyoo"
club	o clube	"kloob"
▷ **a night club**	um clube nocturno	"oom kloob noh**toor**noo"
▷ **a set of golf clubs**	um conjunto de paus de golfe	"oom kon**joon**too duh **pows** duh golf"
coach (*bus*)	a camioneta (de passageiros)	"**kah**myoo-nehtuh (duh pasuh-**jay**roosh)"
(*train*)	a carruagem	"karr**wah**-jayng"
▷ **when does the coach leave in the morning?**	a que horas parte a camioneta de manhã?	"uh kee **o**rush part uh **kah**myoo-nehtuh duh **man**yang"
coach station	a estação de camionetas	"shta**sowng** duh **kah**myoo-nehtush"
coach trip	a viagem de camioneta	"vee**ah**-jayng duh **kah**myoo-nehtuh"
coast	a costa	"**kosh**tuh"
coastguard	o guarda fiscal	"**gwar**duh feesh**kal**"
coat	o casaco	"ka**zah**koo"
coat hanger	o cabide	"ka**beed**"
cockroaches	as baratas	"ba**rah**tush"
cocktail	o cocktail	"cocktail"
cocoa	o cacau	"ka**kow**"
coconut	o coco	"**koh**koo"
cod	o bacalhau	"bakuh**lyow**"

ABSOLUTE ESSENTIALS

do you have ...?	tem ...?	"tayng"
is there ...?	há ...?	"ah"
are there ...?	há ...?	"ah"
how much is ...?	quanto custa ...?	"**kwan**too **koosh**tuh"

coffee	o café	"kuh**fe**"
▷ **white coffee**	o café com leite	"kuh**fe** kong layt"
	o galão	"ga**lowng**"
▷ **black coffee**	o café	"kuh**fe**"
coin	a moeda	"**mway**duh"
▷ **what coins do I need?**	de que moedas preciso?	"duh kuh **mway**dush pre**see**zoo"
▷ **a 50 escudos coin**	uma moeda de 50 escudos	"**oo**muh **mway**duh duh seeng**kwen**tuh sh**koo**doosh"
Coke®	a coca-cola	"kokuh**ko**luh"
colander	o coador	"kohuh-**dor**"
cold¹ *n*	o frio	"**free**oo"
▷ **I have a cold**	estou constipado	"shtoh konstee-**pah**doo"
cold² *adj*	frio	"**free**oo"
	fria	"**free**uh"
▷ **I'm cold**	tenho frio	"**ten**yoo **free**oo"
▷ **will it be cold tonight?**	vai estar frio esta noite?	"vy shtar **free**oo **esh**tuh noyt"
cold meat	a carne fria	"**karn free**uh"
Cologne	Colónia	"koo**loh**nya"
▷ **(Eau de) Cologne**	a água de colônia	"uh **ah**gua duh koo**loh**nya"
colour	a cor	"kor"
▷ **I don't like the colour**	não gosto da cor	"nowng **gosh**too duh kor"
▷ **I need a colour film**	preciso de um rolo de fotografias a cores	"pre**see**zoo doom **roh**loo duh footoogruh-**fee**ush uh **kor**ush"
▷ **do you have it in another colour?**	tem isso numa cor diferente?	"tayng **ees**soo **noo**muh **kor** deefuh**rent**"
▷ **a colour TV**	uma televisão a cores	"**oo**muh tuhluh-vee**sowng** uh **kor**uhsh"

comb	o pente	"pent"
to **come**	vir	"veer"
(*arrive*)	chegar	"shuh**gar**"
▷ **what does that come to?**	qual é o total?	"kwal **e** oo too**tal**"
to **come back**	voltar	"vol**tar**"
to **come in**	entrar	"ayn**trar**"
▷ **come in!**	entre!	"**ayn**truh"
comfortable	confortável	"komfoor-**tah**vel"
commission:		
▷ **how much commission do you charge?**	qual é a sua comissão?	"kwal **e** uh soouh koomee**sowng**"
communion	a comunhão	"koomoon**yowng**"
compact disc	o disco compacto	"**deesh**koo kom**pahk**too"
compact disc player	o aparelho de CDs	"apa**rayhl**yoo duh seh **dehsh**"
company	a companhia	"kompan-**yee**uh"
compartment	o compartimento	"kompuhr-tee**men**too"
▷ **I would like a seat in a non-smoking compartment**	queria um lugar num compartimento para não-fumadores	"**kree**uh oom loo**gar** noom kompuhr-tee**men**too paruh **nowng** foomuh**dor**ush"
to **complain**	queixar-se (de)	"kay**shar**-suh (duh)"
▷ **I want to complain about the service** (*in shop etc*)	queria apresentar uma queixa do serviço	"**kree**uh apruh-zen**tar** oomuh **kay**shuh doo ser**vee**soo"

ABSOLUTE ESSENTIALS

I don't understand	não compreendo	"nowng kompree**een**doo"
I don't speak Portuguese	não falo português	"nowng **fah**loo poortoo**gaysh**"
do you speak English?	fala inglês?	"**fah**luh een**glesh**"
could you help me?	podia ajudar-me?	"poo**dee**uh ajoo**dar**muh"

comprehensive insurance cover:

▷ **how much extra is the comprehensive insurance cover?**	qual a diferença a pagar para ter um seguro contra todos os riscos?	"**kwal** deefuh-**ren**suh uh pa**gar** pa**ruh** tehr oom se**goo**roo **kon**truh **toh**duzoosh **reesh**koosh"
compulsory	obrigatório(a)	"ohbree-guh**tor**yoo(yuh)"
computer	o computador	"kompoo-tuh**dor**"
concert	o concerto	"kon**sehr**too"
condensed milk	o leite condensado	"layt konden-**sah**doo"
conditioner	o creme amaciador	"krem amuhsee-uh**dor**"
condom	o preservativo	"preser-vuh**tee**voo"
▷ **a packet of condoms**	uma caixa de preservativos	"oomuh **ky**shuh duh preser-vuh**tee**voosh"
conductor (on bus etc)	o cobrador	"koobruh**dor**"
conference	a conferência	"komfuh-**ren**syuh"
confession	a confissão	"komfee**sowng**"
▷ **I want to go to confession**	quero-me confessar	"**keh**roomuh komfuh**sar**"
to **confirm**	confirmar	"komfeer**mar**"
congratulations!	parabéns!	"paruh-**baynsh**"
connection	a ligação	"leeguh-**sowng**"
▷ **I missed my connection**	perdi o comboio de ligação	"per**dee** oo kon**boy**oo duh leeguh-**sowng**"
constipated	com prisão de ventre	"kong pree**zowng** duh **ven**truh"
▷ **I am constipated**	tehno prisão de ventre	"**ten**yoo pree**zowng** duh **ven**truh"
constipation	a prisão de ventre	"pree**zowng** duh **ven**truh"

ABSOLUTE ESSENTIALS		
I would like ...	queria ...	"**kree**uh"
I need ...	preciso de ...	"pre**see**zoo duh"
where is ...?	onde fica ...?	"ond **fee**kuh"
I'm looking for ...	procuro ...	"pro**koo**roo"

consulate	o consulado	"konsoo**lah**doo"
▷ **where is the British/ American Consulate?**	onde fica o Consulado Britânico/Americano?	"**ond**uh **fee**kuh oo konsoo**lah**doo bree**tah**nikoo/amuhree-**kah**noo"
to **contact:**		
▷ **where can I contact you?**	onde posso contactá-lo(a)?	"ond **pos**oo kontak**tah**-loo(uh)"
contact lenses	as lentes de contacto	"lentsh duh kon**tak**too"
▷ **contact lens cleaner**	o líquido para as lentes de contacto	"**lee**kidoo prash lentsh duh kon**tak**too"
▷ **hard contact lenses**	lentes de contacto duras	"lentsh duh kon**tak**too **doo**rush"
▷ **soft contact lenses**	lentes de contacto gelatinosas	"lentsh duh kon**tak**too juhluhtee-**noh**zush"
continental breakfast	o pequeno-almoço continental	"puh**kay**noo-al**moh**soo konteenen**tal**"
contraceptive	o anticonceptivo	"antee-konsep**tee**voo"
controls:		
▷ **how do I operate the controls?**	como funcionam os comandos do carro?	"**koh**moo foon-**syoh**nowng oosh koo**man**doosh doo **karr**oo"
to **cook**	cozinhar	"koozeen**yar**"
cooker	o fogão	"foo**gowng**"
▷ **how does the cooker work?**	como funciona o fogão?	"**koo**moo foon-**syoh**nuh oo foo**gowng**"
cool	fresco(a)	"**fresh**koo(uh)"
copy¹ *n* (*photocopy*)	a cópia a fotocópia	"**koh**pyuh" "fohtoh-**koh**pyuh"
▷ **4 copies please**	quatro fotocópias, por favor	"**kwah**troo fohtoh-**koh**pyush poor fa**vor**"
to **copy²** *vb*	copiar fotocopiar	"koop-**yar**" "**foh**toh-koopyar"

▷ **I want to copy this document**	quero fotocopiar este documento	"**kehr**oo **foh**toh-koopyar ehsht dookoo-**men**too"
corkscrew	o saca-rolhas	"sakuh-**rol**yush"
corner	a esquina	"**shkee**nuh"
	o canto	"**kan**too"
▷ **it's round the corner**	é ao virar da esquina	"e ow vee**rar** duh **shkee**nuh"
cornflakes	os cornflakes	"cornflakes"
cortisone	a cortisona	"koortee-**zon**uh"
cosmetics	os cosméticos	"kooj-**met**ikoosh"
to cost	custar	"koosh**tar**"
▷ **how much does it cost to get in?**	quanto custa o bilhete de entrada?	"**kwan**too **koosh**tuh oo beel**yet dayn-trah**duh"
▷ **how much does that cost?**	quanto custa aquilo?	"**kwan**too **koosh**tuh a**kee**loo"
cot	o berço para bebé	"**behr**soo paruh be**be**"
▷ **do you have a cot for the baby?**	tem um berço para o bebé?	"tayng oom **behr**soo proh be**be**"
cotton	o algodão	"algoo**downg**"
cotton wool	o algodão em rama	"algoo**downg** ayng **rah**muh"
couchette	a couchette	"koo**shet**"
▷ **I want to reserve a couchette**	quero reservar uma couchette	"**kehr**oo ruhzer**var** oomuh koo**shet**"
cough	a tosse	"tohss"
▷ **I have a cough**	tenho tosse	"**ten**yoo tohss"
▷ **do you have any cough mixture?**	tem xarope para a tosse?	"tayng shuh**rop** paruh uh tohss"

could:

I could	podia	"poo**dee**uh"
you could (*informal singular*)	podias	"poo**dee**ush"
(*formal singular*)	você podia	"voseh poo**dee**uh"
he/she/it could	ele/ela podia	"**el**/**el**uh poo**dee**uh"
we could	podíamos	"poo**dee**uh-moosh"
you could (*informal plural*)	podíeis	"poo**dee**-aysh"
(*formal plural*)	vocês podiam	"vosehsh poo**dee**-owng"
they could	eles/elas podiam	"**elsh**/**el**ush poo**dee**-owng"

country (*not town*)	o campo	"**kam**poo"
(*nation*)	o país	"pa**eesh**"
couple (*two people*)	o casal	"ka**zal**"
courgette	a courgette	"koor**jet**"
courier	o mensageiro	"mensa-**jay**roo"
▷ **I want to send this by courier**	quero mandar isto por um mensageiro	"**keh**roo man**dar eesh**too poor oom mensa-**jay**roo"
course (*of meal*)	o prato	"**prah**too"
cover charge	o serviço	"ser**vee**soo"
crab	o caranguejo	"karan-**gej**oo"
cramp:		
▷ **I've got cramp (in my leg)**	tenho uma cãimbra (na perna)	"**ten**yo oomuh ka-**een**bruh (nuh **per**nuh)"
crash	o choque	"shok"
	o acidente	"ase**dent**"
▷ **I've crashed my car**	tive um acidente com o carro	"teev oom ase**dent** kong oo **kar**ro"
▷ **there's been a crash**	houve um acidente	"**ohv** oom ase**dent**"
crash helmet	o capacete	"kapuh**set**"

ABSOLUTE ESSENTIALS

I don't understand	não compreendo	"nowng kompree**en**doo"
I don't speak Portuguese	não falo português	"nowng **fah**loo poortoo**gaysh**"
do you speak English?	fala inglês?	"**fah**luh een**glesh**"
could you help me?	podia ajudar-me?	"poo**dee**uh ajoo**dar**muh"

cream (*lotion*)	o creme	"krem"
(*on milk*)	a nata	"**nah**tuh"
cream cheese	o queijo creme	"**kay**joo krem"
credit card	o cartão de crédito	"kar**towng** duh **kred**ito"
▷ can I pay by credit card?	posso pagar com o cartão de crédito?	"**pos**oo pa**gar** kong oo kar**towng** duh **kred**itoo"
▷ I've lost my credit card	perdi o meu cartão de crédito	"per**dee** oo mayoo kar**towng** duh **kred**itoo"
crisps	as batatas fritas	"ba**tah**tush **free**tush"
croissant	o croissant	"croissant"
croquette	o croquete	"kro**ket**"
to cross	(*road*) atravessar	"atruhvuh-**sar**"
cross-country:		
▷ is it possible to go cross-country skiing?	pode ir-se fazer esqui de fundo?	"pod **eer**ss fa**zehr** shkee duh **foon**doo"
crossed line	as linhas cruzadas	"**leen**yush kroo**zah**dush"
crossing	a travessia	"travuh-**see**uh"
▷ how long does the crossing take?	quanto tempo demora a travessia?	"**kwan**too **tem**poo de**mor**uh uh travuh-**see**uh"
crossroads	a encruzilhada	"aynkroo-zeel**yah**duh"
crowded	cheio(a) de gente	"**shay**oo(uh) duh jent"
cruise	o cruzeiro	"kroo**zay**roo"
cucumber	o pepino	"puh**pee**noo"
cup	a chávena	"**shah**vnuh"
▷ could we have another cup of tea/coffee, please?	podia dar-nos outra chávena de chá/café, por favor?	"poo**dee**uh **dar**noosh ohtruh **shah**vnuh duh **sha**/kuhfe poor fa**vor**"
cupboard	o aparador	"apa-ruh**dor**"
currant	a groselha	"gro**zel**yuh"

current	a corrente	"koo**rrent**"
▷ **are there strong currents?**	há correntes fortes?	"a koo**rrentsh** fortsh"
cushion	a almofada	"almoo-**fah**duh"
customs	a alfândega	"alfan-duhguh"
cut[1] *n*	o corte	"kort"
▷ **a cut and blow-dry, please**	cortar e secar, por favor	"koor**tar** ee se**kar** poor fa**vor**"
to **cut**[2] *vb*	cortar	"koor**tar**"
▷ **he has cut himself**	ele cortou-se	"ayl koor**toh**-suh"
▷ **I've been cut off**	foi interrompida a ligação	"foy eenterom-**pee**duh uh leeguh-**sowng**"
cutlery	os talheres	"tal-**yeh**rush"
to **cycle** *vb*	andar de bicicleta	"an**dar** duh beesee-**kle**tuh"
cycle path	o caminho para bicicletas	"ka**meen**yoo paruh beesee-**kle**tush"
cycle helmet	o capacete para andar de bicicleta	"kapuh**seht** paruh an**dar** duh beesee-**kle**tuh"
cycling	o ciclismo	"seek**leej**-moo"
▷ **we would like to go cycling**	gostávamos de ir andar de bicicleta	"goosh**tah**-vuhmoosh duh eer an**dar** duh beesee-**kle**tuh"
daily (*each day*)	cada dia	"**kah**duh **dee**uh"
	diário	"dee**ahr**-yoo"
dairy products	os lacticínios	"lakti-**seen**yoosh"
damage *n*	o prejuízo	"pruh-**jwee**zoo"
damp	húmido(a)	"**oo**meedoo(uh)"
▷ **my clothes are damp**	a minha roupa está húmida	"uh meenya **roh**puh shta **oo**meeduh"

ABSOLUTE ESSENTIALS

do you have ...?	tem ...?	"tayng"
is there ...?	há ...?	"ah"
are there ...?	há ...?	"ah"
how much is ...?	quanto custa ...?	"**kwan**too **koosh**tuh"

dance

dance[1] *n*	o baile	"**by**le"
to **dance**[2] *vb*	dançar	"dan**sar**"
dangerous	perigoso	"peree-**goh**zoo"
	perigosa	"peree- **goh**zuh"
dark	escuro	"**shkoo**roo"
	escura	"**shkoo**ruh"
date	a data	"**dah**tuh"
(*fruit*)	a tâmara	"**tah**muhruh"
▷ **what is the date today?**	a quantos estamos hoje?	"uh **kwan**tosh **shtah**moozohj"
date of birth	a data de nascimento	"**dah**tuh duh nashsee-**men**too"
daughter	a filha	"**feel**yuh"
day	o dia	"**dee**uh"
day trip	o passeio (de um dia)	"pa**say**oo (duh oom **dee**uh)"
dear	caro	"**kah**roo"
	cara	"**kah**ruh"
decaffeinated coffee	o café descafeinado	"kuh**fe** dushkafay-**nah**doo"
December	Dezembro	"duh**zem**broo"
deck	o convés	"kom**vesh**"
▷ **can we go out on deck?**	podemos ir para o convés?	"poo**day**moozeer pro kom**vesh**"
deck chair	a cadeira de lona	"ka**day**ruh duh **lon**uh"
to **declare**	declarar	"duhkla**rar**"
▷ **I have nothing to declare**	não tenho nada a declarar	"nowng **ten**yoo **nah**duh uh duhkla**rar**"
▷ **I have two bottles of wine to declare**	tenho duas garrafas de vinho a declarar	"**ten**yoo **doo**ush gar**rah**fush duh **veen**yoo uh duhkla**rar**"

ABSOLUTE ESSENTIALS

yes (please)	sim (por favor)	"**seeng** (por fa**vor**)"
no (thank you)	não (obrigado/a)	"**nowng** (ohbree**gah**doo/uh)"
hello	olá	"oh**la**"
goodbye	adeus	"a**day**oosh"

deep	fundo	"**foon**doo"
	funda	"**foon**duh"
▷ **how deep is the water?**	qual a profundidade da água?	"**kwal** uh proofoon-dee**dahd** duh **ah**gwuh"
deep freeze	congelador	"konjuhluh**dor**"
to **defrost**	descongelar	"dushkonjuh**lar**"
to **de-ice**	descongelar	"dushkonjuh**lar**"
delay	a demora	"duh**mo**ruh"
▷ **the flight has been delayed (by 6 hours)**	o voo foi atrasado (seis horas)	"oo **voh**oo foy atruh**zah**doo (say**zo**rush)"
delicious	delicioso	"duhlees-**yoh**zoo"
	deliciosa	"duhlees-**yoh**zuh"
dentist	o dentista	"den**teesh**tuh"
	a dentista	"den**teesh**tuh"
▷ **I need to see the dentist (urgently)**	preciso de ir ao dentista (urgentemente)	"pre**see**zoo deer ow den**teesh**tuh (oorjent**ment**)"
dentures	a dentadura postiça	"dentuh-**doo**ruh poosh**tee**suh"
	a placa	"**plah**kuh"
▷ **my dentures need repairing**	a minha placa tem que ser arranjada	"uh **mee**nyuh **plah**kuh tayng kuh sehr arran**jah**duh"
deodorant	o desodorizante	"duzohdo-ree**zant**"
department store	o grande armazém	"grand armuh-**zayng**"
departure lounge	a sala de espera para partidas	"**sah**luh dush**peh**ruh **par**uh per**tee**dush"
departures	partidas	"per**tee**dush"
deposit	o depósito	"duh**po**zitoo"

▷ **what is the deposit?**	de quanto é o depósito?	"duh **kwan**too e oo duh**poz**itoo"
dessert	a sobremesa	"sobruh-**may**zuh"
▷ **we'd like a dessert**	queríamos uma sobremesa	"kehr**ee**-uhmooz oomuh sobruh-**may**zuh"
▷ **the dessert menu please**	a ementa de sobremesas, por favor	"uh ee**men**tuh duh soobruh-**may**zush poor fa**vor**"
details	os pormenores	"poormuh-**nor**ush"
detergent	o detergente	"duhter**jent**"
detour	o desvio	"duj-**vee**oo"
to **develop**	desenvolver	"duzaym-vol**vehr**"
diabetic	diabético	"deeuh-**bet**ikoo"
	diabética	"deeuh-**bet**ikuh"
▷ **I am diabetic**	sou diabético(a)	"soh deeuh-**bet**ikoo(uh)"
dialling code	o indicativo	"eendeekuh-**tee**voo"
▷ **what is the dialling code for the UK?**	qual é o indicativo para o Reino Unido?	"kwal e o eendeekuh-**tee**voo paruh oo **ray**noo oo**nee**doo"
diamond	o diamante	"deeuh-**mant**"
diarrhoea	a diarreia	"deeuh-**rray**uh"
▷ **I need something for diarrhoea**	preciso de alguma coisa para a diarreia	"pre**see**zoo duh algoomuh **koy**zuh paruh uh deeuh-**rray**uh"
diary	o diário	"dee**ar**yoo"
dictionary	o dicionário	"deesyoo-**nar**yoo"
diesel	o gasóleo	"ga**zol**yoo"
diet	a dieta	"dee-**etuh**"
different	diferente	"deefuh**rent**"

▷ I would like something different	gostaria de algo diferente	"gooshtuh-**ree**uh duh **al**goo deefuh**rent**"
difficult	difícil	"dee**fee**seel"
dinghy	o bote	"bot"
dining car	a carruagem-restaurante	"karroo-**ah**jayng rushtow-**rant**"
dining room	a sala de jantar	"**sah**luh duh jan**tar**"
dinner	o jantar	"jan**tar**"
direct (*train etc*)	directo directa	"dee**re**too" "dee**re**tuh"
directory	a lista telefónica	"**leesh**tuh tuhluh-**fon**ikuh"
directory enquiries:		
▷ what is the number for directory enquiries?	qual é o número para as informações?	"kwal **e** oo **noo**muhroo parah-zeenfoor-muh**soynsh**"
dirty	sujo suja	"**soo**joo" "**soo**juh"
▷ the washbasin is dirty	o lavatório está sujo	"oo lavuh**tor**yoo shta **soo**joo"
disabled	deficiente	"duhfees-**yent**"
▷ is there a toilet for the disabled?	há casa de banho para deficientes?	"a **kah**zuh duh **bahn**yoo paruh duhfees-**yentsh**"
▷ do you have facilities for the disabled?	têm instalações para deficientes?	"tayng eenshtaluh-**soynsh** paruh duhfees-**yentsh**"
▷ do you provide access for the disabled?	têm acessos para deficientes?	"tayng a**se**soosh paruh duhfees-**yentsh**"
disco	a discoteca	"deeshkoo**tek**uh"
discount	o desconto	"dush**kon**too"
▷ do you offer a discount for cash?	concedem desconto para pagamentos a dinheiro?	"kon**se**dayng dsh**kon**toosh paruh paguh-**men**toosh uh deen**yay**roo"

ABSOLUTE ESSENTIALS

do you have ...?	tem ...?	"tayng"
is there ...?	há ...?	"ah"
are there ...?	há ...?	"ah"
how much is ...?	quanto custa ...?	"**kwan**too **koosh**tuh"

▷ **are there discounts for students/children?**	há descontos para estudantes/crianças?	"a dsh**kon**toosh paruh shtoo**dantsh**/kree-**an**sush"
dish	o prato	"**prah**too"
▷ **how is this dish cooked?**	como é preparado este prato?	"**koh**moo e pruhpa**rah**doo aysht **prah**too"
▷ **how is this dish served?**	como é servido este prato?	"**koh**moo e ser**vee**doo aysht **prah**too"
▷ **what is in this dish?**	o que é que leva este prato?	"oo kee e kuh **lev**uh aysht **prah**too"
dishtowel	o pano da louça	"**pah**noo duh **loh**suh"
dishwasher	a máquina de lavar louça	"**mah**kinuh duh la**var loh**suh"
disinfectant	o desinfectante	"duzeem-fek**tant**"
distilled water	a água destilada	"**ahg**wuh dushtee**lah**duh"
to dive:		
▷ **where is the best place to dive?**	onde é o melhor sítio para mergulhar?	"ond **e** o muhlyor **see**tyoo paruh muhrgoo**lyar**"
diversion:		
▷ **is there a diversion?**	há um desvio?	"a oom dush**vee**oo"
diving:		
▷ **I'd like to go diving**	queria ir mergulhar	"**kree**uh **eer** muhrgoo**lyar**"
divorced	divorciado	"deevoor-see**ah**doo"
	divorciada	"deevoor-see**ah**duh"
dizzy	tonto	"**ton**too"
	tonta	"**ton**tuh"
▷ **I feel dizzy**	sinto-me tonto	"**seen**toomuh **ton**too"
to do	fazer	"fa**zehr**"

I do	faço	"**fah**soo"
you do (*informal singular*)	fazes	"**fah**zush"
(*formal singular*)	você faz	"voseh **fash**"
he/she/it does	ele/ela faz	"el/eluh **fash**"
we do	fazemos	"fuh**zeh**moos"
you do (*informal plural*)	fazeis	"fuh**zaysh**"
(*formal plural*)	vocês fazem	"vosehsh **fah**zayng"
they do	eles/elas fazem	"elsh/elush **fah**zayng"

dock	a doca	"**do**kuh"
doctor	o médico	"**med**ikoo"
▷ **can I make an appointment with the doctor?**	posso marcar uma consulta com o médico?	"**pos**oo mar**kar** oomuh kon**sool**tuh kong oo **med**ikoo"
▷ **I need a doctor**	preciso de um médico	"pre**see**zoo duh oom **med**ikoo"
▷ **call a doctor**	chame um médico	"**shahm** oom **med**ikoo"
documents	os documentos	"dookoo**men**toosh"
doll	a boneca	"boo**nek**uh"
dollar	o dólar	"**dol**ar"
door	a porta	"**por**tuh"
double	o dobro	"**doh**broo"
double bed	a cama de casal	"**kah**muh duh ka**zal**"
double room	o quarto de casal	"**kwar**too duh ka**zal**"
▷ **I want to reserve a double room**	quero reservar um quarto de casal	"**keh**roo ruhzer**var** oom **kwar**too duh ka**zal**"
doughnut	o donut	"**doh**noot"
down	para baixo	"**par**uh **by**shoo"
▷ **to go down**	descer	"dush**sehr**"

ABSOLUTE ESSENTIALS

I don't understand	não compreendo	"nowng kompree**en**doo"
I don't speak Portuguese	não falo português	"nowng **fah**loo poortoo**gaysh**"
do you speak English?	fala inglês?	"**fah**luh een**glesh**"
could you help me?	podia ajudar-me?	"poo**dee**uh ajoo**dar**muh"

downstairs	lá em baixo	"la ayng **by**shoo"
drain:		
▷ the drain is blocked	o cano está entupido	"oo **kah**noo shta entoo**pee**doo"
draught	a corrente de ar	"koo**rrent** dar"
▷ a draught beer, please	um fino, por favor	"oom **fee**noo poor fa**vor**"
dress¹ *n*	o vestido	"vush**tee**doo"
to dress² *vb*:		
▷ to get dressed	vestir-se	"vush**teer**suh"
dressing (*for food*)	o tempero	"tem**pay**roo"
drink¹ *n*	a bebida	"buh**bee**duh"
▷ would you like a drink?	quer uma bebida?	"kehr oomuh buh**bee**duh"
▷ a cold/hot drink	uma bebida fria/quente	"oomuh buh**bee**duh **free**uh/**kent**"
to drink² *vb*	beber	"buh**behr**"
▷ what would you like to drink?	o que quer beber?	"oo kuh ker buh**behr**"
drinking chocolate	o chocolate	"shookoo**lat**"
	o leite achocolatado	"lait uhshookoo-luh**ta**doo"
drinking water	a água potável	"**ahg**wuh poo**tah**vel"
to drive	conduzir	"kondoo**zeer**"
▷ he was driving too fast	ele conduzia demasiado depressa	"ayl kondoo-**zee**uh duhmuhzee-**ah**doo duh**pre**suh"
driver (*of car*)	o condutor	"kondoo**tor**"
driving licence	a carta de condução	"**kar**tuh duh kondoo-**sowng**"
▷ my driving licence number is ...	o número da minha carta de condução é ...	"oo **noo**meroo duh **meen**yuh **kar**tuh duh kondoo-**sowng** e"

▷ **I don't have my driving licence on me**	não tenho aqui a minha carta de condução	"nowng **teny**oo a**kee** uh **meen**yuh **kar**tuh duh kondoo-**sowng**"
to drown:		
▷ **someone is drowning!**	está uma pessoa a afogar-se!	"shta oomuh puh**soh**uh uh afoo-**gar**suh"
drunk	bêbedo(a)	"**bay**buhdoo(uh)"
dry[1] *adj*	seco(a)	"**say**koo(uh)"
to dry[2] *vb*	secar	"suh**kar**"
▷ **where can I dry my clothes?**	onde é que posso secar a roupa?	"**on**dee e kuh **pos**oo se**kar** uh **roh**puh"
dry-clean:		
▷ **I need this dry-cleaned**	preciso de mandar limpar isto a seco	"pre**see**zoo duh mandar **leem**par eeshtoo uh **say**koo"
dry-cleaner's	a limpeza a seco	"leem**pay**zuh uh **say**koo"
duck	o pato	"**pah**too"
due:		
▷ **when is the train due?**	a que horas chega o comboio?	"uh kuh **o**rush shguh oo kom**boy**oo"
dummy	a chupeta	"shoo**pet**uh"
during	durante	"doo**rant**"
duty-free	isento de direitos	"ee**zent**oo duh dee**ray**toosh"
duty-free shop	a loja franca	"**lo**juh **fran**kuh"
duvet	o edredão	"edruh**downg**"
dynamo	o dínamo	"**dee**namoo"
each	cada	"**kah**duh"
ear	a orelha	"oh**rel**yuh"
earache	as dores de ouvidos	"**dor**ush doh**vee**doosh"

ABSOLUTE ESSENTIALS

do you have ...?	tem ...?	"tayng"
is there ...?	há ...?	"ah"
are there ...?	há ...?	"ah"
how much is ...?	quanto custa ...?	"**kwan**too **koosh**tuh"

earlier	mais cedo	"mysh **say**doo"
▷ **I would prefer an earlier flight**	preferia um voo mais cedo	"pruhfuh-**ree**uh oom **vo**ho mysh **say**doo"
early	cedo	"**say**doo"
earrings	os brincos	"**breen**koosh"
east	o leste	"lesht"
Easter	a Páscoa	"**pashk**wuh"
easy	fácil	"**fah**seel"
to eat	comer	"koo**mehr**"
▷ **I don't eat meat**	(eu) não como carne	"(ayoo) nowng **koh**moo **karn**"
▷ **would you like something to eat?**	quer comer alguma coisa?	"ker koo**mehr** al**goo**muh **koy**zuh"
▷ **have you eaten?**	já comeu?	"ja koo**may**oo"
EC	a CE	"sehe"
egg	o ovo	"**oh**voo"
▷ **fried egg**	ovo estrelado	"**oh**voo shtre**lah**doo"
▷ **hard-boiled egg**	ovo cozido	"**oh**voo coo**zee**doo"
▷ **scrambled eggs**	ovos mexidos	"**oh**voos me**shi**doosh"
eight	oito	"**oy**too"
eighteen	dezoito	"du**zoy**too"
eighty	oitenta	"oy**ten**tuh"
either:		
▷ **either one**	um ou outro	"oom oh **oh**troo"
elastic	elástico	"ee**lash**tikoo"
	elástica	"ee**lash**tikuh"
elastic band	o elástico	"ee**lash**tikoo"
electric	eléctrico	"ee**le**trikoo"
	eléctrica	"ee**le**trikuh"

electrician	o electricista	"eletree-**seesh**tuh"
electricity	a electricidade	"eeletree-see**dahd**"
▷ is the cost of electricity included in the rental?	a despesa de electricidade está incluída na renda?	"uh dsh**pay**-zuh duh eeletree-see**dahd** shta eenklw**ee**duh nuh **ren**duh"
electricity meter	o contador de electricidade	"kontuh**dor** deeletree-see**dahd**"
electric razor	a máquina de barbear	"**mak**inuh duh barb**yar**"
eleven	onze	"onz"
to **embark**:		
▷ when do we embark?	quando embarcamos?	"**kwan**doo aynbuhr-**kah**moosh"
embassy	a embaixada	"aymby-**shah**duh"
emergency	a emergência	"eemer-**jens**yuh"
empty	vazio	"va**zee**oo"
	vazia	"va**zee**uh"
end	o fim	"feeng"
engaged (to be married)	noivo	"**noy**voo"
	noiva	"**noy**vuh"
(phone, toilet)	ocupado	"ohkoo**pah**doo"
	ocupada	"ohkoo**pah**duh"
▷ the line's engaged	está impedido	"shta eempuh**dee**doo"
engine	o motor	"moo**tor**"
England	a Inglaterra	"eengluh**terr**uh"
English	inglês	"een**glesh**"
	inglesa	"een**glez**uh"
▷ do you speak English?	fala inglês?	"**fah**luh een**glesh**"
▷ I'm English	sou inglês/inglesa	"soh een**glesh**/ een**glez**uh"

ABSOLUTE ESSENTIALS

I don't understand	não compreendo	"nowng kompree**en**doo"
I don't speak Portuguese	não falo português	"nowng **fah**loo poortoo**gaysh**"
do you speak English?	fala inglês?	"**fah**luh een**glesh**"
could you help me?	podia ajudar-me?	"poo**dee**uh ajoo**dar**muh"

▷ **do you have any English books/ newpapers?** — tem alguns livros/jornais ingleses? — "tayng al**goom**sh lee**vroosh**/joor**nysh** een**glay**zesh"

to enjoy:

▷ **to enjoy oneself** — divertir-se — "deever**teer**suh"

▷ **I enjoyed the tour** — gostei da viagem — "goos**tay** duh veeah-jayng"

▷ **I enjoy swimming** — gosto de nadar — "**gosh**too duh na**dar**"

▷ **enjoy your meal** — bom apetite! — "bong apuh**teet**"

enough — bastante — "bash**tant**"

enquiry desk — as informações — "eenfoormuh-**soynsh**"

entertainment — a diversão — "deever**sowng**"

▷ **what entertainment is there?** — que diversões há? — "kuh deevuhr**soynz** a"

entrance — a entrada — "ayn**trah**duh"

entrance fee — o bilhete de entrada — "beel**yet** dayn**trah**duh"

entry visa — o visto de entrada — "**veesh**too dayn**trah**duh"

▷ **I have an entry visa** — tenho um visto de entrada — "**ten**yoo oom **veesh**too dayn**trah**duh"

envelope — o envelope — "aymvuh**lop**"

epileptic — epiléptico(a) — "epee-**lep**tikoo(uh)"

equipment — o equipamento — "eekeepuh-**men**too"

▷ **can we rent the equipment?** — podemos alugar o equipamento? — "poo**day**mooz aloo**gar** oo eekeepuh-**men**too"

escalator — a escada rolante — "**shkah**duh roo**lant**"

especially — especialmente — "shpusyal**ment**"

essential — essencial — "eesen**syal**"

Eurocheque — o Eurocheque — "ayooroo-**shek**"

▷ **do you take Eurocheques?** — aceita Eurocheques? — "a**say**tuh ayooroo-**sheksh**"

ABSOLUTE ESSENTIALS		
I would like ...	queria ...	"**kree**uh"
I need ...	preciso de ...	"pre**see**zoo duh"
where is ...?	onde fica ...?	"ond **fee**kuh"
I'm looking for ...	procuro ...	"pro**koo**roo"

Europe	a Europa	"ayoo-**rop**uh"
European	europeu	"ayooroo-**pay**oo"
	europeia	"ayooroo-**pay**uh"
European Community	a Comunidade Européia	"koomoonee-**dahd** ayooroo-**pay**uh"
European Union	União Européia	"ooneeowng ayooroo-**pay**uh"
evening	a noite	"noyt"
▷ **in the evening**	à noite	"a noyt"
▷ **what is there to do in the evenings?**	o que há para fazer à noite?	"oo kee a **par**uh fa**zehr** a noyt"
▷ **what are you doing this evening?**	o que faz esta noite?	"oo kuh **fash esh**tuh noyt"
evening meal	o jantar	"jan**tar**"
every	cada	"**kah**duh"
everyone	toda a gente	"**toh**duh uh jent"
everything	todas as coisas	"**toh**duz ush **koy**zush"
	tudo	"**too**doo"
excellent	excelente	"eeshsuh**lent**"
▷ **the meal was excellent**	a refeição estava excelente	"uh ruhfay-**sowng** sh**tah**vuh ayshsuh-**lent**"
except	excepto	"eesh**set**oo"
excess luggage	o excesso de bagagem	"eesh**ses**oo duh ba**gah**-jayng"
exchange[1] *n*	a troca	"**trok**uh"
	o câmbio	"**kamb**yoo"
to exchange[2] *vb*	trocar	"troo**kar**"
	cambiar	"kambee**ar**"
▷ **could I exchange this please?**	posso trocar isto, por favor?	"**pos**oo troo**kar eesh**too poor fa**vor**"
exchange rate	a taxa de câmbio	"**ta**shuh duh **kamb**yoo"

ABSOLUTE ESSENTIALS

do you have ...?	tem ...?	"tayng"
is there ...?	há ...?	"ah"
are there ...?	há ...?	"ah"
how much is ...?	quanto custa ...?	"**kwant**oo **koosh**tuh"

▷ **what is the exchange rate?**	qual é a taxa de câmbio?	"kwal e uh **ta**shuh duh **kamb**yo"
excursion	a excursão	"shkoor**sowng**"
▷ **what excursions are there?**	que excursões há?	"kuh ayshkoor-**soynz** a"
to excuse:		
▷ **excuse me!** (*sorry!*)	desculpe!	"dush**koolp**"
(*when passing*)	com licença	"kong lee**sen**suh"
exhaust pipe	o tubo de escape	"**too**boo dush**kap**"
exhibition	a exposição	"shpoozee-**sowng**"
exit	a saída	"su**hee**duh"
▷ **where is the exit?**	onde é a saída?	"ond e uh su**hee**duh"
▷ **which exit for ...?**	qual é a saída para ...?	"**kwal** e a su**hee**duh **paruh**"
expensive	caro	"**kah**roo"
	cara	"**kah**ruh"
▷ **I want something more expensive**	quero uma coisa mais cara	"**keh**roo **oom**uh **koy**zuh mysh **kah**ruh"
▷ **it's too expensive**	é demasiado caro(a)	"e duhmuhzee-**ah**doo **kar**oo(uh)"
expert	o perito	"pe**ree**too"
	a perita	"pe**ree**tuh"
to expire (*ticket, passport*)	expirar	"shpee**rar**"
express[1] *n* (*train*)	o rápido	"**ra**pidoo"
express[2] *adj* (*parcel etc*)	expresso	"eesh-**pres**oo"
	expressa	"eesh-**pres**uh"
extra (*spare*)	sobresselente	"sobruh-se**lent**"
(*more*)	mais	"mysh"
eye	o olho	"**ohl**yoo"
▷ **I have something in my eye**	tenho alguma coisa no olho	"**ten**yoo al**goo**muh **koy**zuh noo **ohl**yoo"

eyeliner	o eyeliner	"eyeliner"
eye shadow	a sombra	"**som**bruh"
face	a cara	"**kah**ruh"
face cream	o creme da cara	"krem duh **kah**ruh"
facilities	as instalações	"een-shtaluh-**soynsh**"
▷ **do you have any facilities for the disabled?**	têm instalações para deficientes?	"tayng een-shtaluh-**soynsh** paruh duhfees-**yent**sh"
▷ **what facilities do you have here?**	que instalações têm aqui?	"kuh een-shtaluh-**soynsh** tayng a**kee**"
▷ **do you have facilities for children?**	têm instalações para crianças?	"tayng een-shtaluh-**soynsh** paruh kree-**an**sush"
▷ **are there facilities for mothers with babies?**	há instalações para mães com bebés?	"a een-shtaluh-**soynsh** paruh mynsh kong be**besh**"
▷ **what sports facilities are there?**	que instalações desportivas há?	"kuh een-shtaluh-**soynsh** dshpoor-**tee**vuz a"
factor:		
▷ **factor 8/15 suntan lotion**	bronzeador de factor 8/15	"bronzeeu**dor** duh fah**tor** oytoo/**keenz**"
factory	a fábrica	"**fa**breeka"
▷ **I work in a factory**	trabalho numa fábrica	"tra**bal**yoo **noo**muh **fa**breeka"
to faint	desmaiar	"duj**myar**"
▷ **she has fainted**	ela desmaiou	"eluh **duj**mayoh"
fair (*fun fair*)	a feira	"**fay**ruh"
to fall	cair	"ca**eer**"
family	a família	"fa**meel**-yuh"
famous	famoso	"fa**moh**zoo"
	famosa	"fa**moh**zuh"
fan (*electric*)	a ventoinha	"ventoo-**een**yuh"

ABSOLUTE ESSENTIALS

I don't understand	não compreendo	"nowng kompree**een**doo"
I don't speak Portuguese	não falo português	"nowng **fah**loo poortoo**gaysh**"
do you speak English?	fala inglês?	"**fah**luh een**glesh**"
could you help me?	podia ajudar-me?	"poo**dee**uh ajoo**dar**muh"

fan belt	a correia da ventoinha	"koo-**rray**uh duh ventoo-**een**yuh"
far	longe	"lonj"
▷ is it far?	é longe?	"e lonj"
▷ how far is it to ...?	a que distância fica ...?	"uh kuh deesh**tan**-syuh **fee**kuh"
fare	o bilhete	"bee**lyet**"
▷ what is the fare to the town centre?	quanto custa o bilhete para o centro da cidade?	"**kwan**too **koosh**tuh oo bee**lyet** pro **sen**troo duh see**dahd**"
farm	a quinta	"**keen**tuh"
farmhouse	a casa de quinta	"**kah**zuh duh **keen**tuh"
fast	rápido	"**rap**idoo"
	rápida	"**rap**iduh"
▷ he was driving too fast	ele conduzia demasiado depressa	"ayl kondoo-**zee**uh duhmuhzee-**ah**doo duh**pre**suh"
fast food	a fast food	"fast food"
fat	gordo	"**gor**doo"
	gorda	"**gor**duh"
father	o pai	"py"
fault (*defect*)	o defeito	"duh**fay**too"
▷ it's not my fault	a culpa não é minha	"uh **kool**puh nowng e **meen**yuh"
favourite	favorito	"favoo**ree**too"
	favorita	"favoo**ree**tuh"
▷ what's your favourite drink?	qual é a sua bebida favorita?	"kwal e uh **soo**uh buh**bee**duh favoo**ree**tuh"
fax	o fax	"fax"
▷ can I send a fax from here?	posso enviar um fax daqui?	"**pos**oo ayn-vee**ar** oom fax duh**kee**"

▷ **what is the fax number?**	qual é o número de fax?	"kwal **e** oo **noo**muhroo duh fax"
February	Fevereiro	"fuhvuh-**ray**roo"
to feed	alimentar	"aleemen**tar**"
▷ **where can I feed the baby?**	onde é que posso dar de comer ao bebé?	"**on**dee e kuh **pos**oo dar duh koo**mehr** ow be**be**"
to feel	apalpar	"apal**par**"
	sentir-se	"sen**teer**suh"
▷ **I don't feel well**	não me sinto bem	"nowng muh **seen**too bayng"
▷ **I feel sick**	tenho náuseas	"**ten**yoo **nowz**-yush"
ferry	o ferry-boat	"ferryboat"
festival	o festival	"fushtee**val**"
to fetch (*bring*)	trazer	"tra**zehr**"
(*go and get it*)	ir buscar	"eer boosh**kar**"
fever	a febre	"**feb**ruh"
▷ **he has a fever**	ele tem febre	"**ayl** tayng **feb**ruh"
few	poucos	"**poh**koosh"
	poucas	"**poh**kush"
▷ **a few**	alguns	"al**goonsh**"
	algumas	"al**goo**mush"
fiancé(e)	o noivo	"**noy**voo"
	a noiva	"**noy**vuh"
field	o campo	"**kam**poo"
fifteen	quinze	"keenz"
fifty	cinquenta	"seen**kwen**tuh"
to fill	encher	"en**shehr**"
to fill up (*container*)	encher	"en**shehr**"
▷ **fill it up, please**	encha o depósito, por favor	"**en**shuh oo duh**pozi**too poor fa**vor**"

ABSOLUTE ESSENTIALS

do you have ...?	tem ...?	"tayng"
is there ...?	há ...?	"ah"
are there ...?	há ...?	"ah"
how much is ...?	quanto custa ...?	"kwantoo **koosh**tuh"

fillet	o filete	"fee**let**"
filling:		
▷ **a filling has come out**	caíu-me um chumbo	"ka**yoo**muh oom **shoom**boo"
▷ **could you do a temporary filling?**	podia pôr-me massa no dente?	"poo**dee**uh **pohr**muh **mah**suh noo dent"
film	o filme	"feelm"
(*photography*)	o rolo	"**roh**loo"
▷ **can you develop this film?**	pode-me revelar este rolo?	"**pod**muh ruhvuh**lar** aysht **roh**loo"
▷ **the film has jammed**	o rolo está preso	"oo **roh**loo shta **pray**zoo"
▷ **I need a colour/black and white film**	preciso de um rolo de fotografias a cores/a preto e branco	"pre**see**zoo doom **roh**loo duh footoogruh-**fee**ush uh **ko**rush/uh **pray**too ee **bran**koo"
▷ **which film is on at the cinema?**	que filme está no cinema?	"kuh feelm shta noo see**nay**muh"
▷ **am I allowed to film here?**	é permitido filmar aqui?	"e puhrmee-**tee**doo feel**mar** a**kee**"
filter	o filtro	"**feel**troo"
filter coffee	o café de saco	"kuh**fe** duh **sah**koo"
filter-tipped	com filtro	"kong **feel**troo"
fine[1] *n*	a multa	"**mool**tuh"
▷ **how much is the fine?**	de quanto é a multa?	"duh **kwan**too e uh **mool**tuh"
fine[2] *adj*:		
▷ **is it going to be fine?** (*weather*)	vai estar bom tempo?	"vy shtar bong **tem**poo"
to finish	acabar	"akuh**bar**"
▷ **when does the show finish?**	quando acaba o espectáculo?	"kwand a**kah**buh oo shpe**tah**-kooloo"
▷ **when will you have finished?**	quando é que você vai acabar?	"kwand e kuh vo**seh** vy akuh**bar**"

fire	o fogo	"**foh**goo"
fire brigade	os bombeiros	"bom**bay**roosh"
fire extinguisher	o extintor	"shteen**tor**"
firework display	o espectáculo de fogo de artifício	"shpe**tah**-kooloo duh **foh**goo duh artee-**fees**yoo"
fireworks	o fogo de artifício	"**foh**goo dartee-**fees**yoo"
first	o primeiro	"pree**may**roo"
	a primeira	"pree**may**ruh"
first aid	os primeiros-socorros	"pree**may**roosh soo**korr**oosh"
first class	de primeira classe	"duh pree**may**ruh klass"
▷ **a first class return to ...**	um bilhete de ida e volta em primeira classe para ...	"oom bee**lyet** duh **ee**duh ee **vol**tuh ayng pree**may**ruh klass **pa**ruh"
first floor	o primeiro andar	"pree**may**ruh an**dar**"
first name	o nome próprio	"nom **prop**reeoo"
fish[1] *n*	o peixe	"paysh"
to **fish**[2] *vb*	pescar	"push**kar**"
▷ **can we fish here?**	podemos pescar aqui?	"poo**day**moosh push**kar** a**kee**"
▷ **can we go fishing?**	podemos ir à pesca?	"poo**day**moosh eer a **pesh**kuh"
▷ **where can I go fishing?**	onde é que posso ir à pesca?	"**ond** e kuh **pos**oo eer a **pesh**kuh"
fishing rod	a cana de pesca	"**kah**nuh duh **pesh**kuh"
fit[1] *n (medical)*	o ataque	"a**tak**"
fit[2] *adj*:		
▷ **to be fit** *(healthy)*	estar em forma	"sh**tar** ayng **for**muh"

ABSOLUTE ESSENTIALS

I don't understand	não compreendo	"nowng kompree**en**doo"
I don't speak Portuguese	não falo português	"nowng **fah**loo poortoo**gaysh**"
do you speak English?	fala inglês?	"**fah**luh een**glesh**"
could you help me?	podia ajudar-me?	"poo**dee**uh ajoo**dar**muh"

to fit³ *vb*:

▷ it doesn't fit me	não me serve	"nowng muh **serv**"
five	cinco	"**seen**koo"
to fix	reparar	"ruhpa**rar**"
▷ where can I get this fixed?	onde posso mandar reparar isto?	"ond poss man**dar** repuh**rar** **eesh**too"
fizzy	gasoso	"ga**zoh**zoo"
	gasosa	"ga**zoh**zuh"
▷ a fizzy drink	uma bebida com gás	"oomuh buh**bee**duh kong **gash**"
flash	o flash	"flash"
▷ the flash is not working	o flash não funciona	"oo flash nowng foonsee-**o**nuh"
flask	a garrafa de termus	"ga**rrah**fuh duh **ter**moosh"
▷ a flask of coffee	uma garrafa de termus com café	"oomuh ga**rrah**fuh duh **ter**moosh kong kuh**fe**"
flat (*apartment*)	o apartamento	"apartuh-**men**too"
flat tyre	o furo	"**foo**roo"
flavour	o sabor	"sa**bor**"
▷ what flavours do you have?	que sabores tem?	"kuh sa**bor**ush **tayng**"
flight	o voo	"**voh**oo"
▷ I've missed my flight	perdi o avião	"per**dee** oo avee**owng**"
▷ my flight has been delayed	o meu avião atrasou-se	"oo **me**oo avee**owng** atra**zoh**suh"
▷ are there any cheap flights?	há alguns voos baratos?	"a al**goomsh voh**oosh ba**rah**toosh"
flint	a pedra de isqueiro	"**pe**druh duh eesh-**kay**roo"
flippers	as barbatanas	"barbuh-**tah**nush"

ABSOLUTE ESSENTIALS		
I would like ...	queria ...	"**kree**uh"
I need ...	preciso de ...	"pre**see**zoo duh"
where is ...?	onde fica ...?	"ond **fee**kuh"
I'm looking for ...	procuro ...	"pro**koo**roo"

flooded:

▷ **the bathroom is flooded** — a casa de banho está inundada — "uh **kah**zuh duh **bah**nyoo shta eenoon**dah**duh"

floor (*of building*) — o andar — "an**dar**"
(*of room*) — o chão — "**showng**"

▷ **what floor is it on?** — em que andar é? — "**ayng** kuh an**dar** e"

▷ **on the top floor** — no último andar — "noo **ool**teemoo an**dar**"

flour — a farinha — "fuh**reen**yuh"

▷ **plain flour** — farinha de trigo — "fuh**reen**yuh duh **tree**goo"

▷ **self-raising flour** — farinha com fermento — "fuh**reen**yuh kong fuh**rmen**too"

▷ **wholemeal flour** — farinha integral — "fuh**reen**yuh **een**tuhgral"

flower — a flor — "flor"

▷ **a bunch/bouquet of flowers** — um ramo de flores — "oom **rah**moo duh **flor**ush"

flu — a gripe — "greep"

▷ **I've got flu** — tenho gripe — "**ten**yoo **greep**"

to flush:

▷ **the toilet won't flush** — o autoclismo não trabalha — "oo owtoo-**kleej**moo nowng tra**bal**yuh"

fly (*insect*) — a mosca — "**mosh**kuh"

flying:

▷ **I hate flying** — detesto andar de avião — "duh**tesh**too an**dar** duh avee**owng**"

fly sheet — o tecto duplo — "**tet**oo **doo**ploo"

foggy — enevoado(a) — "eenuh-**vwah**doo(uh)"

▷ **it's foggy** — está nevoeiro — "shta nuhvoo-**ayroo**"

to follow — seguir — "suh**geer**"

▷ **follow me!** — venha comigo! — "**vay**nyuh koo**mee**goo"

food — a comida — "koo**mee**duh"

> *ABSOLUTE ESSENTIALS*
>
> | do you have ...? | tem ...? | "tayng" |
> | is there ...? | há ...? | "ah" |
> | are there ...? | há ...? | "ah" |
> | how much is ...? | quanto custa ...? | "**kwan**too **koosh**tuh" |

▷ **where is the food department?**	onde fica a secção de comidas?	"**on**duh **fee**kuh uh sek**sowng** duh koo**mee**dush"
food poisoning	a intoxicação alimentar	"eentoxee-ka**sowng** aleemen**tar**"
foot	o pé	"pe"
(*measure: metric equiv = 0.30 m*)	o pé	"pe"
football (*game*)	o jogo de futebol	"**joh**goo duh foot**bol**"
(*ball*)	a bola de futebol	"**bol**uh duh foot**bol**"
▷ **let's play football**	vamos jogar futebol	"**vah**moosh joo**gar** foot**bol**"
for (*in exchange for*)	por	"poor"
foreign	estrangeiro	"shtran-**jay**roo"
	estrangeira	"shtran-**jay**ruh"
forest	a floresta	"floo**resh**tuh"
to **forget**	esquecer-se de	"shkuh-**sehr**suh duh"
▷ **I've forgotten my passport/the key**	esqueci-me do meu passaporte/da chave	"shke**see**-muh doo mayoo pahsuh**port**/duh **shahv**"
fork	o garfo	"**gar**foo"
(*in road*)	a bifurcação	"beefoor-kuh**sowng**"
fortnight	a quinzena	"keen**zen**uh"
forty	quarenta	"kwuh**ren**tuh"
fountain	a fonte	"font"
four	quatro	"**kwat**roo"
fourteen	catorze	"ka**tohrz**"
France	a França	"**fran**suh"
free (*not occupied*)	livre	"**leev**ruh"
▷ **I am free tomorrow morning/for lunch**	amanhã estou livre de manhã/à hora do almoço	"ahman**yang** shtoh **leev**ruh duh man**yang**/a **or**uh doo al**moh**soo"

▷ is this seat free?	este lugar está vago?	"aysht loo**gar** shta **vah**goo"
freezer	o congelador	"konjuh-luh**dor**"
French	francês	"fran**sesh**"
	francesa	"fran**say**zuh"
French beans	o feijão-verde	"fayjowng-**vehrd**"
frequent	frequente	"fruh**kwent**"
▷ how frequent are the buses?	com que frequência é que há autocarros?	"kong kuh fruh-**kwayn**syuh e kuh **a** owto**karr**oosh"
fresh	fresco	"**fresh**koo"
	fresca	"**fresh**kuh"
▷ are the vegetables fresh or frozen?	os legumes são frescos ou congelados?	"oosh luh**goo**mush sowng **fresh**koosh oh konjuh-**lah**doosh"
fresh air	o ar fresco	"ar **fresh**koo"
fresh vegetables	os legumes frescos	"luh**goo**mush **fresh**koosh"
Friday	sexta-feira	"**saish**tuh-fairuh"
fridge	o frigorífico	"freegoo-**ree**fikoo"
fried	frito	"**free**too"
	frita	"**free**tuh"
friend	o amigo	"a**mee**goo"
	a amiga	"a**mee**guh"
from	de	"duh"
▷ I want to stay three nights/from ... till ...	quero ficar três noites/ do dia ... ao dia ...	"**keh**roo fee**kar** traysh noytsh/doo **dee**uh ... ow **dee**uh"
front	a frente	"frent"
frozen (*food*)	congelado	"konjuh-**lah**doo"
	congelada	"konjuh-**lah**duh"

ABSOLUTE ESSENTIALS

I don't understand	não compreendo	"nowng kompree**en**doo"
I don't speak Portuguese	não falo português	"nowng **fah**loo poortoo**gaysh**"
do you speak English?	fala inglês?	"**fah**luh een**glesh**"
could you help me?	podia ajudar-me?	"poo**dee**uh ajoo**dar**muh"

fruit	a fruta	"**froo**tuh"
fruit juice	o sumo de frutas	"**soo**moo duh **froo**tush"
fruit salad	a salada de frutas	"sa**lah**duh duh **froo**tush"
frying pan	a frigideira	"freejee-**day**ruh"
fuel	o combustível	"komboosh-**tee**vel"
fuel pump	a bomba de gasolina	"**bom**buh duh gazoo**lee**nuh"
full	cheio	"**shay**oo"
	cheia	"**shay**uh"
▷ **I'm full (up)**	estou cheio(a)	"sh**toh shay**oo(uh)"
full board	a pensão completa	"pen**sowng** kom**ple**tuh"
full fat milk	o leite gordo	"layt **gor**doo"
funny (*amusing*)	engraçado	"aym-gra**sah**doo"
	engraçada	"aym-gra**sah**duh"
(*strange*)	estranho	"**shtrahn**-yoo"
	estranha	"**shtrahn**-yuh"
fur	a pele	"pel"
fuse	o fusível	"foo**zee**vel"
▷ **a fuse has blown**	queimou-se um fusível	"kay**moh**suh oom foo**zee**vel"
▷ **can you mend a fuse?**	sabe arranjar fusíveis?	"**sahb** arran**jar** foo**see**vaysh"
gallery	o museu	"moo**zay**oo"
gallon (*metric equiv = 9.09 l*)	o galão	"guh**lowng**"
gambling	o jogo	"**joh**goo"
game	o jogo	"**joh**goo"
▷ **a game of chess**	um jogo de xadrez	"oom **joh**goo duh sha**draysh**"

ABSOLUTE ESSENTIALS

I would like ...	queria ...	"**kree**uh"
I need ...	preciso de ...	"pre**see**zoo duh"
where is ...?	onde fica ...?	"ond **fee**kuh"
I'm looking for ...	procuro ...	"pro**koo**roo"

gammon	o gamão	"gamowng"
garage	a garagem	"garah-jayng"
▷ can you tow me to a garage?	pode rebocar-me para uma garagem?	"pod ruhbookar-muh paruh oomuh garah-jayng"
garden	o jardim	"jardeeng"
▷ can we visit the gardens?	podemos visitar os jardins?	"poodehmoosh veezeetar oosh jardeengs"
garlic	o alho	"alyoo"
▷ is there any garlic in it?	contém alho?	"kontayng alyoo"
gas	o gás	"gash"
▷ I can smell gas	cheira a gás aqui	"shayruh uh gash akee"
gas cylinder	a botija de gás	"booteejuh duh gash"
gear	a velocidade	"vuhloo-seedahd"
▷ first/third gear	primeira/segunda velocidade	"preemayruh/ suhgoonduh vuhloo-seedahd"
gentleman	o cavalheiro	"kavalyayroo"
gents'	Homens	"omaynsh"
▷ where is the gents?	onde é a casa de banho dos homens?	"onduh shta uh kahzuh duh bahnyoo dooz omaynsh"
genuine (leather, silver)	genuíno genuína	"junweenoo" "junweenuh"
(antique, picture)	autêntico autêntica	"owtentikoo" "owtentikuh"
German	alemão alemã	"aluhmowng" "aluhmang"
German measles	a rubéola	"roobay-ooluh"
Germany	a Alemanha	"aluh-mahnyuh"

ABSOLUTE ESSENTIALS

do you have ...?	tem ...?	"tayng"
is there ...?	há ...?	"ah"
are there ...?	há ...?	"ah"
how much is ...?	quanto custa ...?	"kwantoo kooshtuh"

to get (*obtain*)	obter	"ob**tehr**"
(*receive*)	receber	"ruhsuh**behr**"
(*fetch*)	ir buscar	"eer boos**kar**"
▷ **please tell me when we get to ...**	por favor diga-me quando chegarmos a ...	"poor favor **dee**guhmuh kwandoo shuh**gar**moosh uh"
▷ **I must get there by 8 o'clock**	tenho de chegar lá até às 8 horas	"**ten**yoo duh shuh**gar** lah ate ash **oy**too orush"
▷ **please get me a taxi**	arranje-me um táxi, por favor	"**arran**-juhmuh oom **ta**xi poor fa**vor**"
▷ **when do we get back?**	quando é que voltamos?	"**kwan**doo e kuh vol**tah**moosh"
to get into (*vehicle*)	entrar em	"ayn**trar** ayng"
to get off (*bus etc*)	descer de	"dush**sehr** duh"
▷ **where do I get off?**	onde é que desço?	"**on**dee e kuh **desh**soo"
▷ **will you tell me where to get off?**	por favor, diz-me onde descer?	"poor favor **deesh**muh ond desh**sehr**"
gift	o presente	"pruh**zent**"
gift shop	a loja de lembranças	"**lo**juh duh laym**brayn**-sush"
giftwrap:		
▷ **please giftwrap it**	podia embrulhar, por favor?	"poo**dee**uh aymbrool**yar** poor fa**vor**"
gin	o gin	"jeen"
▷ **I'll have a gin and tonic**	quero um gin tónico	"**keh**roo oom jeen **ton**ikoo"
ginger	o gengibre	"jen**jeeb**ruh"
girl	a rapariga	"ruhpuh**ree**guh"
girlfriend	a namorada	"namoo**rah**duh"
to give	dar	"dar"
to give back	devolver	"duhvol**vehr**"
to give way	dar prioridade	"dar preeo-ree**dahd**"

▷ he did not give way	ele não deu prioridade	"ayl nowng **day**oo preeo-ree**dahd**"
glass (*for drinking*)	o copo	"**kop**oo"
(*substance*)	o vidro	"**vee**droo"
▷ a glass of lemonade	uma limonada	"**oom**uh leemoo**nah**duh"
▷ broken glass	o vidro partido	"**vee**droo per**tee**doo"
glasses	os óculos	"**ok**ooloosh"
▷ can you repair my glasses?	podia consertar-me os óculos?	"poo**dee**uh konsuhr-**tar**muh oo**zok**ooloosh"
gloves	as luvas	"**loo**vush"
glucose	a glucose	"gloo**koz**"
glue	a cola	"**kol**uh"
gluten	o glúten	"**gloo**ten"
to go	ir	"eer"

I go	vou	"vo"
you go (*informal singular*)	vais	"vysh"
(*formal singular*)	você vai	"vo**seh vy**"
he/she/it goes	ele/ela vai	"el/eluh **vy**"
we go	vamos	"**vah**moosh"
you go (*informal plural*)	ides	"**ee**dush"
(*formal plural*)	vocês vão	"vo**sehsh vowng**"
they go	eles/elas vão	"elsh/elush **vowng**"

▷ **I'm going to the beach**	vou para a praia	"**voh** paruh uh **pry**uh"
▷ **you go on ahead**	vá indo à frente	"va **een**doo a **fren**tuh"
to go back	voltar	"**vol**tar"
▷ **I must go back now**	tenho de voltar agora	"**ten**yoo duh voltar a**go**ruh"
to go down (*downstairs etc*)	descer	"dush**sehr**"

ABSOLUTE ESSENTIALS

i don't understand	não compreendo	"nowng kompree**een**doo"
I don't speak Portuguese	não falo português	"nowng **fah**loo poortoo**gaysh**"
do you speak English?	fala inglês?	"**fah**luh een**glesh**"
could you help me?	podia ajudar-me?	"poo**dee**uh ajoo**dar**muh"

to **go in**	entrar	"aym**trar**"
to **go out** (*leave*)	sair	"sa**eer**"
goggles	os óculos de protecção	"**o**kooloosh duh proote**sowng**"
gold	o ouro	"**oh**roo"
gold-plated	dourado	"doh**rah**doo"
	dourada	"doh**rah**duh"
golf	o golfe	"golf"
▷ **where can we play golf?**	onde podemos jogar golfe?	"**on**duh poo**day**moosh joo**gar** golf"
golf ball	a bola de golfe	"**bol**uh duh golf"
golf club (*stick*)	o pau de golfe	"pow duh golf"
(*association*)	o clube de golfe	"kloob duh golf"
golf course	o campo de golfe	"**kam**poo duh golf"
▷ **is there a public golf course near here?**	há um campo de golfe público perto daqui?	"a oom **kam**poo duh golf **poo**blikoo **per**too duh**kee**"
good	bom	"bong"
	boa	"**boh**uh"
good afternoon	boa tarde	"**boh**uh tard"
goodbye	adeus	"a**day**oosh"
good evening	boa noite	"**boh**uh noyt"
Good Friday	a Sexta-Feira Santa	"**say**shtuh fayruh **san**tuh"
good-looking	bonito	"boo**nee**too"
	bonita	"boo**nee**tuh"
good morning	bom dia	"bong **dee**uh"
good night	boa noite	"**boh**uh noyt"
goose	o ganso	"**gan**soo"
gram	a grama	"**grah**muh"

ABSOLUTE ESSENTIALS

I would like ...	queria ...	"**kree**uh"
I need ...	preciso de ...	"pre**see**zoo duh"
where is ...?	onde fica ...?	"ond **fee**kuh"
I'm looking for ...	procuro ...	"pro**koo**roo"

▷ **500 grams of minced meat**	500 gramas de carne picada	"keen-**yen**toosh **grah**mush duh **karn** peekahduh"
grandfather	o avô	"a**voh**"
grandmother	a avó	"a**vo**"
grapefruit	a toranja	"too**ran**juh"
grapefruit juice	o sumo de toranja	"**soo**moo duh too**ran**juh"
grapes	as uvas	"**oov**ush"
▷ **a bunch of grapes**	um cacho de uvas	"oom **kah**shoo duh **oov**ush"
▷ **seedless grapes**	uvas sem semente	"**oov**ush sayng suh**ment**"
grass	a erva	"**ehr**vuh"
gravy	o molho	"**mohl**yoo"
greasy	oleoso	"ol**yoh**zoo"
	oleosa	"ol**yoh**zuh"
▷ **the food is very greasy**	a comida tem muita gordura	"uh koo**mee**duh tayng **mween**tuh goor**doo**ruh"
▷ **shampoo for greasy hair**	o champô para cabelos oleosos	"oo sham**poh** paruh ka**bay**loosh olee-o**zoosh**"
Greece	a Grécia	"**gres**-yuh"
Greek	grego	"**gray**goo"
	grega	"**gray**guh"
green	verde	"**vehrd**"
green card	a carta verde	"**kar**tuh vehrd"
green pepper	a pimenta verde	"pee**men**tuh vehrd"
grey	cinzento	"seen**zen**too"
	cinzenta	"seen**zen**tuh"
grilled	grelhado	"grel**yah**doo"
	grelhada	"grel**yah**duh"

ABSOLUTE ESSENTIALS

do you have ...?	tem ...?	"tayng"
is there ...?	há ...?	"ah"
are there ...?	há ...?	"ah"
how much is ...?	quanto custa ...?	"**kwan**too **koosh**tuh"

grocer's	a mercearia	"mersee-uh**ree**uh"
ground	a terra	"**terr**uh"
ground floor	o rés-do-chão	"resh-doo-**showng**"
▷ could I have a room on the ground floor?	podia dar-me um quarto no rés-do-chão?	"poo**dee**uh **dar**muh oom **kwar**too noo resh-doo-**showng**"
groundsheet	o pano de chão de tenda	"**pah**noo duh showng duh **ten**duh"
group	o grupo	"**groo**poo"
▷ do you give discounts for groups?	concedem descontos a grupos?	"kon**se**dayng dsh**kon**toosh uh **groo**poosh"
group passport	o passaporte colectivo	"pahsuh**port** koole**tee**voo"
guarantee	a garantia	"garan**tee**uh"
▷ it's still under guarantee	ainda está na garantia	"a**een**duh shta nuh garan**tee**uh"
▷ a five-year guarantee	uma garantia de cinco anos	"oomuh garan**tee**uh duh **seen**koo **ahn**oosh"
guard (on train)	o/a guarda	"**gwar**duh"
▷ have you seen the guard?	viu o/a guarda?	"veew oo/uh **gwar**duh"
guest (house guest)	o convidado	"komvee**dah**doo"
	a convidada	"komvee**dah**duh"
(in hotel)	o/a hóspede	"**osh**ped"
guesthouse	a pensão	"pen**sowng**"
guide n	o/a guia	"**ghee**uh"
▷ is there an English-speaking guide?	têm um guia que fale inglês?	"tayng oom **ghee**uh kuh fahl **een**glaysh"
guidebook	o roteiro	"roo**tay**roo"
▷ do you have a guidebook in English?	tem um roteiro em inglês?	"tayng oom roo**tay**roo ayng een**glesh**"

▷ do you have a guidebook to the cathedral?	tem um folheto desta catedral?	"tayng oom fool-**yet**oo **desh**tuh katuh**dral**"
guided tour	a excursão guiada	"shkoor**sowng** ghee**ah**duh"
▷ what time does the guided tour begin?	a que horas começa a excursão guiada?	"uh kuh **o**rush koo**me**suh uh shkoor**sowng** ghee**ah**duh"
gum	a gengiva	"jen**jee**vuh"
▷ my gums are bleeding/are sore	as minhas gengivas estão a sangrar/a doer	"ush **meen**yush jen**jee**vush shtowng uh san**grar**/uh doo**ehr**"
gym	o ginásio	"jee**nahz**-yoo"
gym shoes	os ténis	"**tay**neesh"
haddock	o eglefim	"**egl**uhfeeng"
haemorrhoids	as hemorróidas	"emoo-**rroy**dush"
▷ I need something for haemorrhoids	preciso de algo para as hemorróidas	"pre**see**zoo duh **al**goo paruh uz emoo-**rroy**dush"
hair	o cabelo	"ka**bay**loo"
▷ my hair is naturally curly/straight	o meu cabelo é encaracolado/liso de natureza	"oo **may**oo ka**bay**loo e ayng-karahkoo-**lah**doo/ **lee**zoo duh nuhtoo**rayz**uh"
▷ I have greasy/dry hair	tenho cabelo oleoso/seco	"**tenyoo** ka**bay**loo ohlee-**oh**zoo/**say**koo"
hairbrush	a escova de cabelo	"**shkoh**vuh duh ka**bay**loo"
haircut	o corte de cabelo	"kort duh ka**bay**loo"
hairdresser (*male*) (*female*)	o cabeleireiro a cabeleireira	"kuhbuh-lay**ray**roo" "kuhbuh-lay**ray**ruh"
hair dryer	o secador de cabelo	"sekuh**dor** duh ka**bay**loo"
hairgrip	o gancho de cabelo	"**gan**shoo duh ka**bay**loo"

hair spray	a laca para o cabelo	"**lah**kuh pro ka**bay**loo"
hake	a abrótea	"**abro**tyuh"
half	a metade	"muh**tahd**"
▷ **half past two/three**	duas/três e meia	"**doo**ush/**traysh** ee **may**uh"
half board	a meia pensão	"**may**uh pen**sowng**"
half bottle	a meia garrafa	"**may**uh ga**rah**fuh"
half fare	o meio bilhete	"**may**oo beel**yet**"
half-price	a metade do preço	"muh**tahd** doo **pray**soo"
ham	o presunto	"pruh**zoon**too"
hamburger	o hamburger	"am**boor**ger"
hand	a mão	"mowng"
handbag	o saco de mão	"**sah**koo duh mowng"
▷ **my handbag's been stolen**	o meu saco de mão foi roubado	"oo **may**oo **sah**koo duh mowng foy roh**bah**doo"
handbrake	o travão de mão	"tra**vowng** duh **mowng**"
handicap:		
▷ **my handicap is ...**	o meu handicap é ...	"oo **may**oo handicap e"
▷ **what's your handicap?**	qual é o teu handicap?	"**kwal** e o **tay**oo handicap"
handicapped	deficiente	"duhfees-**yent**"
handkerchief	o lenço	"**len**soo"
handle (*of door*)	o puxador	"pooshuh**dor**"
(*of pan*)	a asa	"**ah**zuh"
▷ **the door handle has come off**	o puxador da porta saiu	"oo pooshuh**dor** duh **por**tuh sa**yoo**"
hand luggage	a bagagem de mão	"ba**gah**-jayng duh mowng"
handmade	feito à mão	"**fay**too a mowng"
	feita à mão	"**fay**tuh a mowng"

▷ is this handmade?	isto é feito à mão?	"**eesh**too e **fay**too a mowng"
hang-glider	a asa-delta	"**ah**zuh-**del**tuh"
hang-gliding:		
▷ I'd like to go hang-gliding	gostava de ir andar de asa-delta	"goosh**tah**vuh duh eer an**dar** duh **ah**zuh-**del**tuh"
hangover	a ressaca	"re**sah**kuh"
to **happen**	acontecer	"akontuh**sehr**"
▷ what happened?	o que aconteceu?	"oo kuh akontuh**say**oo"
▷ when did it happen?	quando é que aconteceu?	"kwand e kuh akonte**say**oo"
happy	feliz	"fuh**leesh**"
	contente	"kon**tent**"
▷ I'm not happy with ...	não estou contente com ...	"nowng sht**oh** kon**tent** kong"
harbour	o porto	"**por**too"
hard	duro	"**doo**roo"
	dura	"**doo**ruh"
hat	o chapéu	"sha**pay**oo"
to **have**	ter	"tehr"

I have	tenho	"**ten**yoo"
you have (*informal singular*)	tens	"**tayng**sh"
(*formal singular*)	você tem	"voseh **tayng**"
he/she/it has	ele/ela tem	"el/eluh **tayng**"
we have	temos	"**teh**moosh"
you have (*informal plural*)	tendes	"**ten**dush"
(*formal plural*)	vocês têm	"vosehsh **tay**ayng"
they have	eles/elas têm	"elsh/**el**ush **tay**ayng"

ABSOLUTE ESSENTIALS

do you have ...?	tem ...?	"**tayng**"
is there ...?	há ...?	"ah"
are there ...?	há ...?	"ah"
how much is ...?	quanto custa ...?	"**kwan**too **koosh**tuh"

▷ do you have ...?	tem ...?	"tayng"
hay fever	a febre dos fenos	"**feb**ruh doosh **fay**noosh"
hazelnut	a avelã	"avuh**lang**"
he	ele	"el"
head	a cabeça	"ka**bay**suh"
headache	a dor de cabeça	"dor duh ka**bay**suh"
▷ I have a headache	dói-me a cabeça	"**doy**muh uh ka**bay**suh"
▷ I want something for a headache	quero qualquer coisa para as dores de cabeça	"**keh**roo kwal**kehr koy**zuh prash **dor**ush duh ka**bay**suh"
headlights	os faróis	"fa**roysh**"
head waiter	o empregado chefe	"aympruh**gah**doo shef"
health food shop	a loja de comida natural	"**lo**juh duh koo**mee**duh natoo**ral**"
to hear	ouvir	"oh**veer**"
heart	o coração	"kooruh**sowng**"
heart attack	o ataque de coração	"a**tak** duh kooruh**sowng**"
heart condition:		
▷ I have a heart condition	tenho um problema de coração	"**ten**yoo oom pro**blay**muh duh kooruh**sowng**"
heater	o aquecedor	"akusuh**dor**"
▷ the heater isn't working	o aquecedor não funciona	"oo akusuh**dor** nowng foonsee-**o**nuh"
heating	o aquecimento	"akusee-**men**too"
▷ I can't turn the heating off/on	não consigo desligar/ligar o aquecimento	"nowng kon**see**goo duj-lee**gar**/lee**gar** oo akusee-**men**too"
heavy	pesado(a)	"puh**zah**doo(uh)"

ABSOLUTE ESSENTIALS		
yes (please)	sim (por favor)	"**seeng** (por fa**vor**)"
no (thank you)	não (obrigado/a)	"**nowng** (ohbree**gah**doo/uh)"
hello	olá	"**ohla**"
goodbye	adeus	"a**day**oosh"

▷ this is too heavy	isto é demasiado pesado	"**eesh**too e duhmuhsee-**ah**doo puh**zah**doo"
hello	olá	"oh**la**"
(on telephone)	está?	"sh**tah**"
help[1] n	a ajuda	"a**joo**duh"
▷ help!	socorro!	"soo**korr**oo"
▷ fetch help quickly!	procure ajuda depressa!	"proo**koor** a**joo**duh de**pres**uh"
to **help**[2] vb	ajudar	"ajoo**dar**"
▷ can you help me?	pode-me ajudar?	"**pod**muh ajoo**dar**"
▷ help yourself!	ajude-se a si próprio/a	"a**joo**duh-suh uh see **pro**pryoo/uh"
herb	a erva	"**ehr**vuh"
here	aqui	"a**kee**"
▷ here you are!	aqui está!	"a**kee** sh**ta**"
herring	o arenque	"a**renk**"
hers (singular)	seu	"**seoo**"
	sua	"**soo**uh"
	dela	"**del**uh"
(plural)	seus	"**seoo**sh"
	suas	"**soo**ush"
	delas	"**del**ush"
high	alto	"**al**too"
	alta	"**al**tuh"
▷ how high is it?	que altura tem?	"kuh al**too**ruh tayng"
▷ 200 metres high	200 metros de altura	"doo**zen**toosh **me**troosh duh al**too**ruh"
high blood pressure	a tensão alta	"ten**sowng al**tuh"
high chair	a cadeira de bebé	"ka**day**ruh duh be**be**"
highlights (in hair)	as mechas	"**me**shush"
high tide	a maré-cheia	"mare-**shay**uh"

ABSOLUTE ESSENTIALS

I don't understand	não compreendo	"nowng kompree**en**doo"
I don't speak Portuguese	não falo português	"nowng **fah**loo poortoo**gaysh**"
do you speak English?	fala inglês?	"**fah**luh een**glesh**"
could you help me?	podia ajudar-me?	"poo**dee**uh ajoo**dar**muh"

▷ when is high tide?	quando é a maré-cheia?	"kwand **e** uh mare-**shay**uh"
hill	a colina	"koo**le**nuh"
hill walking	o montanhismo	"montan**yeej**moo"
to hire	alugar	"aloo**gar**"
▷ I want to hire a car	quero alugar um carro	"**keh**roo aloo**gar** oom **kar**roo"
▷ can I hire a deck chair/a boat?	posso alugar uma cadeira de lona/um barco?	"**pos**oo aloo**gar** oomuh ka**day**ruh duh **lon**uh/ oom **bar**koo"
his (*singular*)	seu	"**se**oo"
	sua	"**soo**uh"
	dele	"del"
(*plural*)	seus	"**se**oosh"
	suas	"**soo**ush"
	deles	"delsh"
to hit	atingir	"ateen**jeer**"
to hitchhike	andar à boleia	"an**dar** a boo**lay**uh"
HIV-negative	seronegativo	"**se**ro-nuhguh**tee**voo"
	seronegativa	"**se**ro-nuhguh**tee**vuh"
HIV-positive	seropositivo	"**se**ro-poosee**tee**voo"
	seropositiva	"**se**ro-poosee**tee**vuh"
to hold	segurar	"suhgoo**rar**"
(*contain*)	conter	"con**tehr**"
▷ could you hold this for me?	pode segurar-me nisto?	"pod suhgoo**rar**muh **neesh**too"
hold-up (*traffic jam*)	o engarrafamento	"aym-garruhfuh-**men**too"
▷ what is causing this hold-up?	qual é a causa deste engarrafamento?	"kwal e uh **kow**zuh **desht** aym-garruhfuh-**men**too"
hole	o buraco	"boo**rah**koo"
holiday	o feriado	"fuhre**ah**doo"
▷ on holiday	em/de férias	"ayng/duh **fehr**yush"

▷ I'm on holiday here	estou aqui de férias	"shtoh **akee** duh **fehr**yush"
holiday resort	a estância de férias	"eesh**tans**syuh duh **fehr**yush"
holiday romance	o romance de férias	"roo**man**suh duh **fehr**yush"
home	a casa	"**kah**zuh"
▷ **when do you go home?**	quando vai para casa!	"kwandoo **vy** paruh **kah**zuh"
▷ **I'm going home tomorrow/on Tuesday**	vou para casa amanhã/ na terça-feira	"**voh** paruh **kah**zuh ahman**yang**/nuh **tehr**suh-fayruh"
▷ **I want to go home**	quero ir para casa	"keroo **eer** paruh **kah**zuh"
homesick:		
▷ **to be homesick**	ter saudades	"tehr sow**dah**dush"
honey	o mel	"mel"
honeymoon	a lua-de-mel	"**loo**uh-duh-mel"
▷ **we are on our honeymoon**	estamos em lua-de-mel	"**shtah**moosh ayng **loo**uh-duh-mel"
to hope	esperar	"shpuh**rar**"
▷ **I hope so/not**	espero que sim/não	"**shpeh**roo kuh seeng/ nowng"
hors d'oeuvre	a entrada	"aym-**trah**duh"
horse	o cavalo	"ka**vah**loo"
horse riding	andar a cavalo	"andar uh ka**vah**loo"
▷ **to go horse riding**	ir andar a cavalo	"**eer** andar a ka**vah**loo"
hose	o tubo	"**too**boo"
hospital	o hospital	"oshpee**tal**"
▷ **we must get him to hospital**	temos que o levar ao hospital	"**tay**moosh kee oo le**var** ow oshpee**tal**"

ABSOLUTE ESSENTIALS

do you have ...?	tem ...?	"tayng"
is there ...?	há ...?	"ah"
are there ...?	há ...?	"ah"
how much is ...?	quanto custa ...?	"**kwan**too **koosh**tuh"

▷ where's the nearest hospital?	onde fica o hospital mais próximo?	"ond **feek**uh oo oshpee**tal** mysh **pro**seemoo"

hot — quente — "kent"

▷ I'm hot	tenho calor	"**ten**yoo ka**lor**"
▷ it's hot (*weather*)	está calor	"shta ka**lor**"
▷ a hot curry	um caril picante	"oom ka**reel** pee**kant**"

hotel — o hotel — "oh**tel**"

| ▷ can you recommend a (cheap) hotel? | pode recomendar-me um hotel (barato)? | "pod rekoomen**dar**muh oom oh**tel** (ba**rah**too)" |

hour — a hora — "**or**uh"

▷ an hour ago	há uma hora	"a **oo**muh **or**uh"
▷ in two hours time	daqui a duas horas	"duh**kee** uh **doo**ush **or**ush"
▷ the journey takes 2 hours	a viagem demora 2 horas	"uh vee**ah**jayng duh**mor**uh **doo**ush **or**ush"

house — a casa — "**kah**zuh"

house wine — o vinho da casa — "**veen**yoo duh **kah**zuh"

| ▷ a bottle/carafe of house wine | uma garrafa/um jarro de vinho da casa | "**oo**muh ga**rrah**fuh/oom **jah**rroo duh **veen**yoo duh **kah**zuh" |

hovercraft — o hovercraft — "hovercraft"

| ▷ we came by hovercraft | viemos de hovercraft | "**vye**moosh duh **over**kraft" |

how (*in what way*) — como — "**koh**moo"

▷ how are you?	como está?	"**koh**moo shta"
▷ how are you feeling now?	como se sente agora?	"**koo**moo suh sent a**gor**uh"
▷ how much?	quanto?	"**kwan**too"
▷ how many?	quantos	"**kwan**toosh"
	quantas	"**kwan**tush"

hungry:

| ▷ I am hungry | tenho fome | "**ten**yoo fom" |

ABSOLUTE ESSENTIALS

yes (please)	sim (por favor)	"**seeng** (por fa**vor**)"
no (thank you)	não (obrigado/a)	"**nowng** (ohbree**gah**doo/uh)"
hello	olá	"oh**la**"
goodbye	adeus	"a**day**oosh"

hurry:

▷ **I'm in a hurry**	tenho pressa	"**ten**yoo **pres**uh"

to hurt	doer	"doo**er**"
▷ **he is hurt**	ele está ferido	"ayl sh**ta** fuh**ree**doo"
▷ **that hurts**	isso dói	"**ee**soo doy"
▷ **he has hurt himself**	ele feriu-se	"ayl fuh**ryoo**suh"
▷ **he has hurt his leg/ arm**	ele feriu-se na perna/no braço	"ayl fuh**ryoo**suh nuh **per**nuh/noo **brah**soo"

husband	o marido	"ma**ree**doo"
hydrofoil	o hidrofoil	"**ee**drofoyl"
I	eu	"**ay**oo"
ice	o gelo	"**jay**loo"
ice cream	o gelado	"juh**lah**doo"
iced	gelado(a)	"juh**lah**doo(uh)"
ice lolly	o gelado	"juh**lah**doo"
ice rink	a pista de patinagem	"**pee**shtuh duh patee**nah**jayng"
ice skates	os patins de gelo	"pat**eengs** duh **jay**loo"
ice skating	a patinagem artística	"patee**nah**jayng ar**tee**shtikuh"
▷ **can we go ice skating?**	podemos ir fazer patinagem?	"poodeh**moosh** **eer** fa**zehr** patee**nah**jayng"
icy	com gelo	"kong **jay**loo"
▷ **icy roads**	as estradas com gelo	"ush sh**trah**dush kong **jay**loo"
if	se	"suh"
ignition	a ignição	"eegnee**sowng**"
ill	doente	"doo**ent**"
immediately	imediatamente	"eemudee-ahtuh**ment**"

ABSOLUTE ESSENTIALS

I don't understand	não compreendo	"nowng kompree**en**doo"
I don't speak Portuguese	não falo português	"nowng **fah**loo poortoo**gaysh**"
do you speak English?	fala inglês?	"**fah**luh een**glesh**"
could you help me?	podia ajudar-me?	"poo**dee**uh ajoo**dar**muh"

important	importante	"eempoor**tant**"
impossible	impossível	"eempoo**see**vel"
in	**den**tro de	"**den**troo duh"
inch (*metric equiv = 2.54 cm*)	a polegada	"pool**gah**duh"
included	incluído	"een**klwee**doo"
	incluída	"een**klwee**duh"
▷ **is service included?**	o serviço está incluído?	"oo ser**vee**soo shta een**klwee**doo"
indicator (*on car*)	o pisca-pisca	"**pee**shkuh-**pee**shkuh"
▷ **the indicator isn't working**	o pisca-pisca não funciona	"oo **pee**shkuh-**pee**shkuh nowng foonsee**o**nuh"
indigestion	a indigestão	"eendee-jesh**towng**"
indoor:		
▷ **indoor swimming pool/indoor tennis**	a piscina coberta/o ténis em recinto coberto	"uh peesh-**see**nuh koo**ber**tuh/oo **tay**neesh ayng ruh**seen**too koo**ber**too"
indoors	em casa	"ayng **kah**zuh"
infectious	infeccioso	"eemfes-**yoh**zoo"
	infecciosa	"eemfes-**yoh**zuh"
▷ **is it infectious?**	é infeccioso?	"e eemfes-**yoh**zoo"
information	a informação	"eemfoor-muh**sowng**"
▷ **I'd like some information about ...**	gostaria de informação sobre ...	"gooshtuh**ree**uh duh eenfoor-muh**sowng** sohbruh"
information office	as informações	"eemfoor-muh**soynsh**"
injection	a injecção	"eenje**sowng**"
▷ **please give me an injection**	por favor, dê-me uma injecção	"poor fa**vor day**muh **oom**uh eenje**sowng**"
injured	ferido(a)	"fe**ree**doo(uh)"

ABSOLUTE ESSENTIALS		
I would like ...	queria ...	"**kree**uh"
I need ...	preciso de ...	"pre**see**zoo duh"
where is ...?	onde fica ...?	"ond **fee**kuh"
I'm looking for ...	procuro ...	"pro**koo**roo"

▷ he is seriously injured	ele está gravemente ferido	"**ayl** shta **grah**vment fe**ree**doo"
ink	a tinta	"**teen**tuh"
insect	o insecto	"een**set**oo"
insect bite	a mordedura de insecto	"moorduh-**door**uh deen**set**oo"
insect repellent	o repelente	"ruhpuh**lent**"
inside	o interior	"eentuh-ree**or**"
▷ let's go inside	vamos lá para dentro	"**vah**moosh la paruh **den**troo"
instant coffee	o café instantâneo	"kuh**fe** eenshtan-**tah**nyoo"
instead	em vez disso	"aym vesh **dee**soo"
instructor	o instrutor	"eenshtroo**tor**"
	a instrutora	"eenshtroo**tor**uh"
insulin	a insulina	"eensoo**lee**nuh"
insurance	o seguro	"suh**goo**roo"
▷ will the insurance pay for it?	o seguro vai pagar?	"oo suh**goo**roo vy pa**gar**"
insurance certificate	o certificado de seguros	"suhrteefee-**kah**doo duh suh**goo**roosh"
▷ can I see your insurance certificate?	posso ver o seu seguro?	"**pos**oo vehr oo **say**oo suh**goo**roo"
to **insure**:		
▷ can I insure my luggage?	posso fazer um seguro para a minha bagagem?	"**pos**oo fa**zehr** oom suh**goo**roo **paru**h uh **meen**yuh ba**gah**jayng"
interesting	interessante	"eentuh-re**sant**"

ABSOLUTE ESSENTIALS

do you have ...?	tem ...?	"tayng"
is there ...?	há ...?	"ah"
are there ...?	há ...?	"ah"
how much is ...?	quanto custa ...?	"**kwan**too **koosh**tuh"

▷ **can you suggest somewhere interesting to go?**	pode sugerir-me algum sítio interessante onde ir?	"pod soojuh**reer**-muh algoom **see**tyoo eentuhruh-**sant** ond **eer**"
international	internacional	"eenter-nasyoo**nal**"
interpreter	o/a intérprete	"een**tehr**pret"
▷ **could you act as an interpreter for us please?**	podia ser nosso/nossa intérprete, por favor?	"pod sehr **nos**oo/**nos**uh een**tehr**pret poor fa**vor**"
into	em	"ayng"
invitation	o convite	"kom**veet**"
to invite	convidar	"komvee**dar**"
▷ **it's very kind of you to invite me**	é muito amável em convidar-me	"e **mween**too a**mah**vel ayng konvee**dar**-muh"
invoice	a factura	"fak**too**ruh"
Ireland	a Irlanda	"eer**lan**duh"
▷ **Northern Ireland**	a Irlanda do Norte	"uh eer**lan**duh doo **nort**"
▷ **Republic of Ireland**	a República da Irlanda	"uh re**poo**blikuh duh eer**lan**duh"
Irish	irlandês irlandesa	"eerlan**desh**" "eerlan**day**zuh"
iron[1] *n (for clothes)*	o ferro	"**fer**roo"
▷ **I need an iron**	preciso dum ferro	"pre**see**zoo doom **fer**roo"
▷ **I want to use my iron**	quero utilizar o meu ferro	"**ker**oo ooteelee**zar** oo meoo **fer**roo"
to iron[2] *vb*	passar a ferro	"pa**sar** uh **fer**roo"
▷ **where can I get this skirt ironed?**	onde é que posso passar a ferro esta saia?	"**on**dee e kuh **pos**oo pa**sar** uh **fer**roo **esh**tuh **sy**uh"
ironmonger's	a loja de ferragens	"**lo**juh duh fe**rah**jaynsh"
is	é está	"e" "sh**ta**"
▷ **he/she/it is**	ele/ela é	"el/eluh **e**"

island	a ilha	"**eel**yuh"
it	o	"oo"
	a	"uh"
Italian	italiano	"eetal**yah**noo"
	italiana	"eetal**yah**nuh"
Italy	a Itália	"eet**al**yuh"
itch	a comichão	"koomee**showng**"
jack *(for car)*	o macaco	"ma**kah**koo"
jacket	o casaco	"ka**zah**koo"
jam *(food)*	a compota	"kom**pot**uh"
▷ **strawberry jam/** **apricot jam**	compota de morango/ damasco	"kom**pot**uh duh moo**rang**oo/ da**mahsh**koo"
jammed	encravado	"aymkra-**vah**doo"
	encravada	"aymkra-**vah**duh"
▷ **the drawer is jammed**	a gaveta está encravada	"uh ga**veh**tuh shta aymkra-**vah**duh"
▷ **the controls have** **jammed**	os comandos encravaram	"oosh koo**man**doosh aymkra-**vah**rowng"
January	Janeiro	"juh**nay**roo"
jar *(container)*	o jarro	"**jar**roo"
▷ **a jar of coffee**	um jarro de café	"oom **jar**roo duh kuh**fe**"
jazz	o jazz	"jaz"
jazz festival	o festival de jazz	"fuhstee**val** duh jaz"
jeans	as jeans	"jeans"
	as calças de ganga	"**kal**sush duh **gan**guh"
jelly *(dessert)*	a geleia	"juh**lay**uh"
jellyfish	a medusa	"muh**doo**zuh"
▷ **I've been stung by a** **jellyfish**	fui mordido por uma medusa	"**fooee** moor**dee**doo poor oomuh muh**doo**zuh"

ABSOLUTE ESSENTIALS

I don't understand	não compreendo	"nowng kompree**en**doo"
I don't speak Portuguese	não falo português	"nowng **fah**loo poortoo**gaysh**"
do you speak English?	fala inglês?	"**fah**luh een**glesh**"
could you help me?	podia ajudar-me?	"poo**deeuh** ajoo**dar**muh"

jersey	o pulover	"poo**loh**vehr"
jet lag	o cansaço devido à diferença de fuso horário	"kan**sah**soo duh**vee**doo a deefuh**ren**suh duh **foo**soo o**rahr**yoo"
▷ **I'm suffering from jet lag**	estou cansado(a) devido à diferença do fuso horário	"shtoh kan**sah**doo(uh) duh**vee**doo a deefuh**ren**suh duh **foo**soo o**rahr**yoo"
jet ski	a mota aquática	"motuh a**kwa**tikuh"
jet skiing:		
▷ **I'd like to go jet skiing**	gostava de ir andar de mota aquática	"goo**stah**vuh duh eer an**dar** duh motuh a**kwa**tikuh"
jeweller's	a joalharia	"jwal-yuh**ree**uh"
jewellery	as jóias	"**joy**ush"
▷ **I would like to put my jewellery in a safe**	gostaria de guardar as minhas jóias num cofre	"goostuh**ree**uh duh gwar**dar** ush **meen**yush **joy**ush noom **ko**fruh"
Jewish	judeu	"joo**day**oo"
	judia	"joo**dee**uh"
job	o emprego	"aym**pray**goo"
▷ **what's your job?**	qual é o seu emprego?	"**kwal** e oo sayoo aym**pray**goo"
jog:		
▷ **to go jogging**	ir fazer jogging	"eer fa**zehr** jogging"
joke	a anedota	"anuh**dot**uh"
journey	a viagem	"vee**ah**jayng"
▷ **how was your journey?**	como foi a sua viagem?	"koomoo **foy** uh soouh vee**ah**jayng"
jug	o jarro	"**jar**roo"
▷ **a jug of water**	um jarro de água	"oom **jar**ro **dah**gwuh"

ABSOLUTE ESSENTIALS		
I would like ...	queria ...	"**kree**uh"
I need ...	preciso de ...	"pre**see**zoo duh"
where is ...?	onde fica ...?	"ond **fee**kuh"
I'm looking for ...	procuro ...	"pro**koo**roo"

juice	o sumo	"**soo**moo"
July	Julho	"**joo**lyoo"
jump leads	os cabos de emergência	"**kah**boosh deemer**jens**-yuh"
junction	a bifurcação	"beefoorkuh**sowng**"
(*crossroads*)	o cruzamento	"kroozuh**men**too"
▷ **go left at the next junction**	vire à esquerda no próximo cruzamento	"**vee**ruh a sh**kehr**duh noo **pro**seemoo kroozuh**men**too"
June	Junho	"**joo**nyoo"
just:		
▷ **just two**	apenas dois	"a**pay**nush doysh"
▷ **I've just arrived**	acabo de chegar	"a**kah**boo duh shuh**gar**"
to keep (*retain*)	guardar	"gwar**dar**"
▷ **keep the door locked**	mantenha a porta fechada à chave	"man**tay**nyuh uh **por**tuh fuh**shah**duh a **shahv**"
▷ **may I keep it?**	posso ficar com ele?	"**pos**oo fee**kar** kong **ayl**"
▷ **could you keep me a loaf of bread?**	podia guardar-me um pão de forma?	"poo**dee**uh gwar**dar**muh oom **powng** duh **fohr**muh"
▷ **how long will it keep?**	quanto tempo aguentará?	"**kwan**too **tem**poo agwentuh**rah**"
▷ **keep to the path**	mantenha-se no caminho	"man**tay**nyuh-suh noo ka**mee**nyoo"
kettle	a chaleira	"sha**lay**ruh"
key	a chave	"**shahv**"
▷ **which is the key for the front door?**	qual é a chave da porta da frente?	"kwal e uh shahv duh **por**tuh duh frent"
▷ **I've lost my key**	perdi a minha chave	"per**dee** uh **meen**yuh shahv"
▷ **can I have my key, please?**	pode dar-me a minha chave, por favor?	"pod **dar**muh uh **meen**yuh shahv poor fa**vor**"
kidneys (*as food*)	os rins	"**reensh**"

ABSOLUTE ESSENTIALS

do you have ...?	tem ...?	"tayng"
is there ...?	há ...?	"ah"
are there ...?	há ...?	"ah"
how much is ...?	quanto custa ...?	"**kwan**too **koosh**tuh"

kilo	o quilo	"**kee**loo"
kilometre	o quilómetro	"kee**loo**metroo"
kind[1] *n (sort, type)*	a espécie	"**shpe**see"
▷ **what kind of...?**	que tipo de ...?	"kuh **tee**poo duh"
kind[2] *adj (person)*	amável	"a**mah**vel"
▷ **that's very kind of you**	é muito amável	"e **mween**too a**mah**vel"
to kiss	beijar	"bay**jar**"
kitchen	a cozinha	"koo**zeen**yuh"
knife	a faca	"**fah**kuh"
to know *(facts)*	saber	"sa**behr**"
(be acquainted with)	conhecer	"koonyuh**sehr**"
▷ **do you know a good place to go?**	conhece algum sítio bom para visitar?	"koo**nye**suh algoom **seet**yoo bong paruh veesee**tar**"
▷ **do you know where I can ...?**	sabe onde posso ...?	"**sahb** ond **pos**oo"
▷ **do you know Paul?**	conhece o Paul?	"kon**ye**suh oo paul"
▷ **do you know how to do this?**	sabe como fazer isto?	"**sahb** koomoo fa**zehr** **eesh**too"
▷ **I don't know**	não sei	"nowng **say**"
lace *(of shoes)*	a renda	"**ren**duh"
laces *(for shoes)*	os cordões	"koor**doynsh**"
ladder	a escada	"**shkah**duh"
ladies	Senhoras	"sun**yor**ush"
▷ **where is the ladies?**	onde é a casa de banho das senhoras?	"**ond**uh shta uh **kah**zuh duh **bahn**yoo dush sun**yor**ush"
lady	a senhora	"sun**yor**uh"
lager	a cerveja	"ser**vay**juh"
lake	o lago	"**lah**goo"

lamb	o cordeiro	"koor**dayr**oo"
lamp	o candeeiro	"kandee-**ayr**oo"
▷ the lamp is not working	o candeeiro não funciona	"oo kandee-**ayr**oo nowng foonsy**o**nuh"
lane	a travessa	"tra**ves**uh"
(of motorway)	a faixa	"**fy**shuh"
▷ you're in the wrong lane	está na faixa errada	"shta nuh **fy**shuh eer**rah**duh"
language	a língua	"**leen**gwuh"
▷ what languages do you speak?	que línguas fala?	"kuh **leen**gwush **fah**luh"
large	grande	"grand"
larger	maior	"my**or**"
▷ do you have a larger one?	tem um maior?	"**tayng** oom my**or**"
last	último	"**ool**timoo"
	última	"**ool**timuh"
▷ last week	na semana passada	"nuh se**mah**nuh puh**sah**duh"
▷ how long will it last?	quanto tempo durará?	"**kwan**too **tem**poo dooruh**ra**"
late	tarde	"tard"
▷ it's too late	é demasiado tarde	"e duhmuh-**syah**doo tard"
▷ we went to bed late	fomos para a cama tarde	"**foh**moosh paruh uh **kah**muh tard"
▷ the train is late	o comboio está atrasado	"oo kom**boy**oo shta atruh**zah**doo"
▷ sorry we are late	desculpe o atraso	"dush**koolp** oo a**trah**zoo"
▷ late last night	ontem ao fim da noite	"**on**tayng ow **feeng** duh noyt"
▷ we are 10 minutes late	estamos 10 minutos atrasados(as)	"**shtah**moosh **desh** mee**noo**tooz atruh**zah**doosh(ush)"

ABSOLUTE ESSENTIALS

I don't understand	não compreendo	"nowng kompree**en**doo"
I don't speak Portuguese	não falo português	"nowng **fah**loo poortoo**gaysh**"
do you speak English?	fala inglês?	"**fah**luh een**glesh**"
could you help me?	podia ajudar-me?	"poo**dee**uh ajoo**dar**muh"

later	mais tarde	"mysh tard"
▷ **shall I come back later?**	quer que volte mais tarde?	"ker kuh volt mysh tard"
▷ **see you later**	até logo	"ate logoo"
launderette	a lavandaria automática	"lavanduhreeuh owtoomatikuh"
laundry service	o serviço de lavandaria	"serveesoo duh lavanduhreeuh"
▷ **is there a laundry service?**	há serviço de lavandaria?	"a suhrveesoo duh lavanduhreeuh"
lavatory	o lavabo	"lavahboo"
lawyer	o advogado	"advoogahdoo"
laxative	o laxativo	"lashuhteevoo"
lay-by	o desvio para estacionamento	"dujveeoo paruh shtasyoonuh-mentoo"
lead (*electric*)	o cabo	"kahboo"
▷ **you lead the way**	indique o caminho	"eendeekuh oo kameenyoo"
leader (*guide*)	o guia	"gheeuh"
leak (*of gas, liquid*)	a fuga	"fooguh"
(*in roof*)	a goteira	"gootayruh"
▷ **there is a leak in the radiator/petrol tank**	há uma ruptura no radiador/depósito da gasolina	"a oomuh rooptooruh noo radeeuhdor/duhpozitoo duh gazooleenuh"
to **learn**	aprender	"aprendehr"
least:		
▷ **at least**	pelo menos	"peloo maynoosh"
leather	o couro	"kohroo"
to **leave**	partir	"perteer"
(*leave behind*)	deixar	"dayshar"

▷ when does the train leave?	a que horas parte o comboio?	"uh kee **o**rush part oo kom**boy**oo"
▷ I shall be leaving tomorrow morning	parto amanhã de manhã	"**par**too amanyang duh manyang"
▷ I've been left behind	deixaram-me para trás	"day**shah**ran-muh **pa**ruh trash"
▷ I left my bags in the taxi	deixei as minhas sacas no táxi	"day**shay** ush meenyush **sah**kush noo **ta**xi"
▷ I left the keys In the car	deixei as chaves no carro	"day**shay** ush **shah**vsh noo **ka**rro"
leeks	os alhos-porros	"alyoosh-**por**roosh"
left:		
▷ on/to the left	à esquerda	"a sh**kehr**duh"
▷ take the third street on the left	vire na terceira rua à esquerda	"**vee**ruh nuh tuhr**say**ruh a sh**kehr**duh"
left-luggage (office)	o depósito de bagagens	"duh**po**zitoo duh bagah**jay**nsh"
leg	a perna	"**pehr**nuh"
lemon	o limão	"lee**mowng**"
lemonade	a limonada	"leemoo**nah**duh"
lemon tea	o carioca de limão	"karee-**o**kuh duh lee**mowng**"
to lend	emprestar	"aymprush**tar**"
▷ could you lend me some money?	podia emprestar-me algum dinheiro?	"poo**dee**uh aymprush**tar**-muh al**goom** deen**yay**roo"
▷ could you lend me a towel?	podia emprestar-me uma toalha?	"poo**dee**uh aymprush**tar**-muh oomuh too**ah**lyuh"
lens	a lente	"lent"
▷ I wear contact lenses	uso lentes de contacto	"**oo**zoo **lent**sh duh kon**tak**too"
less	menos	"**may**noosh"

ABSOLUTE ESSENTIALS

do you have ...?	tem ...?	"tayng"
is there ...?	há ...?	"ah"
are there ...?	há ...?	"ah"
how much is ...?	quanto custa ...?	"**kwan**too **koosh**tuh"

lesson	a lição	"leesowng"
▷ **do you give lessons?**	dá lições?	"da leesoynsh"
▷ **can we take lessons?**	podemos ter lições?	"poodaymoosh tehr leesoynsh"
to let (*allow*)	deixar	"dayshar"
(*hire out*)	alugar	"aloogar"
letter	a carta	"kartuh"
▷ **how much is a letter to England?**	quanto custa mandar uma carta para a Inglaterra?	"kwantoo kooshtuh mandar oomuh kartuh pra eengluhterruh"
▷ **are there any letters for me?**	há cartas para mim?	"a kartush paruh meeng"
lettuce	a alface	"alfass"
level crossing	a passagem de nível	"pasahjayng duh neevel"
library	a biblioteca	"beeblee-ootekuh"
licence	a autorização	"owtooree-zuhsowng"
lid	a tampa	"tampuh"
to lie down	deitar-se	"daytar-suh"
lifeboat	o salva-vidas	"salvuh-veedush"
▷ **call out the lifeboat!**	chame o salva-vidas!	"shahmuh oo salvuh-veedush"
lifeguard	o nadador-salvador	"naduhdor-salvuhdor"
▷ **get the lifeguard!**	vá chamar o nadador-salvador!	"va shamar oo naduhdor-salvuhdor"
life jacket	o colete de salvação	"koolet duh salvuhsowng"
lift	o elevador	"eeluhvuhdor"
▷ **is there a lift in the building?**	o edifício tem elevador?	"oo edeefeesyoo tayng eeluhvuhdor"
▷ **can you give me a lift to the garage?**	pode dar-me uma boleia para a garagem?	"pod dar-muh oomuh boolayuh paruh uh garahjayng"

lift pass	o passe de elevador	"**pas** duh eeluhvuh**dor**"
light	a luz	"loosh"
▷ may I take it over to the light?	posso vê-lo à luz?	"**pos**oo **veh**loo a loosh"
▷ do you mind if I turn off the light?	importa-se que eu apague a luz?	"een**por**tuh-suh kuh ayoo a**pah**guh loosh"
▷ have you got a light?	tem lume?	"tayng loom"
▷ light blue/green	luz azul/verde	"loosh a**zool**/vehrd"
light bulb	a lâmpada	"**lahm**paduh"
lighter	o isqueiro	"eesh**kay**roo"
lighter fuel	o gás de isqueiro	"gash duh eesh**kay**roo"
like¹ *prep*	como	"**koo**moo"
▷ like you	como você	"**koo**moo voceh"
▷ like this	assim	"a**seeng**"
to like² *vb*	gostar de	"goosh**tar** duh"
▷ I like coffee	gosto de café	"**gosh**too duh kuh**fe**"
▷ I would like a newspaper	queria um jornal	"**kree**uh oom joor**nal**"
lime *(fruit)*	a lima	"**lee**muh"
line	a linha	"**leen**yuh"
▷ I'd like an outside line, please	quero uma chamada para o exterior, por favor	"**keh**roo **oom**uh sha**mah**duh pro shtuhree**or** poor fa**vor**"
▷ the line's engaged	está impedido	"shta eempuh**dee**doo"
▷ it's a bad line	a ligação está má	"uh leeguh**sowng** shta ma"
lip salve	a manteiga de cacau	"man**tay**guh duh ka**kow**"
lipstick	o bâton	"**bah**tong"
liqueur	o licor	"lee**kor**"
▷ what liqueurs do you have?	que licores tem?	"kuh lee**kor**ush tayng"

Lisbon	Lisboa	"**leesh**bohuh"
to **listen to**	ouvir	"oh**veer**"
litre	o litro	"**lee**troo"

little:

▷ **a little milk**	um pouco de leite	"oom **poh**koo duh layt"
to **live**	viver	"vee**vehr**"
▷ **he lives in London**	ele vive em Londres	"**ayl** veev ayng **lon**drush"
▷ **where do you live?**	onde mora?	"ond **mo**ruh"
liver	o fígado	"**fee**guhdoo"
living room	a sala de estar	"**sah**luh dush**tar**"
loaf	o pão	"powng"
lobby	a entrada	"en**trah**duh"
▷ **I'll meet you in the lobby**	encontramo-nos à entrada	"aym-kon**trah**moo-noosh a en**trah**duh"
lobster	a lagosta	"la**gosh**tuh"
local (*wine, speciality*)	local	"loo**kal**"
▷ **what's the local speciality?**	qual é a especialidade local?	"kwal **e** uh shpuh-syuhlee**dahd** loo**kal**"
▷ **I'd like to order something local**	queria encomendar algo da região	"**kree**uh aymkomen**dar** algoo duh ruhjee-**owng**"
lock[1] *n* (*on door, box*)	a fechadura	"feshuh**doo**ruh"
▷ **the lock is broken**	a fechadura está estragada	"uh feshuh**doo**ruh shta shtruh**gah**duh"
to **lock**[2] *vb* (*door*)	fechar com chave	"fu**shar** kong shav"
▷ **I have locked myself out of my room**	fiquei fechado(a) à chave fora do quarto	"**fee**kay fu**shah**doo(uh) a shav **fo**ruh doo **kwar**too"
locker	o cacifo	"ka**see**foo"

▷ where are the clothes lockers?	onde são os cacifos para guardar a roupa?	"ond **sowng** oosh ka**see**foosh paruh gwar**dar** uh **roh**puh"
▷ are there any luggage lockers?	há compartimentos para a bagagem?	"a konpurtee-**men**toosh paruh uh ba**gah**jayng"
lollipop	o chupa-chupa	"shoopuh-**shoo**puh"
London	Londres	"**lon**drush"
long (*in length*)	comprido	"kom**pree**doo"
	comprida	"kom**pree**duh"
▷ for a long time	durante muito tempo	"doo**rant** m**ween**too **tem**poo"
▷ how long will it take to get there?	quanto tempo demora a chegar lá?	"**kwan**too **tem**poo duh**mor**uh uh shuh**gar** la"
▷ will it be long?	vai demorar muito?	"vy duhmoo**rar** m**ween**too"
▷ how long will it be?	quanto tempo vai demorar?	"**kwan**too **tem**poo vy duhmoo**rar**"
long-sighted:		
▷ I'm long-sighted	vejo bem ao longe	"**vay**joo **bayng** ow lonj"
to **look**	olhar	"ohl**yar**"
(*seem*)	parecer	"paruh**sehr**"
▷ I'm just looking	estou só a ver	"shtoh so uh vehr"
to **look after**	cuidar de	"kwee**dar** duh"
▷ could you look after my case for a minute please?	podia vigiar-me a mala por um minuto, por favor?	"poo**dee**uh veegee**ar**-muh uh **mah**luh poor oom mee**noo**too poor fa**vor**"
▷ I need someone to look after the children tonight	preciso de alguém que me olhe pelas crianças esta noite	"pre**see**zoo duh al**gayng** kuh muh **ohl**yuh **pay**lush kree**an**sush **esh**tuh noyt"
to **look for**	procurar	"prooko**orar**"
▷ we're looking for a hotel/an apartment	estamos à procura de um hotel/apartamento	"sh**tah**moosh a pro**koo**ruh duh oom oh**tel**/apartuh**men**too"

do you have ...?	tem ...?	"tayng"
is there ...?	há ...?	"ah"
are there ...?	há ...?	"ah"
how much is ...?	quanto custa ...?	"kwantoo kooshtuh"

lorry	o camião	"kam**yowng**"
to lose	perder	"per**dehr**"
lost (*object*)	perdido	"per**dee**doo"
	perdida	"per**dee**duh"
▷ **I have lost my wallet**	perdi a minha carteira	"per**dee** uh **meen**yoo kar**tay**ruh"
▷ **I am lost**	perdi-me	"per**dee**-muh"
▷ **my son is lost**	o meu filho perdeu-se	"oo **may**oo **feel**yoo per**day**oo-suh"
lost property office	a secção de perdidos e achados	"sek**sowng** duh per**dee**doozee a**shah**doosh"
lot:		
▷ **a lot**	muitos	"**mween**toosh"
lotion	a loção	"loo**sowng**"
loud	alto	"**al**too"
	alta	"**al**tuh"
▷ **it's too loud**	está demasiado alto	"shta duhmuhsee-**ah**doo **al**too"
lounge (*in hotel*)	a sala de estar	"**sah**luh dush**tar**"
▷ **could we have coffee in the lounge?**	podemos tomar café na sala de estar?	"poo**deh**moosh too**mar** kuh**fe** nuh **sah**luh dush**tar**"
to love (*person*)	amar	"uh**mar**"
(*things*)	adorar	"adoo**rar**"
▷ **I love swimming**	adoro nadar	"a**doo**roo na**dar**"
▷ **I love seafood**	adoro marisco	"a**doo**roo ma**reesh**koo"
lovely	encantador	"aymkantuh**dor**"
	encantadora	"aymkantuh**dor**uh"
▷ **it's a lovely day**	está um dia lindo	"shta oom **dee**uh **leen**doo"
low	baixo	"**by**shoo"
	baixa	"**by**shuh"

low tide	a maré-baixa	"ma**re-by**shuh"
lucky	afortunado	"afortoo**nah**doo"
	afortunada	"afortoo**nah**duh"
luggage	a bagagem	"ba**gah**jayng"
▷ **can you help me with my luggage, please?**	pode ajudar-me com a bagagem, por favor?	"pod ajoo**dar**-muh kon uh ba**gah**jayng poor fa**vor**"
▷ **please take my luggage to a taxi**	por favor, leve-me a bagagem para um táxi	"poor fa**vor le**vuh-muh uh ba**gah**jayng **pa**ruh oom **taxi**"
▷ **I sent my luggage on in advance**	enviei a minha bagagem à frente	"aymvee**ay** uh **mee**nyuh ba**gah**jayng a frent"
▷ **our luggage has not arrived**	a nossa bagagem não chegou	"uh **nos**uh ba**gah**jayng nowng shuh**goh**"
▷ **where do I check in my luggage?**	onde faço o check-in da bagagem?	"**on**duh **fah**soo oo checkin duh ba**gah**jayng"
▷ **could you have my luggage taken up?**	podem levar a minha bagagem para o quarto?	"**pod**ayng le**var** uh **mee**nyuh ba**gah**jayng pro **kwar**too"
▷ **please send someone to collect my luggage**	por favor, mande alguém para levar a minha bagagem	"poor fa**vor** mandal**gayng pa**ruh le**var** uh **mee**nyuh ba**gah**jayng"
luggage allowance	o limite de peso autorizado	"lee**meet** duh **pay**zoo owto-ree**zah**doo"
▷ **what's the luggage allowance?**	qual é o limite de bagagem autorizado?	"kwal **e** oo lee**meet** duh ba**gah**jayng owtoo-ree**zah**doo"
luggage rack (*on car, in train*)	o porta-bagagens	"portuh-ba**gah**jaynsh"
luggage tag	a etiqueta de bagagem	"etee**ket**uh duh ba**gah**jayng"
luggage trolley	o carrinho para a bagagem	"ka**rreen**yoo pra ba**gah**jayng"
▷ **are there any luggage trolleys?**	há carrinhos para a bagagem?	"a ka**rreen**yoosh pra ba**gah**jayng"
lunch	o almoço	"al**moh**soo"

ABSOLUTE ESSENTIALS

I don't understand	não compreendo	"nowng kompree**en**doo"
I don't speak Portuguese	não falo português	"nowng **fah**loo poortoo**gaysh**"
do you speak English?	fala inglês?	"**fah**luh een**glesh**"
could you help me?	podia ajudar-me?	"poo**dee**uh ajoo**dar**muh"

▷ what's for lunch?	o que há para o almoço?	"oo kuh **a** paruh oo al**moh**soo"
luxury	o luxo	"**loo**shoo"
machine	a máquina	"**mak**inuh"
madam	senhora	"sun**yor**uh"
magazine	a revista	"ruh**veesh**tuh"
▷ do you have any English magazines?	tem revistas inglesas?	"tayng ruh**veesh**tush een**glay**zush"
maid (*in hotel*)	a empregada	"aympruh-**gah**duh"
▷ when does the maid come?	quando é que a empregada vem?	"kwande kuh uh aympruh-**gah**duh **vayng**"
main	principal	"preensee**pal**"
▷ the main station	a estação principal	"uh shta**sowng** preensee**pal**"
main course	o prato principal	"**prah**too preensee**pal**"
mains (*electric*)	o quadro da electricidade	"**kwa**dro duh eeletree-see**dahd**"
▷ turn it off at the mains	desligue na tomada	"dush**lee**guh nuh too**mah**duh"
to **make** (*generally*)	fazer	"fa**zehr**"
(*meal*)	preparar	"pruhpa**rar**"

I make	faço	"**fah**soo"
you make (*informal singular*)	fazes	"**fah**zush"
(*formal singular*)	você faz	"voseh **fash**"
he/she/it makes	ele/ela faz	"el/eluh **fash**"
we make	fazemos	"fuh**zeh**moosh"
you make (*informal plural*)	fazeis	"fuh**zaysh**"
(*formal plural*)	vocês fazem	"vosehsh **fah**zayng"
they make	eles/elas fazem	"elsh/elush **fah**zayng"

ABSOLUTE ESSENTIALS

I would like ...	queria ...	"**kree**uh"
I need ...	preciso de ...	"pre**see**zoo duh"
where is ...?	onde fica ...?	"ond **fee**kuh"
I'm looking for ...	procuro ...	"pro**koo**roo"

make-up	a maquilhagem	"makeel-**yah**jayng"
make-up remover	o desmaquilhador	"dushmuh-keelyuh**dor**"
mallet	o maço	"**muh**soo"
man	o homem	"**o**mayng"
manager	o gerente	"juh**rent**"
	a gerente	"juh**rent**"
> **I'd like to speak to the manager**	queria falar com o gerente	"**kree**uh fa**lar** kon oo juh**rent**"
many	muitos	"**mween**toosh"
	muitas	"**mween**tush"
map	o mapa	"**mah**puh"
▷ **can you show me on the map?**	pode-me mostrar no mapa?	"**pod**-muh moosh**trar** noo **mah**puh"
▷ **I want a street map of the city**	quero um mapa com as ruas da cidade	"**keh**roo oom **mah**puh kong ush **roo**ush duh see**dahd**"
▷ **I need a road map of ...**	preciso de um mapa das estradas de ...	"pre**see**zoo doom **mah**puh dush **shtrah**dush duh"
▷ **where can I buy a local map?**	onde posso comprar um mapa local?	"**onduh** **pos**oo kom**prar** oom **mah**puh loo**kal**"
March	Março	"**mar**soo"
margarine	a margarina	"marguh**ree**nuh"
mark	a marca	"**mar**kuh"
market	o mercado	"mer**kah**doo"
market day:		
▷ **when is market day?**	quando é o dia de feira?	"**kwan**doo e oo **dee**uh duh **fay**ruh"

ABSOLUTE ESSENTIALS

do you have ...?	tem ...?	"tayng"
is there ...?	há ...?	"ah"
are there ...?	há ...?	"ah"
how much is ...?	quanto custa ...?	"**kwan**too **koosh**tuh"

marmalade	o doce de laranja	"dohs duh la**ran**juh"
married	casado	"ka**zah**doo"
	casada	"ka**zah**duh"
marzipan	o marçapão	"massuh**powng**"
mascara	o rímel®	"**ree**mel"
mass (*in church*)	a missa	"**mees**uh"
▷ **when is mass?**	quando é a missa	"kwandoo **e** uh **mees**uh"
match	o fósforo	"**fosh**fooroo"
material (*cloth*)	o material	"matuh**ree**al"
▷ **what is the material?**	qual é a fazenda?	"kwal e uh fa**zen**duh"
matter:		
▷ **it doesn't matter**	não tem importância	"nowng tayng eempoor-**tans**yuh"
▷ **what's the matter?**	o que se passa?	"**oo** kuh suh **pah**suh"
May	Maio	"**my**oo"
mayonnaise	a maionaise	"my-oo**nez**"
meal	a refeição	"ruhfay**sowng**"
to **mean** (*signify*)	significar	"seegneefee**kar**"
▷ **what does this mean?**	o que significa isto?	"oo kuh seegnee**fee**kuh **eesh**too"
measles	o sarampo	"sa**ram**po"
to **measure**	medir	"me**deer**"
▷ **can you measure me please?**	pode medir-me, por favor?	"pod me**deer**-muh poor fa**vor**"
meat	a carne	"karn"
▷ **I don't eat meat**	não como carne	"nowng **koh**moo karn"

mechanic	o mecânico	"me**kah**nikoo"
▷ **can you send a mechanic?**	pode mandar um mecânico?	"pod man**dar** oom me**kah**nikoo"
medicine	o medicamento	"medeekuh-**men**too"
medium	médio	"**med**yoo"
	média	"**med**yuh"
medium rare	mal passado	"**mal** pa**sah**do"
	mal passada	"**mal** pa**sah**duh"
to meet	encontrar	"aymkon**trar**"
▷ **pleased to meet you**	prazer em conhecê-lo	"pra**zehr** ayng koonyuh**seh**-loo"
▷ **shall we meet afterwards?**	encontramo-nos depois?	"aymkon**trah**moo-noosh duh**poysh**"
▷ **where can we meet?**	onde nos podemos encontrar?	"ond noosh poo**deh**moosh aymkon**trar**"
melon	o melão	"me**lowng**"
to melt	fundir	"foon**deer**"
member (*of club etc*)	o sócio	"**sos**yoo"
	a sócia	"**sos**yuh"
▷ **do we need to be members?**	temos que ser sócios?	"**tay**moosh kuh sehr **sos**yoosh"
men	os homens	"**o**maynsh"
to mention	mencionar	"**men**syoonar"
▷ **don't mention it**	não tem importância	"nowng tayng eempoor**tans**yuh"
menu	a ementa	"ee**men**tuh"
▷ **may we see the menu?**	pode-nos dar a ementa?	"**pod**noosh dar uh ee**men**tuh"
▷ **do you have a special menu for children?**	tem uma ementa especial para crianças?	"tayng **oom**uh ee**men**tuh shpus**yal** paruh kree**an**sush"
▷ **we'll have the menu at ... escudos**	queremos a ementa de ... escudos	"**kray**moozuh ee**men**tuh duh ... **shkoo**doosh"

ABSOLUTE ESSENTIALS

meringue	o merengue	"muh**reng**uh"
message	o recado	"re**kah**doo"
	a mensagem	"men**sah**jayng"
▷ **can I leave a message with his secretary?**	posso deixar um recado à secretária?	"**pos**oo day**shar** oom re**kah**doo a sekruh**tar**yuh"
▷ **could you take a message please?**	posso deixar um recado, por favor?	"**pos**oo day**shar** oom re**kah**doo poor fa**vor**"
metal	o metal	"muh**tal**"
meter	o contador	"kontuh**dor**"
▷ **the meter is broken**	o contador está avariado	"oo kontuh**dor** shta avuhree-**ah**doo"
▷ **do you have change for the meter?**	tem troco para o contador?	"tayng **troh**koo paruh oo kontuh**dor**"
metre	o metro	"**met**roo"
migraine	a enxaqueca	"aynshuh**kek**uh"
mile (*metric equiv = 1.60 km*)	a milha	"**meel**yuh"
milk	o leite	"layt"
milkshake	o batido de leite	"ba**tee**doo duh layt"
millimetre	o milímetro	"mee**lee**metroo"
million	o milhão	"meel**yowng**"
mince	a carne picada	"karn pee**kah**duh"
to **mind:**		
▷ **do you mind if I ...?**	importa-se que eu ...?	"eem**por**tuh-suh kee **ay**oo"
▷ **I don't mind**	não me importo	"nowng muh eem**por**too"
mine (*singular*)	meu	"**may**oo"
	minha	"**meen**yuh"
(*plural*)	meus	"**may**oosh"
	minhas	"**meen**yush"

▷ **this is not mine**	isto não é meu	"**eesh**too nowng e **me**oo"
mineral water	a água mineral	"**ahg**wuh meenuh**ral**"
minimum	o mínimo	"**mee**nimoo"
minister (*church*)	o pastor	"pash**tor**"
minor road	a estrada secundária	"**shtrah**duh sekoon**dar**yuh"
mint (*herb*)	a hortelã	"ortuh**lang**"
(*sweet*)	a pastilha de mentol	"pash**teel** duh men**tol**"
minute	o minuto	"mee**noo**too"
▷ **wait a minute**	espere um minuto	"**shper** oom mee**noo**too"
mirror	o espelho	"**shpel**yoo"
Miss	Menina	"muh**nee**nuh"
to miss (*train, etc*)	perder	"per**dehr**"
▷ **I've missed my train**	perdi o comboio	"per**dee** oo kom**boy**oo"
missing:		
▷ **my son is missing**	não encontro o meu filho	"nowng ayng**kon**troo oo **may**oo **feel**yoo"
▷ **my handbag is missing**	não encontro o meu saco de mão	"nowng ayng**kon**troo oo **may**oo **sah**koo duh **mowng**"
mistake	o erro	"**err**oo"
▷ **there must be a mistake**	deve haver um engano	"dev a**vehr** oom ayng**gah**noo"
▷ **you've made a mistake in the change**	enganou-se no troco	"ayngga**noh**-suh noo **troh**koo"
misty	enevoado	"eenu-**vwah**doo"
	enevoada	"eenu-**vwah**duh"
misunderstanding:		
▷ **there's been a misunderstanding**	houve um malentendido	"ohv oom malenten-**dee**doo"

ABSOLUTE ESSENTIALS

do you have ...?	tem ...?	"tayng"
is there ...?	há ...?	"ah"
are there ...?	há ...?	"ah"
how much is ...?	quanto custa ...?	"**kwan**too **koosh**tuh"

modern	moderno	"moo**dehr**moo"
	moderna	"moo**dehr**muh"
moisturizer	o creme hidratante	"krem eedruh**tant**"
monastery	o mosteiro	"moosh**tay**roo"
Monday	segunda-feira	"suh**goon**duh-fairuh"
money	o dinheiro	"deen**yay**roo"
▷ **I have run out of money**	fiquei sem dinheiro	"fee**kay** sayng deen**yay**roo"
▷ **I have no money**	não tenho dinheiro	"nowng **ten**yoo deen**yay**roo"
▷ **can I borrow some money?**	pode emprestar-me algum dinheiro?	"pod aymprush**tar**-muh al**goom** deen**yay**roo"
▷ **can you arrange to have some money sent over urgently?**	pode enviar-me algum dinheiro urgentemente?	"pod aynvee**ar**-muh al**goom** deen**yay**roo oorgentuh-**ment**"
money belt	o cinto com porta-moedas	"**seen**too kong **por**tuh moo-**e**dush"
money order	o vale postal	"vahl poosh**tal**"
month	o mês	"mesh"
monument	o monumento	"moonoo**men**too"
mop (for floor)	a esfregona	"shfre**gon**uh"
more	mais	"mysh"
▷ **more wine, please**	mais vinho, por favor	"mysh **veen**yoo poor fa**vor**"
▷ **more than three**	mais de três	"mysh duh tresh"
▷ **more bread**	mais pão	"mysh powng"
morning	a manhã	"man**yang**"
▷ **in the morning**	de manhã	"duh man**yang**"
mosquito	o mosquito	"moosh**kee**too"
mosquito bite	a picada de mosquito	"pee**kah**duh duh moosh**kee**too"

most:

▷ **the most popular discotheque** | a discoteca mais frequentada | "uh deeshkootekuh **mysh** fruhkwen**tah**duh"

mother | a mãe | "**myng**"

motor | o motor | "moo**tor**"

motor boat | o barco a motor | "**bar**koo uh moo**tor**"

▷ **can we rent a motor boat?** | podemos alugar um barco a motor? | "poo**day**mooz aloo**gar** oom **bar**koo uh moo**tor**"

motorcycle | a motocicleta | "mootoo-see**kle**tuh"

motorway | a auto-estrada | "owtoo-**shtrah**duh"

▷ **how do I get onto the motorway?** | como se vai para a auto-estrada? | "**koh**moo suh vy pra owtoo-**shtrah**duh"

▷ **is there a toll on this motorway?** | há portagem nesta auto-estrada? | "a poor**tah**jayng **nesh**tuh owtoo-**shtrah**duh"

mountain | a montanha | "mon**tah**nyuh"

mountain bike | a bicicleta de todo-terreno | "beesee**kle**tuh duh **toh**doo-tuh**rreh**noo"

mouth | a boca | "**boh**kuh"

to move | mexer-se | "mu**shehr**-suh"

▷ **he can't move** | ele não pode mexer-se | "**ayl** nowng pod mu**shehr**-suh"

▷ **I can't move my leg** | não posso mexer a perna | "nowng **pos**oo mu**shehr** uh **pehr**nuh"

▷ **don't move him** | não lhe mexam | "nowng lyuh **mesh**owng"

▷ **could you move your car please?** | podia afastar o seu carro, por favor? | "poo**dee**uh afush**tar** oo **say**oo **kar**roo poor fa**vor**"

Mr | Senhor | "sun**yor**"

Mrs | Senhora | "sun**yor**uh"

much | muito | "**mween**too"
 | muita | "**mween**tuh"

ABSOLUTE ESSENTIALS

I don't understand	não compreendo	"nowng kompree**een**doo"
I don't speak Portuguese	não falo português	"nowng **fah**loo poortoo**gaysh**"
do you speak English?	fala inglês?	"**fah**luh een**glesh**"
could you help me?	podia ajudar-me?	"poo**dee**uh ajoo**dar**muh"

▷ **too much**	demais	"duh**mysh**"
	demasiado	"duhmuhzee-**ah**doo"
▷ **that's too much**	isso é demasiado	"**ee**soo e duhmuhzee-**ah**doo"
▷ **there's too much ... in it**	contém demasiado ...	"kon**tayng** duhmuhzee-**ah**doo"
mumps	a papeira	"pa**payr**uh"
Munich	Munique	"moo**neek**uh"
museum	o museu	"moo**zayoo**"
▷ **the museum is open in the morning/ afternoon**	o museu está aberto de manhã/de tarde	"oo moo**zayoo** shta **abehr**too duh man**yang**/duh tard"
mushroom	o cogumelo	"koogoo**mel**oo"
music	a música	"**moo**zikuh"
▷ **the music is too loud**	a música está demasiado alta	"uh **moo**zikuh shta duhmuhzee-**ah**doo **al**tuh"
Muslim	muçulmano	"moo**sool**manoo"
	muçulmana	"moo**sool**manuh"
mussel	o mexilhão	"musheel-**yowng**"
must	dever	"de**vehr**"
	ter de	"tehr duh"

I must	tenho de	"**ten**yoo duh"
you must (*informal singular*)	tens de	"**tayngsh** duh"
(*formal singular*)	você tem de	"voseh **tayng** duh"
he/she/it must	ele/ela tem de	"el/eluh **tayng** duh"
we must	temos de	"**teh**moosh duh"
you must (*informal plural*)	tendes de	"**ten**dush duh"
(*formal plural*)	vocês têm de	"vosehsh **tay**ayng duh"
they must	eles/elas têm de	"elsh/elush **tay**ayng duh"

ABSOLUTE ESSENTIALS		
I would like ...	queria ...	"**kree**uh"
I need ...	preciso de ...	"pre**see**zoo duh"
where is ...?	onde fica ...?	"ond **feek**uh"
I'm looking for ...	procuro ...	"pro**koo**roo"

▷ **I must make a phone call**	tenho de fazer um telefonema	"**ten**yoo duh fa**zehr** oom tuhluh-foo**neh**muh"
mustard	a mostarda	"moosh**tard**uh"
mutton	o carneiro	"kar**nay**roo"
nail (*metal*)	o prego	"**pray**goo"
nail file	a lima das unhas	"**lee**muh duh**zoon**yush"
nail polish	o verniz das unhas	"ver**neesh** duh**zoon**yush"
nail polish remover	a acetona	"asuh**ton**uh"
naked	nu	"noo"
	nua	"**noo**uh"
name	o nome	"nom"
▷ **what's your name?**	como se chama?	"**koh**moo suh **shah**muh"
▷ **my name is ...**	chamo-me ...	"**shah**moo-muh"
napkin	o guardanapo	"gwarduh**nah**poo"
nappy	a fralda	"**fral**duh"
narrow	estreito	"**shtray**too"
	estreita	"**shtray**tuh"
nationality	a nacionalidade	"nasyoona-lee**dahd**"
navy blue	azul marinho	"**azool** mar**een**yoo"
near	perto	"**pehr**too"
▷ **near the bank/hotel**	perto do banco/hotel	"**pehr**too doo **bank**oo/oh**tel**"
necessary	necessário	"nusuh-**sary**oo"
	necessária	"nusuh-**sary**uh"
neck	o pescoço	"push**koh**soo"

do you have ...?	tem ...?	"tayng"
is there ...?	há ...?	"ah"
are there ...?	há ...?	"ah"
how much is ...?	quanto custa ...?	"**kwan**too **koosh**tuh"

necklace	o colar	"koo**lar**"
to need:		
▷ **I need an aspirin**	preciso duma aspirina	"pre**see**zoo **doom**uh ashpee**ree**nuh"
▷ **do you need anything?**	precisa de alguma coisa?	"pre**see**zuh duh al**goo**muh **koy**zuh"
needle	a agulha	"a**gool**yuh"
▷ **a needle and thread**	uma agulha e a linha	"**oom**uh a**gool**yuh ee uh **leen**yuh"
▷ **do you have a needle and thread?**	tem uma agulha e linha?	"**tayng** oomuh a**gool**yuh ee **leen**yuh"
negative (*photography*)	o negativo	"nuhguh**tee**voo"
neighbour	o vizinho	"vee**zeen**yoo"
	a vizinha	"vee**zeen**yuh"
never	nunca	"**noon**kuh"
▷ **I never drink wine**	nunca bebo vinho	"**noon**kuh **be**boo **veen**yoo"
▷ **I've never been to Italy**	nunca fui a Itália	"**noon**kuh **fwee** uh ee**tahl**yuh"
new	novo	"**noh**voo"
	nova	"**no**vuh"
news	a notícia	"noo**tees**yuh"
newsagent	a tabacaria	"tabuh-kuh**ree**uh"
newspaper	o jornal	"joor**nal**"
▷ **do you have any English newspapers?**	tem jornais ingleses?	"tayng joor**nysh** een**glay**zush"
New Year	o Ano Novo	"**ah**noo **noh**voo"
▷ **Happy New Year!**	Feliz Ano Novo	"fuh**leesh ah**noo **noh**voo"
New Zealand	a Nova Zelândia	"**noh**vuh zuh**lan**deeuh"
next	próximo	"**pros**imoo"
	próxima	"**pros**imuh"

▷ the next stop	a próxima paragem	"uh **pros**imuh puhra**jayn**"
▷ next week	na próxima semana	"nuh **pros**imuh se**mah**nuh"
▷ when's the next bus to town?	quando é o próximo autocarro para a cidade	"**kwan**doo e oo **pros**imoo owto**kar**roo paruh uh see**dahd**"
▷ take the next turning on the left	vire na próxima à esquerda	"**vee**ruh nuh **pros**imuh a sh**kehr**duh"
nice	simpático simpática	"seem**pat**ikoo" "seem**pat**ikuh"
▷ we are having a nice time	estamos a divertir-nos	"sh**tah**moosh uh deevuhr**teer**-noosh"
▷ it doesn't taste very nice	não sabe muito bem	"nowng **sahb mween**too bayng"
▷ yes, that's very nice	sim, isso é muito bom	"sayng **ees**oo e **mween**too bong"
▷ nice to have met you	foi bom tê-lo conhecido	"foy bong **tay**loo koonye**seed**oo"
night	a noite	"noyt"
▷ at night	à noite	"a noyt"
▷ on Saturday night	no sábado à noite	"noo **sah**buhdoo a noyt"
▷ last night	ontem à noite	"**on**tayng a noyt"
▷ tomorrow night	amanhã à noite	"ahman**yang** a noyt"
night club	a boite	"bwat"
nightdress	a camisa de noite	"ka**mee**zuh duh noyt"
nine	nove	"nov"
nineteen	dezanove	"duzuh**nov**"
ninety	noventa	"noo**ven**tuh"
no	não	"nowng"
▷ no thank you	não, obrigado	"nowng ohbree**gah**doo"
▷ there's no coffee	não há café	"nowng a kuh**fe**"
nobody	ninguém	"neen**gayng**"

noisy	barulhento	"baroolyentoo"
	barulhenta	"baroolyentuh"
▷ it's too noisy	é demasiado barulhento	"e duhmuhzee-ahdoo baroolyentoo"
non-alcoholic	não-alcoólico	"nowng-alkwolikoo"
	não-alcoólica	"nowng-alkwolikuh"
▷ what non-alcoholic drinks do you have?	que bebidas não-alcoólicas tem?	"kuh buhbeedush nowng-alkwolikush tayng"
none	nenhum	"nunyoom"
	nenhuma	"nunyoomuh"
▷ there's none left	não sobrou nada	"nowng soobroh nahduh"
non-smoking (*compartment*)	para não fumadores	"paruh nowng foomuhdorush"
▷ is this a non-smoking area?	esta zona é para não fumadores?	"eshtuh zonuh e paruh nowng foomuhdorush"
▷ I would like a seat in a non-smoking compartment	queria um lugar num compartimento para não fumadores	"kreeuh oom loogar noom konpuhrtee-mentoo paruh nowng-foomuhdorush"
north	o norte	"nort"
Northern Ireland	a Irlanda do Norte	"eerlanduh doo nort"
not	não	"nowng"
▷ I don't know	não sei	"nowng say"
▷ I am not coming	eu não vou	"ayoo nowng voh"
note	a nota	"notuh"
▷ do you have change of this note?	tem troco para esta nota?	"tayng trohkoo paruh eshtuh notuh"
note pad	o bloco de notas	"blokoo duh notush"
nothing	nada	"nahduh"
▷ nothing to declare	nada a declarar	"nahduh uh dekluhrar"
notice (*sign*)	o aviso	"aveezoo"
November	Novembro	"noovembroo"

now	agora	"**ago**ruh"
number	o número	"**noo**meroo"
▷ car number	matrícula do carro	"ma**tree**kooluh doo **kar**roo"
▷ what's your room number?	qual é o número do seu quarto?	"kwal **e** oo **noo**meroo doo sayoo **kwar**too"
▷ what's the telephone number?	qual é o número de telefone?	"kwal **e** oo **noo**meroo duh tuhluh**fon**"
▷ sorry, wrong number	desculpe, foi engano	"dsh**kool**p foy aym**gah**noo"
Nuremberg	Noremberga	"**noo**raymbehrguh"
nurse	a enfermeira	"aymfer-**may**ruh"
nursery slope	a rampa para principiantes	"**ram**puh paruh **preen**seepee-antsh"
nut (*to eat*)	a noz	"nosh"
(*for bolt*)	a porca	"**por**kuh"
o'clock:		
▷ at 2 o'clock	às 2 horas	"ash **doo**ush **o**rush"
▷ it's 10 o'clock	são 10 horas	"sowng **desh o**rush"
▷ it's 1 o'clock	é 1 hora	"e **oo**muh **o**ruh"
occasionally	às vezes	"ash **vay**zush"
October	Outubro	"oh**too**broo"
of	de	"duh"
of course	claro	"**klah**roo"
off (*machine etc*)	desligado	"dujlee**gah**doo"
	desligada	"dujlee**gah**duh"
(*rotten*)	pôdre	"**poh**druh"
▷ let me off here, please	deixe-me sair aqui, por favor	"**day**shuh-muh sa**eer** a**kee** poor fa**vor**"
▷ the lights are off	as luzes estão apagadas	"ush **loo**zush shtowng apuh**gah**dush"

do you have ...?	tem ...?	"tayng"
is there ...?	há ...?	"ah"
are there ...?	há ...?	"ah"
how much is ...?	quanto custa ...?	"**kwan**too **koosh**tuh"

to **offer**	oferecer	"ofuhruh**sehr**"
office	o escritório	"shkree**tor**yoo"
▷ **I work in an office**	trabalho num escritório	"tra**bal**yoo noom shkree**tor**yoo"
often	muitas vezes	"**mween**tush **vay**zush"
oil	o óleo	"**ol**yoo"
oil filter	o filtro do óleo	"**feel**troo doo **ol**yoo"
ointment	a pomada	"poo**mah**duh"
O.K.	está bem	"shta bayng"
old	velho	"**vel**yoo"
	velha	"**vel**yuh"
▷ **how old are you?**	que idade tem?	"kuh ee**dahd** tayng"
▷ **old-age pensioner**	o reformado	"ruhfoor**mah**do"
	a reformada	"ruhfoor**mah**duh"
olive	a azeitona	"azay**ton**uh"
olive oil	o azeite	"a**zayt**"
omelette	a omeleta	"omuh**let**uh"
on[1] *adj (light, engine)*	aceso	"a**say**zoo"
	acesa	"a**say**zuh"
on[2] *prep*	na	"nuh"
	em cima de	"ayng **see**muh duh"
▷ **on the bed**	em cima da cama	"ayng **see**mah duh **kah**muh"
▷ **on the table**	na mesa	"nuh **may**zuh"
once	uma vez	"**oom**uh vesh"
▷ **once a day/year**	uma vez por dia/ano	"**oom**uh vesh poor **dee**uh/**ah**noo"
one	um	"oom"
	uma	"**oom**uh"
one hundred	cem	"sayng"

one hundred and one	cento e um	"**sen**toee**oom**"
one hundred and twenty one	cento e vinte e um	"**sen**to-ee**veen**tee-**oom**"
one thousand	mil	"meel"
one-way street	rua de sentido único	"**roo**uh duh sen**tee**doo **oo**nikoo"
onion	a cebola	"suh**bo**luh"
only	só	"so"
▷ we only want 3	só queremos três	"so ke**reh**moosh trehsh"
open¹ *adj*	aberto aberta	"a**behr**too" "a**behr**tuh"
▷ is the castle open to the public?	o castelo está aberto ao público?	"oo kash**te**loo shta a**behr**too ow **poob**likoo"
▷ are you open?	está aberto?	"shta a**behr**too"
to open² *vb*	abrir	"a**breer**"
▷ what time does the museum open?	a que horas é que abre o museu?	"uh kee **o**ruz e kee **ah**bruh oo moo**zay**oo"
▷ I can't open the window	não posso abrir a janela	"nowng **pos**oo a**breer** uh ja**ne**luh"
opera	a ópera	"**o**peruh"
operator	o operador	"ohperuh**dor**"
opposite (*house etc*)	em frente	"aym frent"
or	ou	"oh"
orange¹ *n*	a laranja	"la**ran**juh"
orange² *adj*	cor de laranja	"kor duh la**ran**juh"
orange juice	o sumo de laranja	"**soo**moo duh la**ran**juh"
to order	encomendar	"ayngkoomen**dar**"
▷ can you order me a taxi, please?	pode chamar-me um táxi?	"pod sha**mar**-muh oom **tax**ee"

ABSOLUTE ESSENTIALS

I don't understand	não compreendo	"nowng kompree**een**doo"
I don't speak Portuguese	não falo português	"nowng **fah**loo poortoo**gaysh**"
do you speak English?	fala inglês?	"**fah**luh een**glesh**"
could you help me?	podia ajudar-me?	"poo**dee**uh ajoo**dar**muh"

▷ **can I order now please?**	posso pedir agora, por favor?	"**pos**oo pe**deer** a**gor**uh poor fa**vor**"
oregano	o oregão	"oruh**gowng**"
original	original	"ohreejee**nal**"
other:		
▷ **the other one**	o outro	"oo **oh**troo"
	a outra	"uh **oh**truh"
▷ **do you have any others?**	tem mais?	"tayng mysh"
▷ **where are the others?**	onde estão os outros?	"ond sh**towng** oosh **oh**troosh"
ounce (*metric equiv = 28.35 g*)	a onça	"**on**suh"
ours (*singular*)	nosso	"**nos**oo"
	nossa	"**nos**uh"
(*plural*)	nossos	"**nos**oosh"
	nossas	"**nos**ush"
out (*light*)	apagado	"apuh**gah**doo"
	apagada	"apuh**gah**duh"
▷ **he's out**	ele saiu	"ayl sa**yoo**"
outdoor (*pool etc*)	ao ar livre	"ow ar **leev**ruh"
▷ **what are the outdoor activities?**	quais são as actividades ao ar livre?	"kwysh **sowng** ush akteevee-**dah**dsh ow ar **leev**ruh"
outside	lá fora	"lah **for**uh"
▷ **let's go outside**	vamos lá para fora	"**vah**moos **lah** puhruh **for**uh"
▷ **an outside line please**	uma ligação exterior, por favor	"**oo**muh leeguh**sowng** **ays**tuhryor poor fa**vor**"
oven	o forno	"**for**noo"
over (*on top of*)	sobre	"**soh**bruh"
to **overcharge**	cobrar demais	"koo**brar** duh**mysh**"

ABSOLUTE ESSENTIALS

I would like ...	queria ...	"**kree**uh"
I need ...	preciso de ...	"pre**see**zoo duh"
where is ...?	onde fica ...?	"ond **fee**kuh"
I'm looking for ...	procuro ...	"pro**koo**roo"

▷ **I've been overcharged**	cobraram-me dinheiro a mais	"koo**brah**rowng-muh deen**yay**roo uh **mysh**"
overheating:		
▷ **the engine is overheating**	o motor aquece demais	"oo moo**tor** a**kes** duh**mysh**"
overnight	durante a noite	"doo**rant** uh noyt"
to owe	dever	"de**vehr**"
▷ **you owe me ...**	deve-me ...	"**dev**-muh"
▷ **what do I owe you?**	quanto lhe devo?	"**kwan**too lye **deh**voo"
owner	o dono	"**doh**noo"
▷ **could I speak to the owner please?**	eu podia falar com o dono, por favor?	"**ay**oo poo**dee**uh fa**lar** kong oo **doh**noo poor fa**vor**"
oyster	a ostra	"**osh**truh"
to pack (luggage)	fazer as malas	"fa**zehr** ush **mah**lush"
▷ **I need to pack now**	preciso de fazer as malas agora	"pre**see**zoo duh fa**zehr** ush **mah**lush a**gor**uh"
package	o embrulho	"aym**brool**yoo"
package tour	a viagem organizada	"vee**ah**jayng organee-**zah**duh"
packed lunch	o almoço embalado	"al**moh**soo aymba**lah**doo"
packet	o pacote	"pa**kot**"
▷ **a packet of cigarettes**	um maço de cigarros	"oom **mah**soo duh see**gar**roosh"
paddling pool	a piscina para crianças	"peesh-**see**nuh **par**uh kree**an**sush"
▷ **is there a paddling pool for the children?**	há uma piscina para crianças?	"a **oom**uh peesh-**see**nuh **par**uh kree**an**sush"
paid	pago	"**pahg**oo"
	paga	"**pahg**uh"
pain	a dor	"dohr"

ABSOLUTE ESSENTIALS

do you have ...?	tem ...?	"tayng"
is there ...?	há ...?	"ah"
are there ...?	há ...?	"ah"
how much is ...?	quanto custa ...?	"**kwan**too **koosh**tuh"

▷ I have a pain here/in my chest	dói-me aqui/o peito	"**doy**-muh a**kee**/oo **pay**too"
painful	doloroso	"dooloo**roh**zoo"
	dolorosa	"dooloo**roh**zuh"
painkiller	o analgésico	"anal**jez**ikoo"
painting	a pintura	"pin**too**ruh"
pair	o par	"par"
▷ a pair of sandals	um par de sandálias	"**oom par** de san**dah**leeush"
palace	o palácio	"pa**las**yoo"
▷ is the palace open to the public?	o palácio está aberto ao público?	"oo pa**las**yoo shta a**behr**too ow **poo**blikoo"
pan	a panela	"pa**nel**uh"
pancake	a panqueca	"pan**kek**uh"
pants	as cuecas	"**kwek**ush"
paper	o papel	"puh**pel**"
paraffin	a parafina	"paruh**fee**nuh"
paragliding:		
▷ where can we go paragliding?	onde podemos ir fazer paraquedismo?	"**ond** poo**deh**moosh eer fa**zehr** pahruhkuh-**deesh**moo"
parascending:		
▷ we'd like to go parascending	gostávamos de ir fazer parascending	"**goosh**tah-vuhmoosh duh eer fa**zehr** parascending"
parasol	o guarda-sol	"gwarduh**sol**"
parcel	a encomenda	"ayngkoo**men**duh"
▷ I want to send this parcel	quero enviar esta encomenda	"**ke**roo **aym**veeahr eshta ayngkoo**men**duh"

pardon (*I didn't understand*)	desculpe?	"dush**koolp**"
▷ **I beg your pardon?**	como disse?	"**koh**moo dees"
parents	os pais	"pysh"
Paris	Paris	"puh**reesh**"
park¹ *n*	o parque	"park"
to **park**² *vb*	estacionar	"shtasyoo**nar**"
▷ **can we park our caravan there?**	podemos estacionar a caravana ali?	"poo**day**moosh shtasyoo**nar** uh kara**vah**nuh a**lee**"
▷ **where can I park?**	onde posso estacionar?	"**on**duh **pos**oo shtasyoo**nar**"
▷ **can I park here?**	posso estacionar aqui?	"**pos**oo shtasyoo**nar** a**kee**"
parking disc	o disco de estacionamento	"**deesh**koo dushtasyoo-nuh**men**too"
parking meter	o parcómetro	"pur**koh**muhtroo"
parsley	a salsa	"**sal**suh"
part	a parte	"part"
party (*group*)	o grupo	"**groo**poo"
passenger	o passageiro	"pasuh**jay**roo"
passport	o passaporte	"pasuh**port**"
▷ **I have forgotten my passport**	esqueci-me do passaporte	"shkuh**see**-muh doo pasuh**port**"
▷ **please give me my passport back**	por favor, devolva-me o passaporte	"poor fa**vor** duh**vol**vuh-muh oo pasuh**port**"
▷ **my wife/husband and I have a joint passport**	a minha mulher/o meu marido e eu temos um passaporte familiar	"uh **meen**yuh mool**yehr**/oo **may**oo ma**ree**doo ee **ay**oo **tay**mooz oom pasuh**port** fameel**yar**"
▷ **the children are on this passport**	as crianças estão neste passaporte	"ush kree**an**sush shtowng naysht pasuh**port**"

ABSOLUTE ESSENTIALS

I don't understand	não compreendo	"nowng kompree**en**doo"
I don't speak Portuguese	não falo português	"nowng **fah**loo poortoo**gaysh**"
do you speak English?	fala inglês?	"**fah**luh een**glesh**"
could you help me?	podia ajudar-me?	"poo**dee**uh ajoo**dar**muh"

▷ my passport number is ...	o número do meu passaporte é ...	"oo **noo**meroo doo **may**oo pasuh**port** e"
▷ I've lost my passport	perdi o meu passaporte	"per**dee** oo **may**oo pasuh**port**"
▷ my passport has been stolen	o meu passaporte foi roubado	"oo **may**oo pasuh**port** foy rohbah**doo**"
▷ I've got a visitors' passport	tenho um passaporte temporário	"**ten**yoo oom pasuh**port** tempoo**rah**ryoo"
passport control	o controle de passaportes	"kon**trol** duh pasuh**portsh**"
pasta	as massas	"**mas**ush"
pastry (*cake*)	a massa / o bolo	"**mas**uh" / "**boh**loo"
pâté	o paté	"pa**tay**"
path	o caminho	"ka**meen**yoo"
▷ where does this path lead?	onde vai dar este caminho?	"**ond** vy **dar** esht ka**meen**yoo"
to **pay**	pagar	"pa**gar**"
▷ do I pay now or later?	pago agora ou mais tarde?	"**pah**goo a**gor**uh oh mysh **tard**"
payment	o pagamento	"paguh**men**too"
peach	o pêssego	"**pay**suhgoo"
peanut	o amendoim	"amendoo-**eeng**"
pear	a pêra	"**pay**ruh"
peas	as ervilhas	"ehr**veel**yush"
to **peel** (*fruit*)	descascar	"dushkash**kar**"
peg (*for clothes*) (*for tent*)	o cabide / a mola	"ka**beed**" / "**mol**uh"
pen	a caneta	"ka**net**uh"

▷ do you have a pen I could borrow?	tem uma caneta que me podia emprestar?	"**tayng** oomuh ka**ne**tuh **kuh** muh poodeeuh aymprush**tar**"
pencil	o lápis	"**lah**peesh"
penicillin	a penicilina	"puneesee-**lee**nuh"
▷ I am allergic to penicillin	sou alérgico à penicilina	"soh a**lehr**jikoo a puneesee-**lee**nuh"
penknife	o canivete	"kanee**vet**"
pensioner	o reformado a reformada	"ruhfoor**mah**doo" "ruhfoor**mah**duh"
▷ are there reductions for pensioners?	fazem descontos para reformados?	"**fah**zayng dsh**kon**toosh paruh refoor**mah**doosh"
pepper (*spice*) (*vegetable*)	a pimenta o pimentão	"pee**men**tuh" "pee**men**too"
per:		
▷ per hour	por hora	"poor **o**ruh"
▷ per week	por semana	"poor se**mah**nuh"
▷ 60 miles per hour	60 milhas por hora	"se**sen**tuh **meel**yush poor **o**ruh"
perfect	perfeito perfeita	"per**fay**too" "per**fay**tuh"
performance (*actors'*)	a representação o espectáculo	"rupruhzen-tuh**sowng**" "shpe**tah**kooloo"
▷ what time does the performance begin?	a que horas começa o espectáculo?	"**uh** kuh **o**rush koo**me**suh oo shpe**tah**kooloo"
▷ how long does the performance last?	quanto tempo demora o espectáculo?	"**kwan**too tempoo duh**mo**ruh oo shpe**tah**kooloo"
perfume	o perfume	"per**foom**"
perhaps	talvez	"tal**vesh**"
period (*menstruation*)	a menstruação	"menshtroo-uh**sowng**"

ABSOLUTE ESSENTIALS

do you have ...?	tem ...?	"tayng"
is there ...?	há ...?	"ah"
are there ...?	há ...?	"ah"
how much is ...?	quanto custa ...?	"**kwan**too **koosh**tuh"

perm	a permanente	"permuh**nent**"
▷ **my hair is permed**	tenho uma permanente	"ten**yoo oom**uh permuh**nent**"
permit	a licença	"lee**sen**suh"
▷ **do I need a fishing permit?**	preciso de uma licença de pesca?	"pre**see**zoo duh oomuh lee**sen**suh duh **pesh**kuh"
person	a pessoa	"puh**soh**uh"
petrol	a gasolina	"gazoo**lee**nuh"
▷ **20 litres of unleaded petrol**	20 litros de gasolina sem chumbo	"**veent leet**roosh duh gazoo**lee**nuh sayng **shoom**boo"
▷ **I have run out of petrol**	acabou-se-me a gasolina	"akuh**boh**-suh-muh uh gazoo**lee**nuh"
petrol station	a bomba de gasolina	"**bom**buh duh gazoo**lee**nuh"
pheasant	o faisão	"**fy**zawng"
phone[1] n	o telefone	"tuhluh**fon**"
to **phone**[2] vb	telefonar	"tuhluhfoo**nar**"
▷ **can I phone from here?**	posso telefonar daqui?	"**pos**oo tuhluhfoo**nar** da**kee**"
phone box	a cabine telefónica	"kah**been** tuhluh**fon**ikuh"
phone card	o cartão de telefone	"kar**towng** duh tuhluh**fon**"
▷ **do you sell phone cards?**	vende cartões para o telefone?	"**vend** kar**toyns** paruh oo tuhluh**fon**"
photocopy	a fotocópia	"footoo**kop**yuh"
▷ **where can I get some photocopying done?**	onde é que eu posso fazer fotocópias?	"**on**dee e kee **ay**oo **pos**oo fa**zehr** footoo**kop**yush"
▷ **I'd like a photocopy of this please**	queria uma fotocópia disto, por favor	"**kree**uh oomuh foto**kop**yuh **deesh**too poor fa**vor**"

photograph	a fotografia	"footoo-gruh**fee**uh"
▷ **when will the photos be ready?**	quando é que as fotografias estão prontas?	"**kwan**doo e kee ush footoo-gruh**fee**ush shtowng prontsh"
▷ **can I take photos in here?**	posso tirar fotografias aqui?	"**pos**oo tee**rar** footoo-gruh**fee**ush a**kee**"
▷ **would you take a photo of us?**	tirava-nos uma fotografia?	"tee**rah**vuh-noosh **oo**muh footoo-gruh**fee**uh"
picnic	o piquenique	"peekuh**neek**"
▷ **a picnic lunch**	um almoço de piquenique	"oom al**moh**soo duh peekuh**neek**"
picture (*painting*) (*photo*)	o quadro a fotografia	"**kwad**roo" "footoo-gruh**fee**uh"
pie	o pastel	"pash**tel**"
piece	o bocado	"boo**kah**doo"
▷ **a piece of cake**	uma fatia de bolo	"**oo**muh fuh**tee**uh duh **boh**loo"
pillow	a almofada	"almoo**fah**doo"
▷ **I would like an extra pillow**	queria outra almofada	"**kree**uh **oh**truh almoo**fah**duh"
pillowcase	o travesseiro	"travuh**say**roo"
pin	o alfinete	"alfee**net**"
pineapple	o ananás	"anuh**nash**"
pink	cor-de-rosa	"korduh**roz**uh"
pint (*metric equiv = 0.56 l*)	o pinto	"**peen**to"
▷ **a pint of beer**	uma caneca de cerveja	"ka**neh**kuh duh ser**vay**juh"
pipe	o cachimbo	"ka**sheem**boo"
pipe tobacco	o tabaco de cachimbo	"ta**bah**koo duh ka**sheem**boo"
pistachio	o pistacho	"peesh**tah**shoo"

ABSOLUTE ESSENTIALS

I don't understand	não compreendo	"nowng kompree**en**doo"
I don't speak Portuguese	não falo português	"nowng **fah**loo poortoo**gaysh**"
do you speak English?	fala inglês?	"**fah**luh een**glesh**"
could you help me?	podia ajudar-me?	"poo**dee**uh ajoo**dar**muh"

plane	o avião	"av**ee**ow**ng**"
▷ **my plane leaves at ...**	o meu avião parte às ...	"oo **may**oo av**ee**ow**ng** part **ash**"
▷ **I've missed my plane**	perdi o avião	"per**dee** oo av**ee**ow**ng**"
plaster (*sticking plaster*)	o adesivo	"aduh**zee**voo"
plastic	o plástico	"**plash**tikoo"
plate	o prato	"**prah**too"
platform	a linha	"**leen**yuh"
▷ **which platform for the train to ...?**	qual é a linha do comboio para ...?	"kwal e uh **leen**yuh doo kom**boy**oo paruh"
to play (*games*)	jogar	"joo**gar**"
▷ **we'd like to play tennis**	queríamos jogar ténis	"kree**uh**moosh joo**gar tay**neesh"
playroom	a sala de jogos	"**sah**luh duh **jog**oosh"
please	por favor	"poor fa**vor**"
▷ **yes, please**	sim, por favor	"seeng poor fa**vor**"
pleased:		
▷ **pleased to meet you**	prazer em conhecê-lo	"pra**zehr** ayng koonyuh**seh**-loo"
pliers	o alicate	"alee**kat**"
plug (*electrical*)	a ficha	"**fee**shuh"
(*for sink*)	a tampa	"**tam**puh"
plum	a ameixa	"a**may**shuh"
plumber	o canalizador	"kanalee-zuh**dor**"
points (*in car*)	os platinados	"plateen**ah**doosh"
police	a polícia	"poo**lee**syuh"
▷ **we will have to report it to the police**	temos que comunicá-lo à polícia	"**tay**moosh kuh koomoo-nee**kah**-loo a poo**lee**syuh"
▷ **get the police!**	chame a polícia!	"shahm uh poo**lee**syuh"

ABSOLUTE ESSENTIALS

I would like ...	queria ...	"**kree**uh"
I need ...	preciso de ...	"pre**see**zoo duh"
where is ...?	onde fica ...?	"ond **fee**kuh"
I'm looking for ...	procuro ...	"pro**koo**roo"

policeman	o polícia	"pooleesyuh"
police station	a esquadra	"shkwahdruh"
▷ where is the police station?	onde fica a esquadra?	"onduh feekuh uh shkwahdruh"
polish (for shoes)	a pomada para o calçado	"poomahduh prokalsahdoo"
polluted	poluído poluída	"poolweedoo" "poolweeduh"
pony trekking	o passeio de pónei	"pasayoo duh ponay"
▷ we'd like to go pony trekking	queríamos dar um passeio de pónei	"kreeuhmoosh dar oom pasayoo duh ponay"
pool (swimming)	a piscina	"peesh-seenuh"
▷ is there a children's pool?	há uma piscina para crianças?	"a oomuh peesh-seenuh paruh kreeansush"
▷ is the pool heated?	a piscina é aquecida?	"uh peesh-seenuh e akuhseeduh"
▷ is it an outdoor pool?	a piscina é descoberta?	"uh peesh-seenuh e dushkoo-behrtuh"
popular	popular	"poopoolar"
pork	a carne de porco	"karn duh porkoo"
port (seaport, wine)	o porto	"portoo"
porter (in hotel) (in station)	o porteiro o carregador	"poortayroo" "karruh-guhdor"
Portugal	Portugal	"poortoogal"
Portuguese	português portuguesa	"poortoogaysh" "poortoogayzuh"
possible	possível	"pooseevel"
▷ as soon as possible	o mais cedo possível	"oo mysh saydoo pooseevel"
to post	pôr no correio	"pohr noo koorayoo"

do you have ...?	tem ...?	"tayng"
is there ...?	há ...?	"ah"
are there ...?	há ...?	"ah"
how much is ...?	quanto custa ...?	"kwantoo kooshtuh"

▷ where can I post these cards?	onde posso enviar estes postais por correio?	"ond **pos**oo aymvee**ar** eshtsh poosh**tysh** poor koo**rray**oo"
postbox	o marco do correio	"**mar**koo do koo**rray**oo"
postcard	o postal	"poosh**tal**"
▷ do you have any postcards?	vende postais?	"**vend** poosh**tysh**"
▷ where can I buy some postcards?	onde posso comprar postais?	"ond **pos**oo kom**prar** poosh**tysh**"
postcode	o código postal	"**kod**igoo poosh**tal**"
post office	os correios	"koo**rray**oosh"
pot (for cooking)	a panela	"pa**nel**uh"
potato	a batata	"ba**tah**tuh"
pottery	a cerâmica	"suh**rah**mikuh"
pound (weight, money)	a libra	"**lee**bruh"
powdered milk	o leite em pó	"layt ayng po"
pram	o carrinho de bebé	"ka**reen**yoo duh be**be**"
prawn	o lagostim	"lagoosh**teeng**"
to **prefer**	preferir	"prefuh**reer**"
▷ I'd prefer to go ...	preferia ir para ...	"prefuh**ree**uh **eer** paruh"
▷ I prefer ... to ...	prefiro ... a ...	"pre**fee**roo ... **uh**"
pregnant	grávida	"**gra**viduh"
to **prepare**	preparar	"pruhpa**rar**"
prescription	a receita médica	"ruh**say**tuh **med**ikuh"
▷ where can I get this prescription made up?	onde posso aviar esta receita?	"ond **pos**oo avee**ar** eshtuh re**say**tuh"
present (gift)	o presente	"pruh**zent**"

▷ I want to buy a present for my husband/my wife	quero comprar um presente para o meu marido/a minha mulher	"**keh**roo komprar oom pruh**zent** pro **may**oo mar**ee**doo/uh **meen**yuh mool**yehr**"
pretty	bonito bonita	"bon**ee**too" "bon**ee**tuh"
price	o preço	"**pray**soo"
price list	a lista de preços	"**leesh**tuh duh **pray**soosh"
priest	o padre	"**pad**ruh"
▷ I want to see a priest	quero falar com um padre	"**keh**roo fa**lar** kong oom **pad**ruh"
print (*photo*)	a fotografia	"footoo-gruh**fee**uh"
private	privado privada	"pree**vah**doo" "pree**vah**duh"
▷ can I speak to you in private?	posso falar-lhe em particular?	"**pos**oo fa**lar**-lye ayng partee**koo**lar"
▷ this is private	isto é privado	"**eesh**too e pree**vah**doo"
▷ I have private health insurance	tenho seguro de saúde particular	"**ten**yoo suh**goo**roo duh sa**ood** parteekoo**lar**"
probably	provavelmente	"proovahvel**ment**"
problem	o problema	"proo**blem**uh"
programme	o programa	"proo**grah**muh"
to pronounce	pronunciar	"proonoons**yar**"
▷ how do you pronounce this?	como se pronuncia isto?	"**koh**moo suh proonoon**see**uh **eesh**too"
Protestant	protestante	"prootush**tant**"
prunes	as ameixas secas	"a**may**shush **say**kush"
public	público pública	"**poo**blikoo" "**poo**blikuh"

▷ is the castle open to the public?	o castelo está aberto ao público?	"oo kash**tel**oo shta a**behr**too ow **poob**likoo"
public holiday	o feriado	"fuhree**ah**doo"
pudding	o pudim	"poo**deeng**"
to pull	puxar	"poo**shar**"
pullover	o pulover	"poo**loh**vehr"
puncture	o furo	"**foo**roo"
▷ I have a puncture	tenho um furo	"**ten**yoo oom **foo**roo"
purple	roxo	"**roh**shoo"
	roxa	"**roh**shuh"
purse	a bolsa	"**bohl**suh"
▷ my purse has been stolen	a minha carteira foi roubada	"uh **meen**yuh kar**tay**ruh foy roh**bah**duh"
▷ I've lost my purse	perdi a minha carteira	"per**dee** uh **meen**yuh kar**tay**ruh"
to push	empurrar	"aympoo**rrar**"
▷ my car's broken down, can you give me a push?	o meu carro foi abaixo. Pode dar um empurrão?	"oo **may**oo **kar**roo foy a**by**shoo. pod **dar** oom aympoo**rrowng**"
to put	pôr	"pohr"
▷ put it down over there please	pouse ali, por favor	"**poh**zuh a**lee** poor fa**vor**"
pyjamas	o pijama	"pee**jah**muh"
quarter:		
▷ quarter to 10	um quarto para as 10	"oom **kwar**too **puh**ruh ush **desh**"
▷ quarter past 3	3 e um quarto	"**tray**sh ee oom **kwar**too"
queue	a fila	"**fee**luh"
▷ is this the end of the queue?	é aqui o fim da fila?	"e a**kee** oo **feeng** duh **fee**luh"
quick	rápido(a)	"**ra**pidoo(uh)"

quickly	depressa	"duh**pres**uh"
quiet (*place*)	sossegado	"soosuh**gah**doo"
	sossegada	"soosuh**gah**duh"
quilt	o edredão	"edruh**downg**"
quite:		
▷ **it's quite good**	é bastante bom	"**e** bash**tant** bong"
▷ **it's quite expensive**	é muito caro	"**e** **mween**too **kah**roo"
rabbit	o coelho	"koo**el**yoo"
racket	a raqueta	"rah**ket**uh"
▷ **can we hire rackets?**	podemos alugar raquetes?	"**poo**deh**moosh** aloo**gar** rah**ket**ush"
radiator	o radiador	"rahdee-uh**dor**"
radio	o rádio	"**rahd**yoo"
▷ **is there a radio/radio cassette in the car?**	o carro tem rádio/leitor de cassetes?	"oo **karr**oo tayng **rahd**yoo/**lay**tor duh kah**set**ush"
radish	o rabanete	"rabuh**net**"
railway station	a estação de comboio	"shta**sowng** duh kom**boy**oo"
rain	a chuva	"**shoo**vuh"
▷ **is it going to rain?**	vai chover?	"vy shoo**vehr**"
raincoat	a gabardine	"gabar**dee**nuh"
	o impermeável	"eempermee-**ah**vel"
raining:		
▷ **it's raining**	está a chover	"shta uh shoo**vehr**"
raisin	a passa	"**pas**uh"
rare (*unique*)	raro	"**rah**roo"
	rara	"**rah**ruh"
(*steak*)	mal passado	"mal pa**sah**doo"
	mal passada	"mal pa**sah**duh"

ABSOLUTE ESSENTIALS

do you have ...?	tem ...?	"tayng"
is there ...?	há ...?	"ah"
are there ...?	há ...?	"ah"
how much is ...?	quanto custa ...?	"**kwan**too **koosh**tuh"

rash:

▷ I have a rash · tenho uma erupção cutânea · "**ten**yoo **oom**uh eeroop**sowng** koo**tan**yuh"

raspberry · a framboesa · "framb**way**zuh"

rate · a taxa · "**tash**uh"

▷ what is the daily/ weekly rate? · qual é a diária?/quanto custa por semana? · "kwal e uh dee**ar**yuh/ **kwan**too **koosh**tuh poor se**mah**nuh"

▷ do you have a special rate for children? · há um preço especial para crianças? · "a oom **pray**soo shpus**yal pa**ruh kree**an**sush"

▷ what is the rate for sterling/dollars? · qual é o câmbio da libra/do dólar? · "kwal e oo **kamb**yoo duh **lee**bruh/doo **do**lar"

▷ rate of exchange · o câmbio · "**kamb**yoo"

raw · cru · "kroo"
· crua · "**kroo**uh"

razor · a navalha de barbear · "na**val**yuh duh barbee**ar**"

razor blades · as lâminas de barbear · "**lah**minush duh barbee**ar**"

ready · pronto · "**pron**too"
· pronta · "**pron**tuh"

▷ are you ready? · está pronto(a)? · "shta **pron**too(uh)"

▷ I'm ready · estou pronto(a) · "shtoh **pron**too(uh)"

▷ when will lunch/dinner be ready? · quando é que o almoço/jantar estará pronto? · "**kwan**doo e kuh **oo** al**moh**soo/jan**tar** shtuh**ra pron**too"

real · real · "ree**al**"

receipt · o recibo · "ruh**see**boo"

▷ I'd like a receipt, please · quero um recibo, por favor · "**keh**roo oom ruh**see**boo poor fa**vor**"

recently · há pouco · "ah **poh**koo"

reception (desk) · a recepção · "ruhsep**sowng**"

recipe	a receita	"ruh**say**tuh"
recommend	recomendar	"ruhkoomen**dar**"
▷ **what do you recommend?**	o que recomenda?	"oo kuh ruhkoo**men**duh"
▷ **can you recommend a cheap hotel/a good restaurant?**	pode recomendar um hotel barato/um restaurante bom?	"**pod** ruhkoomen**dar** oom oh**tel** ba**rah**too/oom rushtow**rant bong**"
record (*music etc*)	o disco	"**deesh**ko"
red	vermelho vermelha	"ver**mel**yoo" "ver**mel**yuh"
reduction	o desconto	"dush**kon**too"
▷ **is there a reduction for children/senior citizens/a group?**	há um desconto para crianças/reformados/ grupos?	"**a** oom dush**kon**too **pa**ruh kree**an**sush/ ruhfoor**mah**doosh/ **groo**poosh"
refill (*for pen, for lighter*)	a carga	"**kar**guh"
▷ **do you have a refill for my gas lighter?**	tem uma carga para o meu isqueiro a gás?	"**tayng** oomuh **kar**guh **pa**ruh oo **may**oo eesh**kay**roo uh **gash**"
refund	o reembolso	"reeaym**bol**soo"
▷ **I'd like a refund**	queria um reembolso	"**kree**uh oom reeaym**bol**soo"
to **register**:		
▷ **where do I register?**	onde registo o meu nome?	"**ond** ru**jeesh**too oo **may**oo **nohm**"
registered	registado registada	"ru**jeesh-tah**doo" "ru**jeesh-tah**duh"
registered delivery	o correio registado	"koo**rray**oo ru**jeesh-tah**doo"
regulations	os regulamentos	"ruhgooluh-**men**toosh"
▷ **I'm very sorry, I didn't know the regulations**	lamento muito, não conhecia as regras	"la**men**too **mween**too, nowng koonyuh**see**uh ush **reg**rush"

I don't understand	não compreendo	"nowng kompree**een**doo"
I don't speak Portuguese	não falo português	"nowng **fah**loo poortoo**gaysh**"
do you speak English?	fala inglês?	"**fah**luh een**glesh**"
could you help me?	podia ajudar-me?	"poo**dee**uh ajoo**dar**muh"

to **reimburse**	reembolsar	"reeaymbol**sar**"
relation (*family*)	o parente	"par**ent**"
to **relax**	repousar	"ruhpoh**zar**"
reliable (*company, service*)	de confiança	"duh komfee-**an**suh"
to **remain**	ficar	"fee**kar**"
to **remember**	lembrar-se de	"laym**brar**-suh duh"
to **rent** (*house, car*)	alugar	"aloo**gar**"
▷ I'd like to rent a room/villa	queria alugar um quarto/uma casa de campo	"**kree**uh aloo**gar** oom **kwar**too/oomuh **kah**zuh duh **kam**poo"
rental (*house, car*)	o aluguer	"aloo**gehr**"
to **repair**	reparar consertar	"ruhpa**rar**" "konsur**tar**"
▷ can you repair this?	pode arranjar isto?	"pod arran**jar** **eesh**too"
to **repeat**	repetir	"ruhpuh**teer**"
▷ please repeat that	pode repetir isso, por favor?	"pod ruhpuh**teer** **ee**soo poor fa**vor**"
reservation	a reserva	"ruh**zehr**vuh"
▷ I'd like to make a reservation for 7.30/ for 2 people	queria reservar uma mesa para as 7.30/para duas pessoas	"**kree**uh ruh**zehr**var oomuh **meh**zuh parash **set** ee **treen**tuh/pruh **doo**ush puh**soh**ush"
to **reserve**	reservar	"ruhzehr**var**"
▷ we'd like to reserve two seats for tonight	queremos reservar dois lugares para esta noite	"**kray**moosh ruhzehr**var** doysh loo**ga**rush **pa**ruh **esh**tuh noyt"
▷ I have reserved a room in the name of ...	reservei um quarto em nome de ...	"ruhzehr**vay** oom **kwar**too ayng nom duh"

▷ **I want to reserve a hotel room/a single room/a double room**	room queria reservar um quarto/um quarto individual/um quarto de casal	"**kree**uh ruhzehr**var** oom **kwar**too/oom **kwar**too eendee-vee**dwal**/oom **kwar**too duh ka**zal**"
reserved	reservado reservada	"ruhzehr**vah**doo" "ruhzehr**vah**duh"
rest[1] *n (repose)*	o descanso	"dush**kan**soo"
▷ **the rest of the wine**	o resto do vinho	"oo **resh**too doo **veen**yoo"
to **rest**[2] *vb*	descansar	"dushkan**sar**"
restaurant	o restaurante	"rushtoh**rant**"
restaurant car	o vagão restaurante	"va**gowng** rushtoh**rant**"
to **return** *(go back)* *(give back)*	voltar devolver	"vol**tar**" "duhvol**vehr**"
return ticket	o bilhete de ida e volta	"beel**yet** duh **ee**duh ee **vol**tuh"
▷ **a return ticket to ..., first-class**	um bilhete de ida e volta para ..., primeira classe	"oom beel**yet** duh **ee**duh ee **vol**tuh **par**uh ..., pree**may**ruh klass"
reverse-charge call	a chamada à cobrança	"sha**mah**duh a koo**bran**suh"
▷ **I'd like to make a reverse-charge call**	queria fazer uma chamada à cobrança	"**kree**uh fa**zehr oo**muh sha**mah**duh a koo**bran**suh"
rheumatism	o reumatismo	"rayoomuh-**teej**moo"
rhubarb	o ruibarbo	"rwee**bar**boo"
rice	o arroz	"a**rosh**"
to **ride** *(on horse)*	montar a cavalo	"mon**tar** uh ka**vah**loo"
▷ **to go for a ride**	ir andar a cavalo	"eer an**dar** uh ka**vah**loo"
riding:		
▷ **can we go riding?**	podemos andar a cavalo?	"poo**day**moosh an**dar** uh ka**vah**loo"

ABSOLUTE ESSENTIALS

do you have ...?	tem ...?	"tayng"
is there ...?	há ...?	"ah"
are there ...?	há ...?	"ah"
how much is ...?	quanto custa ...?	"**kwan**too **koosh**tuh"

right¹ *n*:

▷ **on/to the right**	à direita	"a deer**ray**tuh"
▷ **right of way**	prioridade	"pryooree**dahd**"

right² *adj (correct)*

	certo	"**sehr**too"
	certa	"**sehr**tuh"

ring	o anel	"**a**nel"

ripe	maduro	"ma**doo**roo"
	madura	"ma**doo**ruh"

river	o rio	"**ree**oo"
▷ **can one swim in the river?**	pode-se nadar no rio?	"**pod**-suh na**dar** noo **ree**oo"
▷ **am I allowed to fish in the river?**	é permitido pescar no rio?	"e permee**tee**doo push**kar** noo **ree**oo"

road	a estrada	"**shtrah**duh"
▷ **is the road to ... snowed up?**	a estrada para ... está cheia de neve?	"uh **shtrah**duh **pa**ruh ... sh**ta shay**uh duh nev"
▷ **which is the road to ...?**	qual a estrada que vai para ...?	"kwal uh **shtrah**duh kuh vy **pa**ruh ..."
▷ **when will the road be clear?**	quando é que a estrada vai ficar livre?	"**kwan**doo e kee uh **shtrah**duh vy fee**kar leev**ruh"

road map	o mapa das estradas	"**mah**puh dush **shtrah**dush"

roast	assado	"a**sah**doo"
	assada	"a**sah**duh"

to rob	roubar	"**roh**bar"
▷ **I've been robbed**	fui roubado	"fwee roh**bah**doo"

rock climbing:

▷ **let's go rock climbing**	vamos escalar montanhas	"**vah**moosh shkuh**lar** mon**tahn**yush"

roll *(bread)*	o papo-seco	"pahpoo-**say**koo"

roller skates	os patins de rodas	"pa**teengsh** duh **ro**dush"

roller skating:

▷ **where can we go roller skating?** — onde podemos ir andar de patins? — "**ond** poo**deh**moosh eer an**dar** duh pa**teengs**"

Rome — Roma — "**roh**muh"

roof — o telhado — "tul**yah**doo"

▷ **the roof leaks** — o telhado verte — "oo tul**yah**doo **vert**"

roof rack — o tejadilho — "tejuh**deel**yoo"

room (in house, hotel) — o quarto — "**kwar**too"
(space) — o espaço — "**shpah**soo"

room service — o serviço de quarto — "ser**vee**soo duh **kwar**too"

rope — a corda — "**kor**duh"

rosé (wine) — o vinho rosé — "**vee**nyoo ro**zay**"

rough (sea) — bravo — "**brah**voo"
— brava — "**brah**vuh"

▷ **is the sea rough today?** — o mar está bravo, hoje? — "oo **mar** shta **brah**voo **ohj**"

▷ **the crossing was rough** — a travessia foi má — "uh trav**see**uh foy **ma**"

round — redondo — "ruh**don**doo"
— redonda — "ruh**don**duh"

▷ **round the corner** — ao virar da esquina — "**ow** vee**rar** duh sh**kee**nuh"

▷ **whose round is it?** — de quem é a vez? — "duh **kayng** e uh **vaysh**"

▷ **a round of golf** — uma partida de golf — "**oo**muh par**tee**duh duh golf"

route — a rota — "**roo**tuh"

▷ **is there a route that avoids the traffic?** — há outra estrada para evitar o trânsito? — "a **oh**truh **shtrah**duh **pa**ruh eevee**tar** oo **tranz**eetoo"

rowing boat — o barco a remos — "**bar**koo uh **ray**moosh"

ABSOLUTE ESSENTIALS

I don't understand	não compreendo	"nowng kompree**een**doo"
I don't speak Portuguese	não falo português	"nowng **fah**loo poortoo**gaysh**"
do you speak English?	fala inglês?	"**fah**luh een**glesh**"
could you help me?	podia ajudar-me?	"poo**dee**uh ajoo**dar**muh"

▷ can we rent a rowing boat?	podemos alugar um barco a remos?	"poo**day**mooz aloo**gar** oom **bar**koo uh **ray**moosh"
rubber	a borracha	"boo**rah**shuh"
rubber band	o elástico	"eela**sh**tikoo"
rubbish	o lixo	"**lee**shoo"
rucksack	a mochila	"moo**shee**luh"
rug	o tapete	"ta**peht**"
rugby	o râguebi	"**rayg**bee"
ruin[1] *n*	a ruína	"r**wee**na"
to **ruin**[2] *vb*	arruinar	"arwee**nar**"
rum	o rum	"roong"
run[1] *n*	a corrida	"koo**rree**duh"
▷ which are the easiest runs?	quais são as corridas mais fáceis?	"kwysh **sowng** ush koo**rree**dush mysh **fah**saysh"
to **run**[2] *vb*	correr	"koo**rrehr**"
rush hour	a hora de ponta	"**o**ruh duh **pon**tuh"
saccharine	a sacarina	"suhka**ree**na"
safe[1] *n*	o cofre	"**koh**fruh"
▷ please put this in the hotel safe	por favor, guarde-me isto no cofre do hotel	"poor fa**vor** g**war**duhmuh **eesh**too noo **ko**fruh doo oh**tel**"
safe[2] *adj* (*beach, medicine*)	seguro segura	"suh**goo**roo" "suh**goo**ruh"
▷ is it safe to swim here?	não há perigo de nadar aqui?	"nowng a pe**ree**goo duh na**dar** a**kee**"
▷ is it safe for children? (*medicine*)	não é perigoso para as crianças?	"nowng e peree**goh**zoo prash kree**an**sush"

safe sex	o sexo com protecção	"**se**ksoo kong proote**sowng**"
▷ **to practise safe sex**	fazer sexo com protecção	"fa**zehr se**ksoo kong proote**sowng**"
safety pin	o alfinete de segurança	"alfee**net** duh suhgoo**ran**suh"
▷ **I need a safety pin**	preciso de um alfinete de segurança	"pre**see**zoo doom alfee**net** duh suhgoo**ran**suh"
sail¹ *n*	a vela	"**vel**uh"
to **sail²** *vb*:		
▷ **when do we sail?**	quando é que navegamos?	"**kwan**doo e kuh nave**gah**moosh"
sailboard	a prancha	"**pran**shuh"
sailboarding:		
▷ **I'd like to go sailboarding**	gostava de ir andar de prancha	"goos**tah**vuh duh **eer** an**dar** duh **pran**shuh"
sailing (*sport*)	a vela	"**vel**uh"
▷ **I'd like to go sailing**	gostava de ir andar à vela	"goos**tah**vuh duh **eer** an**dar** a **vel**uh"
▷ **what time is the next sailing?**	a que horas parte o próximo barco?	"uh kee **o**rush part oo **pros**imoo **bar**koo"
salad	a salada	"sa**lah**duh"
▷ **a mixed salad**	uma salada mista	"**oo**muh sa**lah**duh **meesh**tuh"
salad dressing	o tempero para a salada	"tem**pay**roo pra sa**lah**duh"
saline solution (*for contact lenses*)	a solução salina	"sooloo**sowng** sa**lee**nuh"
salmon	o salmão	"sal**mowng**"
salt	o sal	"sal"
▷ **pass the salt, please**	passe-me o sal, por favor	"**pah**suh-muh oo **sal** poor fa**vor**"

ABSOLUTE ESSENTIALS

do you have ...?	tem ...?	"tayng"
is there ...?	há ...?	"ah"
are there ...?	há ...?	"ah"
how much is ...?	quanto custa ...?	"**kwan**too **koosh**tuh"

same	mesmo	"**mej**moo"
	mesma	"**mej**muh"
▷ **I'll have the same**	eu como/bebo o mesmo	"**ay**oo **koh**moo/**beh**boo oo **mej**moo"
sand	a areia	"**aray**uh"
sandals	as sandálias	"san**dahl**yush"
sandwich	a sanduíche	"sand**weesh**"
	a sande	"sand"
▷ **what kind of sandwiches do you have?**	que tipo de sanduíches tem?	"kuh **tee**poo duh sand**wee**shush **tayng**"
sandy:		
▷ **a sandy beach**	uma praia com muita areia	"**oo**muh **pry**uh kong **mween**tuh **aray**uh"
sanitary towel	o penso higiénico	"**pen**soo eej**yen**ikoo"
sardine	a sardinha	"sar**deen**yuh"
Saturday	sábado	"**sah**buhdoo"
sauce	o molho	"**mohl**yoo"
saucepan	a caçarola	"kasuh**rol**uh"
saucer	o pires	"**peer**ush"
sauna	a sauna	"**sow**nuh"
sausage	a salsicha	"sal**see**shuh"
savoury (not sweet)	saboroso	"saboo**roh**zoo"
	saborosa	"saboo**ro**zuh"
to **say**	dizer	"dee**zehr**"
scallop	o escalope	"shkuh**lop**"
scampi	os camarões fritos	"kamuh**royns free**toosh"
scarf (long)	o cachecol	"kashuh**kol**"

(*square*)	o lenço (de pescoço)	"**len**soo (duh push**koh**soo)"
school	a escola	"**shkol**uh"
scissors	a tesoura	"tuh**zoh**ruh"
Scotland	a Escócia	"**shkos**yuh"
Scottish	escocês	"shkoo**sesh**"
	escocesa	"shkoo**say**zuh"
▷ **I'm Scottish**	sou escocês/escocesa	"soh shkoo**sesh**/shkoo**say**zuh"
screw	o parafuso	"paruh**foo**zoo"
▷ **the screw has come loose**	o parafuso está solto	"oo paruh**foo**zoo sh**ta sol**too"
screwdriver	a chave de parafusos	"shahv duh paruh**foo**zoosh"
scuba diving:		
▷ **where can we go scuba diving?**	onde é que podemos ir mergulhar?	"**ond e** kuh poo**deh**moosh **eer** mergool**yar**"
sculpture (*object*)	a escultura	"shkool**too**ruh"
sea	o mar	"mar"
seafood	o marisco	"ma**reesh**koo"
▷ **do you like seafood?**	gosta de marisco?	"**gosh**tuh duh ma**reesh**koo"
seasickness	o enjoo	"en**joh**oo"
seaside	a praia	"**pry**uh"
	a beira-mar	"**bay**ruh mar"
season ticket	o passe	"pass"
seat (*chair*)	cadeira	"ka**day**ruh"
(*in train, theatre*)	o lugar	"loo**gar**"
▷ **is this seat free?**	este lugar está vago?	"aysht loo**gar** sh**ta vah**goo"

ABSOLUTE ESSENTIALS

I don't understand	não compreendo	"nowng kompree**en**doo"
I don't speak Portuguese	não falo português	"nowng **fah**loo poortoo**gaysh**"
do you speak English?	fala inglês?	"**fah**luh een**glesh**"
could you help me?	podia ajudar-me?	"poo**dee**uh ajoo**dar**muh"

▷ **is this seat taken?**	este lugar está ocupado?	"aysht loo**gar** shta okoo**pah**doo"
▷ **we'd like to reserve two seats for tonight**	queríamos reservar dois lugares para esta noite	"kuh**ree**uhmoosh ruhzehr**var** doysh loo**gar**ush **par**uh **esh**tuh noyt"
▷ **I have a seat reservation**	eu tenho um lugar marcado	"**ay**oo **ten**yoo oom loo**gar** mar**kah**doo"
second	segundo	"suh**goon**doo"
	segunda	"suh**goon**duh"
second class	de segunda classe	"duh suh**goon**duh klass"
to see	ver	"vehr"
▷ **see you soon**	até breve	"ate brev"
▷ **what is there to see here?**	o que há para ver aqui?	"oo kee a **par**uh vehr a**kee**"
self-service	o self-service	"**self**-service"
to sell	vender	"ven**dehr**"
▷ **do you sell stamps/ hair spray?**	vende selos/laca do cabelo?	"vend **seh**loosh/**lah**kuh doo ka**bay**loo"
Sellotape®	a fita-cola	"feetuh-**ko**luh"
semi-skimmed milk	o leite meio-gordo	"layt **may**oo-**gor**doo"
to send	mandar	"man**dar**"
▷ **please send my mail/ luggage on to this address**	por favor, mande o meu correio/a minha bagagem para esteendereço	"poor fa**vor man**duh oo **may**oo koo**rray**oo/uh **meen**yuh ba**gah**jayng **par**uh esht ayngduh-**reh**soo"
senior citizen	o reformado	"ruhfoor**mah**doo"
	a reformada	"ruhfoor**mah**duh"
▷ **is there a reduction for senior citizens?**	há um desconto para os reformados?	"a oom dush**kon**too prosh ruhfoor**mah**doosh"
separate	separado	"suhpa**rah**doo"
	separada	"suhpa**rah**duh"

September	Setembro	"suhtembroo"
serious	grave	"grahv"
seriously:		
▷ he is seriously injured	ele está gravemente ferido	"ayl shta grahvment fereedoo"
to serve	servir	"serveer"
▷ we are still waiting to be served	ainda estamos à espera que nos sirvam	"aeenduh shtahmooz a shpehruh kuh noosh seervowng"
service (in restaurant)	o serviço	"serveesoo"
▷ is service included?	o serviço está incluído?	"oo serveesoo shta eenklweedoo"
▷ what time is the service? (church)	a que horas é a missa?	"uh kee oruz e uh meesuh"
service charge	o serviço	"serveesoo"
service station	a estação de serviço	"shtuhsowng duh serveesoo"
set menu	a ementa fixa	"eementuh feeksuh"
▷ do you have a set menu?	tem uma ementa fixa?	"tayng oomuh eementuh feeksuh"
▷ how much is the set menu?	quanto custa a ementa fixa?	"kwantoo kooshtuh uh eementuh feeksuh"
▷ we'll take the set menu	queremos a ementa fixa	"kraymooz uh eementuh feeksuh"
seven	sete	"set"
seventeen	dezassete	"duzuhset"
seventy	setenta	"suhtentuh"
shade	o tom	"tong"
	a sombra	"songbruh"
▷ in the shade	à sombra	"a songbruh"
shallow	pouco profundo	"pohkoo proofoondoo"

ABSOLUTE ESSENTIALS

do you have ...?	tem ...?	"tayng"
is there ...?	há ...?	"ah"
are there ...?	há ...?	"ah"
how much is ...?	quanto custa ...?	"kwantoo kooshtuh"

	pouco profunda	"**poh**koo proo**foon**duh"
shampoo	o champô	"sham**poh**"
▷ a shampoo and set, please	lavar e fazer mise, por favor	"la**var** ee fa**zehr** meez, poor fa**vor**"
shandy	a cerveja e limonada	"ser**vay**juh ee leemoo**nah**duh"
to share	repartir	"ruhpar**teer**"
	dividir	"deevee**deer**"
▷ we could share a taxi	podíamos dividir um táxi	"poo**dee**uhmoosh **dee**veedeer oom **taxi**"
to shave	fazer a barba	"fa**zehr** uh **bar**buh"
shaving brush	o pincel da barba	"peen**sel** duh **bar**buh"
shaving cream	o creme de barbear	"krem duh barbee**ar**"
she	ela	"**el**uh"
sheet	o lençol	"len**sol**"
shellfish	o marisco	"ma**reesh**koo"
sherry	o xerez	"shuh**resh**"
ship	o barco	"**bar**koo"
shirt	a camisa	"ka**mee**zuh"
shock absorber	o amortecedor	"amortuh-suh**dor**"
shoe	o sapato	"sa**pah**too"
▷ I have a hole in my shoe	tenho um buraco no sapato	"**ten**yoo oom boo**rah**koo noo sa**pah**too"
▷ can you reheel these shoes?	pode pôr uns saltos nestes sapatos?	"pod por oonsh **sal**toosh **naysh**tush sa**pah**toosh"
shoe laces	os cordões de sapato	"koor**doyns** duh sa**pah**too"
shoe polish	a graxa	"**gra**shuh"
shop	a loja	"**lo**juh"

▷ what time do the shops close?	a que horas fecham as lojas?	"uh kee **o**rush **fesh**owng ush **lo**jush"

shopping:

▷ to go shopping	ir às compras	"eer **ash kom**prush"
▷ where is the main shopping area?	onde fica a zona comercial?	"**on**duh **fee**kuh uh **zo**nuh koomehr-see**al**"

shopping centre   o centro comercial   "**sen**troo koomehr-see**al**"

short   curto   "**koor**too"
     curta   "**koor**tuh"

short cut   o atalho   "a**tal**yoo"

shorts   os calções   "kal**soynsh**"

short-sighted:

▷ I'm short-sighted	não vejo ao longe	"nowng **vay**joo **ow** lonj"

shoulder   o ombro   "**om**broo"

▷ I've hurt my shoulder	magoei-me no ombro	"ma**gway**-muh noo **om**broo"

show¹ *n*   o espectáculo   "shpe**tak**ooloo"

to show² *vb*   mostrar   "moosh**trar**"

▷ could you show me please?	podia mostrar-me, por favor?	"poo**dee**uh moosh**trar**-muh poor fa**vor**"
▷ could you show us around?	podia mostrar-nos as vistas	"poo**dee**uh moosh**trar**-noosh ush **veesh**tush"

shower   o duche   "doosh"
     o chuveiro   "shoo**vay**roo "

▷ how does the shower work?	como é que o chuveiro trabalha?	"**koh**moo e kee oo shoo**vay**roo tra**bal**yuh"
▷ I'd like a room with a shower	queria um quarto com chuveiro	"**kree**uh oom **kwar**too kong shoo**vay**roo"

shrimps   os camarões   "kamuh**roynsh**"

sick (*ill*)   doente   "doo**ent**"

▷ she has been sick	ela vomitou	"eluh voomee**toh**"

ABSOLUTE ESSENTIALS

I don't understand	não compreendo	"nowng kompree**en**doo"
I don't speak Portuguese	não falo português	"nowng **fah**loo poortoo**gaysh**"
do you speak English?	fala inglês?	"**fah**luh een**glesh**"
could you help me?	podia ajudar-me?	"poo**dee**uh ajoo**dar**muh"

▷ **I feel sick**	estou enjoado	"sh**tou** aymjo**ah**do"
sightseeing	a visita a lugares de interesse	"vee**zee**tuh uh loo**gah**rush deentuh**res**"
▷ **are there any sightseeing tours?**	há excursões guiadas?	"a aysh-koor**soynsh** ghee**ah**dush"
sign[1] *n*	a tabuleta	"taboo**le**tuh"
to **sign**[2] *vb*	assinar	"uhsee**nar**"
▷ **where do I sign?**	onde é que assino?	"**ond e** kuh uh**see**noo"
signature	a assinatura	"asseenuh-**too**ruh"
silk	a seda	"**say**duh"
silver	a prata	"**prah**tuh"
similar	similar	"seemee**lar**"
simple	simples	"**seem**plush"
single (*unmarried*)	solteiro	"sol**tay**roo"
	solteira	"sol**tay**ruh"
(*not double*)	individual	"eendee-vee**dwal**"
▷ **a second-class single to ...**	um bilhete de ida de segunda classe para ...	"oom beel**yet dee**duh duh se**goon**duh klass **par**uh ..."
single bed	a cama de solteiro	"**kah**muh duh sol**tay**roo"
single room	o quarto individual	"**kwar**too eendee-vee**dwal**"
▷ **I want to reserve a single room**	quero reservar um quarto individual	"**keh**roo ruhzehr**var** oom **kwar**too eendee-vee**dwal**"
sink	o lava-louça	"lavuh-**loh**suh"
sir	senhor	"sun**yor**"
sister	a irmã	"eer**mang**"
to **sit**	sentar-se	"sen**tar**-suh"

ABSOLUTE ESSENTIALS		
I would like ...	queria ...	"**kree**uh"
I need ...	preciso de ...	"pre**see**zoo duh"
where is ...?	onde fica ...?	"ond **fee**kuh"
I'm looking for ...	procuro ...	"pro**koo**roo"

▷ **please sit down**	sente-se por favor	"**sen**tuh-suh poor fa**vor**"
six	seis	"saish"
sixteen	dezasseis	"duzuh**saish**"
sixty	sessenta	"suh**sen**tuh"
size	o número	"**noo**muhro"
▷ **I take a continental size 40**	o meu número é o quarenta	"oo **may**oo **noo**muhroo e oo kwa**ren**tuh"
▷ **do you have this in a bigger/smaller size?**	tem isto num tamanho maior/menor?	"tayng **eesh**too noong tama**h**nyoo my**or**/muh**nor**"
skate	o patim	"pa**teeng**"
▷ **where can we hire skates?**	onde podemos alugar patins?	"**ond** poo**deh**moosh aloo**gar** pa**teengs**"
skateboard	o skate	"skate"
skateboarding:		
▷ **I'd like to go skateboarding**	gostava de ir andar de skate	"goos**tah**vuh duh eer an**dar** duh skate"
skating	a patinagem	"pateen**ah**jayng"
▷ **where can we go skating?**	onde podemos ir fazer patinagem?	"**ond** poo**deh**moosh eer fa**zehr** pateen**ah**jayng"
ski[1] *n*	o esqui	"sh**kee**"
▷ **can we hire skis here?**	podemos alugar esquis aqui?	"poo**deh**moosh aloo**gar** sh**keesh** a**kee**"
to ski[2] *vb*	esquiar	"shkee**ar**"
ski boot	a bota de esquiar	"**bo**tuh duh shkee**ar**"
skid:		
▷ **the car skidded**	o carro resvalou	"oo **karr**oo **rush**vuhloh"
skiing	o esqui	"sh**kee**"
(*downhill*)	o esqui de descida	"sh**kee** duh dush**see**duh"
(*cross-country*)	o esqui de fundo	"sh**kee** duh **foom**doo"

ABSOLUTE ESSENTIALS

do you have ...?	tem ...?	"tayng"
is there ...?	há ...?	"ah"
are there ...?	há ...?	"ah"
how much is ...?	quanto custa ...?	"**kwan**too **koosh**tuh"

| ▷ I'd like to go skiing | gostava de ir esquiar | "gooshtahvuh duh eer shkeear" |

skiing lessons:

▷ do you organize skiing lessons?	organizam aulas de esqui?	"orguhneezowng owlush duh shkeear"
ski instructor	o treinador de esqui	"traynuhdor duh shkee"
ski jacket	o casaco de esquiar	"kazahkoo duh shkeear"
ski lift	o telesqui	"tehleshkee"
skimmed milk	o leite magro	"layt mahgroo"
skin	a pele	"pel"
skin diving	a caça submarina	"kahsuh soobmuhreenuh"
ski pants	as calças de esqui	"kalsush duh shkee"
ski pass	o passe para esquiar	"pass paruh shkeear"
ski pole	o bastão de esqui	"bushtowng duh shkee"
ski resort	a estância de férias	"eeshtansyuh duh fehryush"
skirt	a saia	"syuh"
ski run	a corrida de esqui	"kooreeduh duh shkee"
ski suit	o fato de esquiar	"fahtoo duh shkeear"
sledge	o trenó	"treno"

sledging:

▷ where can we go sledging?	onde podemos ir andar de trenó?	"ond poodehmoosh eer andar duh trayno"
to sleep	dormir	"doormeer"
▷ I can't sleep for the noise/heat	não consigo dormir por causa do barulho/calor	"nowng konseegoo doormeer poor kowzuh doo baroolyoo/kuhlor"
sleeper (in train)	a carruagem-cama	"karwahjayng-kahmuh"

▷ **can I reserve a sleeper?**	posso reservar um lugar numa carruagem-cama?	"**pos**oo rezer**var** oom loo**gar** noomuh kar**wah**jayng-**kah**muh"
sleeping bag	o saco-cama	"**sah**koo-**kah**muh"
sleeping car	a carruagem-cama	"kar**wah**jayng- **kah**muh"
sleeping pill	o comprimido para dormir	"kompree**mee**doo **par**uh door**meer**"
slice	a fatia	"fa**tee**uh"
slide (*photograph*)	o slide o diapositivo	"shlyd" "dyuhpoo-zee**tee**voo"
slippers	os chinelos	"shee**nel**oosh"
slow	lento lenta	"**len**too" "**len**tuh"
to **slow down** *vb*	abrandar	"uhbran**dar**"
slowly	devagar	"duhvuh**gar**"
▷ **please speak slowly**	podia falar devagar, por favor?	"poo**dee**uh fa**lar** duhvuh**gar** poor fa**vor**"
small	pequeno pequena	"puh**kay**noo" "puh**kay**nuh"
smaller	mais pequeno mais pequena	"mysh puh**kay**noo" "mysh puh**kay**nuh"
smell (*pleasant*) (*unpleasant*)	o cheiro o mau cheiro	"**shay**roo" "mow **shay**roo"
smoke[1] *n*	o fumo	"**foo**moo"
to **smoke**[2] *vb*	fumar	"foo**mar**"
▷ **do you mind if I smoke?**	importa-se que eu fume?	"eem**por**tuh-suh kuh **ayo**o **foo**muh"
▷ **do you smoke?**	fuma?	"**foo**muh"
smoked	fumado fumada	"foo**mah**doo" "foo**mah**duh"

ABSOLUTE ESSENTIALS

I don't understand	não compreendo	"nowng kompree**een**doo"
I don't speak Portuguese	não falo português	"nowng **fah**loo poortoo**gaysh**"
do you speak English?	fala inglês?	"**fah**luh een**glesh**"
could you help me?	podia ajudar-me?	"poo**dee**uh ajoo**dar**muh"

smoking:

▷ I'd like a no smoking room/seat	queria um quarto/lugar para não fumadores	"**kree**uh oom **kwar**too/loo**gar** paruh **nowng** foomuh**dor**ush"
▷ I'd like a seat in the smoking area	queria um lugar na área para fumadores	"**kree**uh oom loo**gar** nuh **a**reeuh paruh foomuh**dor**ush"

smoky:

▷ it's too smoky here	há demasiado fumo aqui	"a duhmuhsee**ah**doo **foo**moo a**kee**"

snack bar	o snack-bar	"snack**bar**"
snorkel	o tubo de ar	"**too**boo dee ar"

snorkelling:

▷ let's go snorkelling	vamos fazer mergulho com tubo de respiração	"**vah**moosh fa**zehr** mergool**yoo** kong **too**boo duh rushpeeruh**sowng**"

snow	a neve	"nev"
▷ the snow is very icy/heavy	a neve tem muito gelo/é muito pesada	"uh **nev** tayng **mween**too **jay**loo/e **mween**too puh**sah**duh"
▷ what are the snow conditions?	em que condição está a neve?	"**ayng** kuh kondee**sowng** shta uh **nev**"
▷ is it going to snow?	vai nevar?	"vy nuh**var**"
snowboard	a prancha para a neve	"**pran**shuh **par**uh uh **nev**"

snowboarding:

▷ where can we go snowboarding?	onde podemos andar de prancha na neve?	"ond poo**deh**moosh an**dar** duh **pran**shuh nuh **nev**"

snowed up	cheio de neve	"**shay**oo duh **nev**"
	cheia de neve	"**shay**uh duh **nev**"

snowing:

▷ it's snowing	está a nevar	"shta uh nuh**var**"

snowplough	o removedor de neve	"ruhmoov**dor** duh **nev**"

ABSOLUTE ESSENTIALS		
I would like ...	queria ...	"**kree**uh"
I need ...	preciso de ...	"pre**see**zoo duh"
where is ...?	onde fica ...?	"ond **fee**kuh"
I'm looking for ...	procuro ...	"pro**koo**roo"

so:

▷ **so much**   tanto   "**tan**too"
                    tanta   "**tan**tuh"

soaking solution (*for contact lenses*)   o líquido para lentes de contacto   "**lee**keedoo **pa**ruh **len**tsh duh kon**tak**too"

soap   o sabão   "sa**bowng**"
          o sabonete   "sa**boo**net"

▷ **there is no soap**   não há sabonete   "nowng a sa**boo**net"

soap powder   o sabão em pó   "sa**bowng** ayng **po**"

sober   sóbrio   "**so**breeoo"
        sóbria   "**so**breeuh"

sock   a meia   "**may**uh"

socket   a tomada   "to**mah**duh"

▷ **where is the socket for my electric razor?**   onde é a tomada para a máquina de barbear eléctrica?   "**ond** e uh to**mah**duh **pa**ruh uh **ma**kinuh duh bur**beear** ee**le**trikuh"

soda   a água bicarbonatada   "**ahg**wuh beekarboo-na**tah**duh"

soft   macio   "ma**see**oo"
       macia   "ma**see**uh"

soft drink   a bebida não alcoólica   "buh**bee**duh nowng al**kwo**likuh"

sole   a solha   "**sol**yuh"

soluble aspirin   a aspirina solúvel   "ushpee**ree**nuh soo**loo**vel"

solution:

▷ **saline solution**   a solução salina   "uh sooloo**sowng** suh**lee**nuh"

▷ **cleansing solution for contact lenses**   líquido de limpeza para lentes de contacto   "**lee**kidoo duh leem**peh**zuh **pa**ruh **len**tsh duh kon**tak**too"

▷ **soaking solution for contact lenses**   líquido para lentes de contacto   "**lee**kidoo **pa**ruh **len**tsh duh kon**tak**too"

ABSOLUTE ESSENTIALS

do you have ...?	tem ...?	"tayng"
is there ...?	há ...?	"ah"
are there ...?	há ...?	"ah"
how much is ...?	quanto custa ...?	"**kwan**too **koosh**tuh"

some	alguns	"al**goonsh**"
	algumas	"al**goom**ush"
someone	alguém	"al**gayng**"
something	alguma coisa	"al**goom**uh **koy**zuh"
sometimes	às vezes	"**ash vay**zush"
son	o filho	"**feel**yoo"
song	a canção	"kan**sowng**"
soon	em breve	"ayng brev"
sore	doloroso	"dooloo**roh**zoo"
	dolorosa	"dooloo**roh**zuh"
▷ **I have a sore throat**	dói-me a garganta	"**doy**muh uh gur**gan**tuh"
▷ **my feet/eyes are sore**	dói-me os pés/olhos	"**doy**muh oosh **pesh**/**ol**yoosh"
sorry:		
▷ **I'm sorry!**	lamento!	"la**men**too"
sort:		
▷ **what sort of cheese?**	que tipo de quejo?	"kuh **tee**poo duh **kay**joo"
soup	a sopa	"**soh**puh"
▷ **what is the soup of the day?**	qual é a sopa do dia?	"kwal e uh **soh**puh doo **dee**uh"
south	o sul	"sool"
souvenir	a recordação	"ruhkoor-duh**sowng**"
space:		
▷ **parking space**	o lugar de estacionamento	"loo**gar** deeshtasyoo-nuh**men**too"
spade	a pá	"pa"
Spain	a Espanha	"**shpan**yuh"
Spanish	espanhol	"shpan**yol**"
	espanhola	"shpan**yol**uh"

spanner	a chave inglesa	"shahv een**glay**zuh"
spare wheel	a roda sobressalente	"**rod**uh sobruhsa**lent**"
sparkling	espumoso	"shpoo**moh**zoo"
	espumosa	"shpoo**moh**zuh"
sparkling wine	o vinho espumoso	"**vee**nyoo shpoo**moh**zo"
spark plug	a vela	"**vel**uh"
to **speak**	falar	"fa**lar**"
▷ can I speak to ...?	posso falar com ...?	"**pos**oo fa**lar** kong"
▷ please speak louder/ (more) slowly	podia falar mais alto/ devagar, por favor?	"poo**dee**uh fa**lar** mysh **al**too/duhvuh**gar** poor fa**vor**"
special	especial	"shpus**yal**"
▷ do you have a special menu for children?	tem uma ementa especial para crianças?	"tayng **oom**uh ee**men**tuh shpus**yal** **par**uh kree**an**sush"
speciality	a especialidade	"shpusya-lee**dahd**"
▷ is there a local speciality?	há alguma especialidade local?	"a al**goo**muh shpusya-lee**dahd** loo**kal**"
▷ what is the chef's speciality?	qual é a especialidade do chefe?	"kwal e uh shpusya-lee**dahd** doo shef"
speed	a velocidade	"vuhloosee**dahd**"
speed limit	o limite de velocidade	"lee**meet** duh vuhloosee**dahd**"
▷ what is the speed limit on this road?	qual é o limite de velocidade nesta estrada?	"kwal e oo lee**meet** duh vuhloosee**dahd** **nesh**tuh shtrahduh"
speedometer	o velocímetro	"vuhloo**see**-muhtroo"
spell:		
▷ how do you spell it?	como se soletra?	"**koh**moo suh soo**leh**truh"
spicy	picante	"pee**kant**"
spinach	o espinafre	"shpee**naf**ruh"

ABSOLUTE ESSENTIALS

I don't understand	não compreendo	"nowng kompree**en**doo"
I don't speak Portuguese	não falo português	"nowng **fah**loo poortoo**gaysh**"
do you speak English?	fala inglês?	"**fah**luh een**glesh**"
could you help me?	podia ajudar-me?	"poo**dee**uh ajoo**dar**muh"

spirits	a bebida alcoólica	"buh**bee**duh al**kwol**ikuh"
sponge	a esponja	"sh**pon**juh"
spoon	a colher	"kool**yehr**"
sport	o desporto	"dush**por**too"
▷ **which sports activities are available here?**	que actividades desportivas se podem fazer aqui?	"kuh ateevee-**dah**dush dushpoor**tee**vush suh **pod**ayng fa**zehr** a**kee**"
spring (*season*)	a primavera	"preemuh**veh**ruh"
square (*in town*)	a praça	"**prah**suh"
squash (*game*) (*drink*)	o squash o sumo	"squash" "**soo**moo"
stain	a nódoa	"**nod**wuh"
▷ **this stain is coffee/ blood**	esta nódoa é de café/ sangue	"**esh**tuh **nod**wuh e duh kuh**fe**/**sang**uh"
▷ **can you remove this stain?**	pode retirar esta nódoa?	"pod ruh**teerar esh**tuh **nod**wuh"
stairs	a escada	"**shkah**duh"
stalls (*theatre*)	a plateia	"plat**ay**uh"
stamp	o selo	"**say**loo"
▷ **do you sell stamps?**	vende selos?	"vend **say**loosh"
▷ **I'd like six stamps for postcards to Great Britain, please**	queria seis selos para postais para a Grã-Bretanha, por favor	"**keh**roo saysh **se**loosh **par**uh poosh**tysh** pra grambruh**tahn**yuh poor fa**vor**"
▷ **twelve 48-escudo stamps, please**	doze selos de quarenta e oito escudos, por favor	"**dohz se**loosh duh kwa**ren**tuh-ee-oitoo **shkoo**doosh poor fa**vor**"
▷ **where can I buy stamps?**	onde posso comprar selos?	"ond **pos**oo kom**prar seh**loosh"
to start	começar	"koomuh**sar**"
▷ **when does the film/ show start?**	quando começa o filme/espectáculo?	"**kwan**doo koo**me**suh oo **feelm**/shpe**tah**kooloo"

ABSOLUTE ESSENTIALS

I would like ...	queria ...	"**kree**uh"
I need ...	preciso de ...	"pre**see**zoo duh"
where is ...?	onde fica ...?	"ond **fee**kuh"
I'm looking for ...	procuro ...	"pro**koo**roo"

starter (*in meal*)	a entrada	"ayn**trah**duh"
(*in car*)	o motor de arranque	"moo**tor** dee a**rank**"
station	a estação	"shta**sowng**"
▷ **to the main station, please**	para a estação principal, por favor	"pra shta**sowng** preensee**pal**, poor fa**vor**"
stationer's	a papelaria	"papuhluh-**ree**uh"
to stay	(*remain*) ficar	"fee**kar**"
▷ **I'm staying at a hotel**	fico num hotel	"**fee**koo noom oh**tel**"
▷ **I want to stay an extra night**	quero ficar mais uma noite	"**keh**roo fee**kar** myz**oom**uh noyt"
▷ **where are you staying?**	onde está hospedado(a)?	"ond shta oshpuh-**dah**doo(uh)"
steak	o bife	"beef"
steep	íngreme	"**een**gremuh"
sterling:		
▷ **pounds sterling**	libras esterlinas	"**lee**brush shtur**lee**nush"
▷ **what is the rate for sterling?**	qual é o câmbio da libra?	"kwal e oo **kamb**yoo duh **lee**bruh"
stew	o guisado	"ghee**zah**doo"
steward	o oficial de bordo	"ofeesee**al** duh **bor**doo"
stewardess	a assistente de bordo	"aseesh**tent** duh **bor**doo"
sticking plaster	o penso adesivo	"**pen**soo ade**zee**voo"
still (*motionless*)	imóvel	"ee**mov**el"
sting	a picada	"pee**kah**duh"
stockings	as meias de senhora	"**may**ush duh sun**yor**uh"
stolen:		
▷ **my passport has been stolen**	o meu passaporte foi roubado	"oo **may**oo pasuh**port** foy rohb**ah**doo"
stomach	o estômago	"**shtoh**magoo"

ABSOLUTE ESSENTIALS

do you have ...?	tem ...?	"tayng"
is there ...?	há ...?	"ah"
are there ...?	há ...?	"ah"
how much is ...?	quanto custa ...?	"**kwan**too **koosh**tuh"

stomach ache	a dor de estômago	"dor dee**shtoh**magoo"
stomach upset	o mal-estar de estômago	"mal-sh**tar** duh **shtoh**magoo"
▷ **I have a stomach upset**	dói-me o estômago	"**doy**-muh oo **shtoh**magoo"
to stop	parar	"pa**rar**"
▷ **stop here/at the corner**	pare aqui/na esquina	"**par** a**kee**/nuh sh**kee**nuh"
▷ **do we stop at ...?**	paramos em ...?	"pa**rah**mooz ayng ..."
▷ **where do we stop for lunch?**	onde paramos para almoçar?	"**on**duh pa**rah**moosh **pa**ruh almoo**sar**"
▷ **please stop the bus, ...**	por favor, páre o autocarro ...	"poor fa**vor** pahr oo owtoo**kar**roo"
stopover	a interrupção de viagem	"eenterroop-**sowng** duh vee**ah**jayng"
storm	a tempestade	"tempush**tahd**"
stormy:		
▷ **it's (very) stormy**	está (muito) tempestoso	"sh**ta** (**mween**too) tempush**toh**zoo"
straight on	sempre em frente	"**sem**pruh ayng frent"
strap:		
▷ **I need a new strap**	preciso duma tira nova	"pre**see**zoo **doo**muh **tee**ruh **no**vuh"
straw (for drinking)	a palha	"**pal**yuh"
strawberry	o morango	"moo**rang**oo"
street	a rua	"**roo**uh"
street map	o mapa das ruas	"**mah**puh dush **roo**ush"
string	o cordel	"koor**del**"
striped	às riscas	"ash **reesh**kush"
strong	forte	"fort"

stuck	bloqueado	"blookyahdoo"
	bloqueada	"blookyahduh"
▷ **it's stuck**	está preso	"shta **pray**zoo"
student	o estudante	"shtoo**dant**"
stung	picado	"pee**kah**doo"
	picada	"pee**kah**duh"
▷ **he has been stung**	ele foi picado	"**ayl** foy pee**kah**doo"
stupid	estúpido	"**shtoop**ldoo"
	estúpida	"**shtoop**iduh"
suddenly	de repente	"duh ruh**pent**"
suede	a camurça	"ka**moor**suh"
sugar	o açúcar	"a**soo**kar"
suit	o fato	"**fah**too"
suitcase	a mala	"**mah**luh"
▷ **my suitcase was damaged in transit**	a minha mala estragou-se na viagem	"uh **mee**nyuh **mah**luh shtra**goh**-suh nuh veeah**jayng**"
▷ **my suitcase is missing**	falta a minha mala	"**fal**tuh uh **mee**nyuh **mal**uh"
summer	o verão	"vuh**rowng**"
sun	o sol	"sol"
to **sunbathe**	tomar banhos de sol	"too**mar bahn**yoosh duh **sol**"
sunbed	a espreguiçadeira	"shpruhgee-suh**day**ruh"
sunburn	a queimadura de sol	"kaymuh**doo**ruh duh **sol**"
▷ **can you give me anything for sunburn?**	pode dar-me alguma coisa para queimaduras de sol?	"pod **dar**-muh al**goo**muh **koy**zuh **pa**ruh kaymuh**doo**rush duh **sol**"
▷ **I am sunburnt**	estou queimado do sol	"sh**tou** kay**mah**doo doo **sol**"

ABSOLUTE ESSENTIALS

I don't understand	não compreendo	"nowng kompree**en**doo"
I don't speak Portuguese	não falo português	"nowng **fah**loo poortoo**gaysh**"
do you speak English?	fala inglês?	"**fah**luh een**glesh**"
could you help me?	podia ajudar-me?	"poo**dee**uh ajoo**dar**muh"

Sunday	domingo	"doo**meen**goo"
sunglasses	os óculos de sol	"**ok**ooloosh duh **sol**"
sun lounger	a espreguiçadeira	"shpruhgee-suh**day**ruh"
sunny	soalheiro	"swal**yay**roo"
	soalheira	"swal**yay**ruh"
sunshade	o guarda-sol	"gwarduh-**sol**"
sunstroke	a insolação	"eensooluh**sowng**"
suntan lotion	a loção de bronzear	"loo**sowng** duh bronzee**ar**"
supermarket	o supermercado	"soopermer**kah**doo"
supper (*dinner*)	a ceia	"**say**uh"
supplement	o suplemento	"soopluh**men**too"
▷ is there a supplement to pay?	é preciso pagar um suplemento?	"e pre**see**zoo pa**gar** oom soopluh**men**too"
sure	seguro	"suh**goo**roo"
	segura	"suh**goo**ruh"
surface mail:		
▷ by surface mail	por correio de superfície	"poor koo**rray**oo duh sooper**fee**see"
surfboard	a prancha de surf	"**pran**shuh duh surf"
▷ can I rent a surfboard?	posso alugar uma prancha de surf?	"**pos**oo uhloo**gar** oomuh **pran**shuh duh surf"
surfer	o surfer	"**sur**fer"
surfing	o surf	"surf"
▷ I'd like to go surfing	gostava de ir fazer surf	"goosh**tah**vuh duh eer fa**zehr** surf"
surname	o apelido	"apuh**lee**doo"
suspension	a suspensão	"sooshpen**sowng**"
sweater	o pulover	"poo**loh**vehr"

sweet	doce	"dohs"
sweetener	o adoçante	"adoo**sant**"
sweets	os rebuçados	"reboo**sah**doosh"
to swim	nadar	"na**dar**"
▷ **can one swim in the river?**	pode-se nadar no rio?	"**pod**-suh na**dar** noo **ree**oo"
▷ **is it safe to swim here?**	é seguro nadar-se aqui?	"e suh**goo**roo na**dar**-suh a**kee**"
▷ **can you swim?**	sabe nadar?	"**sahb** na**dar**"
swimming:		
▷ **let's go swimming**	vamos nadar	"**vah**moosh na**dar**"
swimming pool	a piscina	"peesh-**see**nuh"
▷ **is there a swimming pool?**	há uma piscina?	"a **oom**uh peesh-**see**nuh"
▷ **where is the public swimming pool?**	onde é a piscina municipal?	"**on**dee e uh peesh-**see**nuh mooneesee**pal**"
swimsuit	o fato de banho	"**fah**too duh **bahn**yoo"
Swiss	suíço	"**swee**soo"
	suíça	"**swee**suh"
switch	o interruptor	"eenteroop**tor**"
to switch off	apagar	"apuh**gar**"
	desligar	"dejlee**gar**"
▷ **can I switch the light/ radio off?**	posso apagar a luz/ desligar o rádio?	"**pos**oo apuh**gar** uh **loosh**/dushlee**gar** oo **rah**dyoo"
to switch on	acender	"asayn**dehr**"
	ligar	"lee**gar**"
▷ **can I switch the light/ radio on?**	posso acender a luz/ ligar o rádio?	"**pos**oo asayn**dehr** uh **loosh**/lee**gar** oo **rah**dyoo"
Switzerland	a Suíça	"**swee**suh"

ABSOLUTE ESSENTIALS

do you have ...?	tem ...?	"tayng"
is there ...?	há ...?	"ah"
are there ...?	há ...?	"ah"
how much is ...?	quanto custa ...?	"**kwan**too **koosh**tuh"

synagogue	a sinagoga	"seenuh**gog**uh"
table	a mesa	"**may**zuh"
▷ **a table for four, please**	uma mesa para quatro, por favor	"**oom**uh **may**zuh **par**uh **kwat**roo poor fa**vor**"
▷ **the table is booked for ... o'clock this evening**	a mesa está reservada para as ... horas da noite	"uh **may**zuh shta ruhzehr**vah**duh praz ... **o**rush duh noyt"
tablecloth	a toalha de mesa	"**twal**yuh duh **may**zuh"
tablespoon	a colher de sopa	"kool**yehr** duh **sop**uh"
tablet	o comprimido	"kompree**mee**doo"
table tennis	o ténis de mesa	"**tay**neesh duh **may**zuh"
to take (*carry*)	levar	"luh**var**"
(*grab, seize*)	tomar	"too**mar**"
▷ **how long does the journey take?**	quanto tempo leva a viagem?	"**kwan**too **tem**poo **lev**uh uh vee**ah**jayng"
▷ **I take a size 40**	o meu número é o quarenta	"oo **may**oo **noo**meroo e oo kwa**ren**tuh"
▷ **I'd like to take a shower**	queria tomar um duche	"**kree**uh too**mar** oom **doosh**"
▷ **could you take a photograph of us?**	podia tirar-nos uma fotografia?	"poo**dee**uh tee**rar**noosh **oom**uh footoo-gruh**fee**uh"
talc	o talco	"**tal**koo"
to talk	conversar	"komver**sar**"
tall	alto	"**al**too"
	alta	"**al**tuh"
▷ **how tall are you/is it?**	que altura tem?	"kuh al**too**ruh **tayng**"
▷ **I am/it is 1m 80/10m tall**	tenho/tem 1 metro e 80/10 metros de altura	"**ten**yoo/**tayng** oom **me**troo ee oy**ten**tuh/ desh **me**troosh duh al**too**ruh"
tampons	os tampões	"tam**poynsh**"

tap	a torneira	"toor**nay**ruh"
tape (*cassette*)	a cassete	"ka**seht**"
(*video*)	a cassete de vídeo	"ka**seht** duh **vee**deeoo"
(*ribbon*)	a fita	"**fee**tuh"
tape-recorder	o gravador	"gravuh**dor**"
tart	a tarte	"tart"
tartar sauce	o molho tártaro	"**mohl**yoo **tar**taroo"
taste[1] *n*	o sabor	"sa**bor**"
to **taste**[2] *vb*:		
▷ **can I taste some?**	posso provar?	"**pos**oo proo**var**"
▷ **can I taste it?**	posso prová-lo	"**pos**oo proo**vah**-loo"
tax	o imposto	"eem**posh**too"
taxi	o táxi	"**tax**ee"
▷ **can you order me a taxi, please?**	pode chamar-me um táxi, por favor?	"pod sha**mar**muh oom **tax**ee poor fa**vor**"
taxi rank	a praça de táxis	"**prah**suh duh **tax**eesh"
tea	o chá	"**sha**"
tea bag	o saquinho de chá	"sa**keen**yoo duh **sha**"
to **teach**	ensinar	"aynsee**nar**"
teacher	o professor	"proofuh**sor**"
	a professora	"proofuh**sor**uh"
team	a equipa	"eh**kee**puh"
team games	os jogos de equipa	"**jog**oosh duh eh**kee**puh"
teapot	o bule	"**bool**"
teaspoon	a colher de chá	"kool**yehr** duh **sha**"
teat	o seio	"**say**oo"
tee shirt	a T-shirt	"teeshirt"

ABSOLUTE ESSENTIALS

I don't understand	não compreendo	"nowng kompree**een**doo"
I don't speak Portuguese	não falo português	"nowng **fah**loo poortoo**gaysh**"
do you speak English?	fala inglês?	"**fah**luh een**glesh**"
could you help me?	podia ajudar-me?	"poo**dee**uh ajoo**dar**muh"

teeth	os dentes	"dentsh"
telegram	o telegrama	"tuhluh**grah**muh"
▷ where can I send a telegram from?	de onde posso enviar um telegrama?	"duh ond **pos**oo aynvee**ar** oom tuhluh**grah**muh"
▷ I want to send a telegram	quero enviar um telegrama	"**ke**roo aynvee**ar** oom tuhluh**grah**muh"
telephone	o telefone	"tuhluh**fon**"
▷ how much is it to telephone Britain/the USA?	quanto custa telefonar para a Grã-Bretanha/ para os Estados-Unidos?	"**kwan**too **koosh**tuh tuhluhfoo**nar** pra grambruh**tahn**yuh/prosh shtahdooz-oo**need**oosh"
telephone book	a lista telefónica	"**leesh**tuh tuhluh- **fon**ikuh"
telephone box	a cabine telefónica	"ka**been** tuhluh- **fon**ikuh"
telephone call	a chamada	"sha**mah**duh"
▷ I'd like to make a telephone call	quero fazer uma chamada	"**keh**roo fa**zehr** **oom**uh sha**mah**duh"
telephone directory	a lista telefónica	"**leesh**tuh tuhluh-**fon**ikuh"
television	a televisão	"tuhluh-vee**zowng**"
television lounge:		
▷ is there a television lounge?	há uma sala de televisão?	"a **oom**uh **sah**luh duh tuhluh-vee**zowng**"
television set	o televisor	"tuhluhvee**zor**"
telex	o telex	"**tel**ex"
to tell	dizer a	"dee**zehr** uh"
temperature	a temperatura	"temperuh-**too**ruh"
▷ to have a temperature	ter febre	"tehr **feb**ruh"
▷ what is the temperature?	qual é a temperatura?	"kwal e uh temperuh-**too**ruh"
temporary	temporário temporária	"tempoo**rar**yoo" "teempoo**rar**yuh"

ten	dez	"desh"
tennis	o ténis	"**tay**neesh"
▷ **where can we play tennis?**	onde podemos jogar ténis?	"**on**duh poo**day**moosh joo**gar tay**neesh"
tennis ball	a bola de ténis	"**boh**luh duh **tay**neesh"
tennis court	o campo de ténis	"**kam**poo duh **tay**neesh"
▷ **how much is it to hire a tennis court?**	quanto custa alugar um campo de ténis?	"**kwan**too **koosh**tuh aloo**gar** oom **kam**poo duh **tay**neesh"
tennis racket	a raqueta de ténis	"ra**ket**uh duh **tay**neesh"
tent	a tenda	"**ten**duh"
▷ **can we pitch our tent here?**	podemos montar a nossa tenda aqui?	"poo**deh**moosh mom**tar** uh **noo**suh **ten**duh a**kee**"
tent peg	a estaca	"**shtah**kuh"
terminus	a estação final	"shta**sowng** fee**nal**"
terrace	a esplanada	"shpla**nah**duh"
▷ **can I eat on the terrace?**	posso comer na esplanada?	"**pos**oo koo**mehr** nuh shpla**nah**duh"
than:		
▷ **better than this**	melhor do que isto	"mul**yor** doo kuh **eesh**too"
thank you	obrigado obrigada	"ohbree**gah**doo" "ohbree**gah**duh"
▷ **thank you very much**	muito obrigado(a)	"mweent ohbree**gah**doo(uh)"
▷ **no thank you**	não, obrigado(a)	"nowng ohbree**gah**doo(uh)"
that (*over yonder*)	aquele aquela	"a**kayl**" "a**kel**uh"
(*there*)	esse essa	"ehs" "**es**uh"

do you have ...?	tem ...?	"tayng"
is there ...?	há ...?	"ah"
are there ...?	há ...?	"ah"
how much is ...?	quanto custa ...?	"**kwan**too **koosh**tuh"

▷ that one	esse	"ehs"
to thaw:		
▷ it's thawing	está a derreter	"shta uh duhrruh**tehr**"
theatre	o teatro	"tee**ah**troo"
theirs (*singular*)	seu	"**se**oo"
	sua	"**soo**uh"
(*plural*)	seus	"**se**oosh"
	suas	"**soo**ush"
then	então	"en**towng**"
there	aí	"a**ee**"
(*over yonder*)	ali	"a**lee**"
▷ there is/there are	há	"a"
thermometer	o termómetro	"termo**metroo**"
these	estes	"**aysh**tush"
	estas	"**esh**tush"
they	eles	"**ay**lush"
	elas	"**e**lush"
thief	o ladrão	"la**drowng**"
	a ladra	"**lah**druh"
thing	a coisa	"**koy**zuh"
▷ my things	as minhas coisas	"ush **mee**nyush **koy**zush"
to think	pensar	"payn**sar**"
third	terceiro	"ter**say**roo"
	terceira	"ter**say**ruh"
thirsty:		
▷ I'm thirsty	tenho sede	"**ten**yoo sed"
thirteen	treze	"trehz"
thirty	trinta	"**treen**tuh"
this	este	"aysht"
	esta	"**esh**tuh"

▷ **this one**	este	"aysht"
those (*over yonder*)	aqueles	"akaylush"
	aquelas	"akelush"
(*there*)	esses	"ehsesh"
	essas	"esush"
thread	a linha	"leenyuh"
three	três	"trehsh"
throat	a garganta	"gargantuh"
▷ **I want something for a sore throat**	quero qualquer coisa para as dores de garganta	"kehroo kwalkehr koyzuh prash dorush duh gargantuh"
throat lozenges	as pastilhas para a garganta	"pashteelyush pra gargantuh"
through	através de	"atruhvesh duh"
▷ **I can't get through**	não consigo fazer a ligação	"nowng konseegoo fazehr uh leeguhsowng"
▷ **is it/this a through train?**	o/este comboio é directo?	"oo/esht komboyoo e deeretoo"
thunder	o trovão	"troovowng"
▷ **I think it's going to thunder**	acho que vai trevojar	"ashoo kuh **vy** truhvoojar"
thunderstorm	a trovoada	"troovwahduh"
▷ **will there be a thunderstorm?**	vai fazer trovoada?	"vy fazehr troovwahduh"
Thursday	quinta-feira	"keentuh-fairuh"
ticket	o bilhete	"beelyet"
▷ **can you book the tickets for us?**	pode marcar-nos os bilhetes?	"pod markar-noozooj beelyetsh"
▷ **where do I buy a ticket?**	onde é que compro um bilhete?	"ondee e kuh komproo oom beelyet"
▷ **can I buy the tickets here?**	posso comprar os bilhetes aqui?	"posoo komprar ooj beelyetzakee"

ABSOLUTE ESSENTIALS

I don't understand	não compreendo	"nowng kompreeendoo"
I don't speak Portuguese	não falo português	"nowng fahloo poortoogaysh"
do you speak English?	fala inglês?	"fahluh eenglesh"
could you help me?	podia ajudar-me?	"poodeeuh ajoodarmuh"

▷ a single ticket	um bilhete de ida	"oom bee**lyet** duh **ee**duh"
▷ a return ticket	um bilhete de ida e volta	"oom bee**lyet** duh **ee**duh ee **vol**tuh"
▷ 2 tickets for the opera/theatre	dois bilhetes para a ópera/o teatro	"**doy**sh bee**lyetsh pa**ruh uh **op**ruh/oo tee**at**roo"
▷ a book of tickets	uma caderneta de senhas	"**oom**uh kadur**neh**tuh duh **sayn**yush"
ticket collector	o revisor	"ruhvee**zor**"
ticket office	a bilheteira	"beelyuh-**tay**ruh"
tide	a maré	"ma**re**"
tie	a gravata	"gruh**vah**tuh"
tights	os collants	"ko**lansh**"
till[1] *n*	a caixa	"**ky**shuh"
till[2] *prep* (*until*)	até	"a**te**"
▷ I want to stay three nights/from ... till ...	quero ficar três noites/ do dia ... ao dia ...	"**keh**roo fee**kar** traysh noytsh/doo **dee**uh ... ow **dee**uh ..."
time	a hora	"**or**uh"
▷ what time is it?	que horas são?	"kee **or**ush sowng"
▷ this time	desta vez	"**desh**tuh vesh"
▷ do we have time to visit the town?	temos tempo para visitar a cidade?	"**tay**moosh **tem**poo **pa**ruh veezee**tar** uh see**dadh**"
▷ what time do we get to ...?	a que horas chegamos a ...?	"uh kee **or**ush shuh**gah**moozuh ..."
▷ is it time to go?	são horas de ir?	"sowng **or**ush duh **eer**"
timetable:		
▷ can I have a timetable?	pode dar-me um horário?	"pod **dar**muh oom o**rar**yoo"
timetable board	o horário	"oh**rar**yoo"
tin	a lata	"**lah**tuh"
tinfoil	a folha de estanho	"**fol**yuh dush**tahn**yoo"

tin-opener	o abre-latas	"ahbruh-**lah**tush"
tinted:		
▷ **my hair is tinted**	tenho o cabelo pintado	"**ten**yoo oo ka**bay**loo peen**tah**doo"
tip (to waiter etc)	a gorjeta	"**goor**jetuh"
▷ **is it usual to tip?**	é costume dar uma gorjeta?	"e koosh**toom** dar **oo**muh **goor**jetuh"
▷ **how much should I tip?**	quanto é que devo dar de gorjeta?	"**kwan**too e kuh **de**voo dar duh **goor**jetuh"
▷ **is the tip included?**	a gorjeta está incluída?	"uh **goor**jetuh shta een**klwee**duh"
tipped	com filtro	"kong **feel**troo"
tired	cansado	"kan**sah**doo"
	cansada	"kan**sah**duh"
tiring	cansativo	"kansa**tee**voo"
	cansativa	"kansa**tee**vuh"
tissue	o lenço de papel	"**len**soo duh pa**pel**"
to	a	"uh"
	para	"**pa**ruh"
▷ **to London**	para Londres	"**pa**ruh **lon**drush"
▷ **to Spain**	para Espanha	"**pa**ruh **shpahn**yuh"
toast	a torrada	"too**rah**duh"
▷ **2 slices of toast**	duas torradas	"**doo**ush too**rah**dush"
tobacco	o tabaco	"ta**bah**koo"
tobacconist's	a tabacaria	"tabuh-ka**ree**uh"
today	hoje	"ohj"
▷ **is it open today?**	está aberto, hoje?	"shta a**ber**too **ohj**"
together	juntos	"**joon**toosh"
toilet	a casa de banho	"**kah**zuh duh **bahn**yoo"

do you have ...?	tem ...?	"tayng"
is there ...?	há ...?	"ah"
are there ...?	há ...?	"ah"
how much is ...?	quanto custa ...?	"**kwan**too **koosh**tuh"

▷ **is there a toilet for the disabled?**	há casa de banho para deficientes?	"a **kah**zuh duh **bahn**yoo **pa**ruh duhfees**yentsh**"
▷ **where are the toilets, please?**	onde são as casas de banho, por favor?	"**ond** sowng ush **kah**zush duh **bahn**yoo poor fa**vor**"
▷ **is there a toilet on board?**	o autocarro tem casa de banho?	"oo owto**karr**oo tayng **kah**zuh duh **bahn**yoo"
▷ **the toilet won't flush**	o autoclismo não funciona	"oo owtoo**kleej**moo nowng foom**syo**nuh"
toilet paper	o papel higiénico	"pa**pel** eej-**yen**ikoo"
▷ **there is no toilet paper**	não há papel higiénico	"nowng a pa**pel** eej-**yen**ikoo"
toll	a portagem	"poor**tah**jayng"
▷ **is there a toll on this motorway?**	há portagem nesta auto-estrada?	"a poor**tah**jayng **nesh**tuh owtoo**shtrah**duh"
tomato	o tomate	"too**mat**"
tomato juice	o sumo de tomate	"**soo**moo duh too**mat**"
tomato soup	a sopa de tomate	"**soh**puh duh too**mat**"
tomorrow	amanhã	"aman**yang**"
▷ **tomorrow morning**	amanhã de manhã	"aman**yang** duh man**yah**"
▷ **tomorrow afternoon**	amanhã de tarde	"aman**yang** duh **tard**"
▷ **tomorrow night**	amanhã à noite	"aman**yang** a noyt"
▷ **is it open tomorrow?**	está aberto, amanhã?	"shta a**ber**too aman**yang**"
tongue	a língua	"**leeng**wuh"
tonic water	a água tónica	"**ahg**wuh **to**nikuh"
tonight	esta noite	"**esh**tuh noyt"
too (*also*)	também	"tam**bayng**"
(*too much*)	demais	"duh**mysh**"
	demasiado	"duhmazee-**ah**doo"
▷ **it's too big**	é demasiado grande	"e duhmuhsee-**ah**doo **grand**"
tooth	o dente	"dent"

▷ **I've broken a tooth**	parti um dente	"par**tee** oom dent"
toothache:		
▷ **I have toothache**	tenho dor de dentes	"**ten**yoo dor duh dentsh"
▷ **I want something for toothache**	quero qualquer coisa para as dores de dentes	"**kehr**oo kwal**kehr koy**zuh prash **dor**ush duh dentsh"
toothbrush	a escova de dentes	"**shko**vuh duh dentsh"
toothpaste	a pasta dentífrica	"**pash**tuh den**tee**frikuh"
toothpick	o palito	"puh**lee**too"
top¹ *n*	a parte de cima	"part duh **see**muh"
▷ **on top of ...**	em cima de ...	"ayng **see**muh duh"
top² *adj*:		
▷ **the top floor**	o último andar	"**ool**timoo an**dar**"
torch	a lanterna	"lahm**ter**nuh"
torn	rasgado	"raj**gah**doo"
	rasgada	"raj**gah**duh"
total	o total	"too**tal**"
tough (*meat*)	duro	"**doo**roo"
	dura	"**doo**ruh"
tour	a excursão	"shkoor**sowng**"
▷ **how long does the tour take?**	quanto tempo demora a visita?	"**kwan**too **tem**poo duh**mor**uh uh vee**zee**tuh"
▷ **when is the bus tour of the town?**	quando é a visita guiada à cidade?	"**kwan**doo e uh vee**zee**tuh ghee-**ah**duh a see**dahd**"
▷ **the tour starts at about ...**	a visita começa cerca da(s) ...	"uh vee**see**tuh koo**me**suh **sehr**kuh duh(dush) ..."
tourist	o turista	"too**reesh**-tuh"
tourist office	o centro de turismo	"**sen**troo duh too**reej**moo"

▷ **I'm looking for the tourist information office**	procuro o centro de turismo	"proo**koo**roo oo **sen**troo duh too**reej**moo"
tourist ticket	o bilhete turístico	"beel**yet** too**reesh**-tikoo"
to tow	rebocar	"ruhboo**kar**"
▷ **can you tow me to a garage?**	pode rebocar-me para uma garagem?	"pod ruhboo**kar**-muh **proo**muh ga**rah**jayng"
towel	a toalha	"**twal**yuh"
▷ **the towels have run out**	já não há toalhas	"jah nowng a **twal**yush"
town	a cidade	"see**dahd**"
town centre	o centro da cidade	"**sen**troo duh see**dahd**"
town plan	o mapa da cidade	"**mah**puh duh see**dahd**"
towrope	o cabo de reboque	"**kah**boo duh ruh**bok**"
toy	o brinquedo	"breen**kay**doo"
toy shop	a loja de brinquedos	"**loh**juh duh breen**kay**doosh"
traditional	tradicional	"tradeesyoo**nal**"
traffic	o trânsito	"**tran**zitoo"
▷ **is the traffic heavy on the motorway?**	há muito trânsito na auto-estrada?	"a **mween**too tran**zee**too nuh owtoo-**shtrah**duh"
▷ **is there a route that avoids the traffic?**	há outra estrada para evitar o trânsito?	"a **oh**truh **shtrah**duh **pa**ruh eevee**tar** oo tran**zee**too"
traffic jam	o engarrafamento	"enguhruh-fuh**men**to"
trailer	o atrelado	"atruh**lah**doo"
train	o comboio	"kom**boy**oo"
▷ **is this the train for ...?**	é este o comboio para ...?	"e aysht oo kom**boy**oo **pa**ruh"

▷ **what times are the trains?**	a que horas são os comboios?	"uh kee **o**rush sowng oosh kom**boy**oosh"
▷ **are there any cheap train fares?**	há alguns bilhetes de comboio baratos?	"a al**goom**sh beel**yet**sh duh kom**boy**oo ba**rah**toosh"
▷ **does this train go to ...?**	este comboio vai para ..?	"aysht kom**boy**oo vy **pa**ruh"
▷ **how frequent are the trains to town?**	com que frequência há comboios para a cidade?	"**kong** kuh fruh**kwem**syuh a kom**boy**oosh paruh uh see**dahd**"
▷ **does this train stop at ...?**	este comboio pára em ...?	"**esh**t kom**boy**oo **pah**ruh ayng ..."
▷ **when is the first/next/ last train to ...?**	quando é o primeiro/ próximo/último comboio para ...?	"**kwan**doo **e** oo pree**may**roo/ **pro**seemoo/**ool**teemoo kom**boy**oo **pa**ruh"

training shoes	os sapatos de treino	"sa**pah**toosh duh **tray**noo"
tram	o eléctrico	"ee**le**trikoo"
trampoline	o trampolim	"tranpoo**leem**"
to **transfer**	transferir	"transhfuh**reer**"
▷ **I should like to transfer some money from my account**	gostava de transferir dinheiro da minha conta	"goosh**tah**vuh duh transhfuh**reer** deen**yay**roo duh **meen**yuh **kon**tuh"
to **translate**	traduzir	"tradoo**zeer**"
▷ **could you translate this for me?**	podia traduzir-me isto, por favor?	"poo**dee**uh truhdoo**zeer**- muh **eesh**too poor fa**vor**"
translation	a tradução	"tradoo**sowng**"
to **travel**	viajar	"veeuh**jar**"
▷ **I am travelling alone**	viajo sozinho	"vee**ah**joo so**zeen**yoo"
travel agent	o agente de viagens	"a**jent** duh vee**ah**jaynsh"

ABSOLUTE ESSENTIALS

do you have ...?	tem ...?	"tayng"
is there ...?	há ...?	"ah"
are there ...?	há ...?	"ah"
how much is ...?	quanto custa ...?	"**kwan**too **koosh**tuh"

traveller's cheques:

▷ **do you accept traveller's cheques?** — aceita traveller cheques? — "a**say**tuh traveller **shek**sh"

▷ **can I change my traveller's cheques here?** — posso trocar os meus traveller cheques aqui? — "**pos**oo troo**kar** oosh **may**oosh traveller **shek**sh a**kee**"

travel-sick:

▷ **I get travel-sick** — eu enjoo nas viagens — "ayoo ayn**joh**oo nush vee**ah**jayngs"

tray — o tabuleiro — "taboo**lay**roo"

tree — a árvore — "**ar**vooruh"

to trim — aparar — "apa**rar**"

▷ **can I have a trim?** — podia espontar-me o cabelo — "poo**dee**uh shpom**tar**muh oo ka**bay**loo"

trip — a viagem — "vee**ah**jayng"

▷ **this is my first trip to ...** — esta é minha primeira viagem a ... — "**esh**tuh e **meen**yuh pree**may**ruh vee**ah**jayng uh"

▷ **a business trip** — uma viagem de negócios — "**oo**muh vee**ah**jayng duh nuh**go**seeooosh"

▷ **do you run day trips?** — fazem excursões de um dia? — "**fa**zayng ayshkoor-**soynsh** doom **dee**uh"

trolley — o carrinho — "kuh**rreen**yoo"

trouble — os problemas — "proo**ble**mush"

▷ **I am in trouble** — tenho problemas — "**ten**yoo proo**ble**mush"

▷ **I'm sorry to trouble you** — desculpe incomodá-lo — "dush**koolp** eemkoomoo**dah**-loo"

▷ **I'm having trouble with the phone/the key** — não consigo usar o telefone/a chave — "nowng kon**see**goo oo**zar** oo tuhluh**fon**/uh **shahv**"

trousers — as calças — "**kal**sush"

trout — a truta — "**troo**tuh"

true	verdadeiro(a)	"verduh**dayroo**(uh)"
trunk (*luggage*)	a mala	"**mah**luh"
▷ **I'd like to send my trunk on ahead**	queria enviar a minha mala à frente	"**kree**uh aynvee**ar** uh **meen**yuh **mah**luh a frent"
trunks	os calções de banho	"kal**soynsh** duh **bahn**yoo"
to try	tentar	"ten**tar**"
to try on	provar	"pro**var**"
▷ **may I try on this dress?**	posso experimentar este vestido?	"**pos**oo shpuhree-men**tar** aysht vush**tee**doo"
T-shirt	a T-shirt	"**tee**shirt"
Tuesday	terça-feira	"**ter**suh-fairuh"
tuna	o atum	"a**toong**"
tunnel	o túnel	"**too**nel"
▷ **the Channel tunnel**	o túnel do Canal da Mancha	"oo **too**nel doo kuh**nal** duh **mayn**shuh"
turkey	o peru	"puh**roo**"
to turn	(*handle, wheel*) voltar	"vol**tar**"
▷ **it's my/her turn**	é a minha/sua vez	"e uh **mee**nyuh/**soo**uh vaysh"
to turn down	(*sound, heating etc*) baixar	"by**shar**"
turning:		
▷ **is this the turning for ...?**	é aqui que se vira para ...?	"e a**kee** kuh suh **vee**ruh **par**uh"
▷ **take the second/third turning on your left**	vire na segunda/terceira rua à esquerda	"**vee**ruh nuh suh**goon**duh/tur**say**ruh **roo**uh a sh**kehr**duh"
turnip	o nabo	"**nah**boo"
to to turn off (*light etc*)	apagar	"apuh**gar**"
(*engine etc*)	desligar	"dejlee**gar**"
(*tap*)	fechar	"fu**shar**"

ABSOLUTE ESSENTIALS

I don't understand	não compreendo	"nowng kompree**een**doo"
I don't speak Portuguese	não falo português	"nowng **fah**loo poortoo**gaysh**"
do you speak English?	fala inglês?	"**fah**luh een**glesh**"
could you help me?	podia ajudar-me?	"poo**dee**uh ajoo**dar**muh"

▷ **I can't turn the heating off** | não consigo desligar o aquecimento | "nowng konseegoo dujleegar oo akusee-mentoo"

to turn on (*light etc*) | acender | "assendehr"
(*engine etc*) | ligar | "leegar"
(*tap*) | abrir | "abreer"

▷ **I can't turn the heating on** | não consigo ligar o aqueciemento | "nowng konseegoo leegar oo akusee-mentoo"

to turn up (*sound, heating etc*) | aumentar | "owmentar"

tweezers | a pinça | "peensuh"

twelve | doze | "doz"

twenty | vinte | "veent"

twenty one | vinte e um | "veenteeoom"

twenty two | vinte e dois | "veenteedoysh"

twice | duas vezes | "dooush vayzush"

twin-bedded room | o quarto com duas camas | "kwartoo kong dooush kahmush"

two | dois | "doysh"

typical | típico | "teepikoo"
| típica | "teepikuh"

▷ **have you anything typical of this town/ region?** | tem alguma coisa típica desta cidade/região? | "tayng algoomuh koyzuh teepikuh deshtuh seedahd/ruhgeeowng"

tyre | o pneu | "pnayoo"

tyre pressure | a pressão dos pneus | "presowng doosh pnayoosh"

▷ **what should the tyre pressure be?** | qual deve ser a pressão dos pneus? | "kwal dev sehr uh presowng doosh pnayoosh"

ABSOLUTE ESSENTIALS

I would like ... | queria ... | "kreeuh"
I need ... | preciso de ... | "preseezoo duh"
where is ...? | onde fica ...? | "ond feekuh"
I'm looking for ... | procuro ... | "prokooroo"

UK	o Reino Unido	"**ray**noo oo**nee**doo"
umbrella (for rain)	o guarda-chuva	"gwarduh-**shoo**vuh"
(on beach)	o guarda-sol	"gwarduh-**sol**"
uncomfortable	incómodo	"een**kom**oodoo"
	incómoda	"een**kom**ooduh"
▷ **the bed is**	a cama é desconfortável	"uh **kah**muh e **dej**kowng-
uncomfortable		foortahvel"
unconscious	inconsciente	"eenkonsh-see**ent**"
under	debaixo de	"duh-**by**shoo duh"
underground	o metro	"**met**roo"
underground	a estação do metro	"uh shta**sowng** doo
station		**met**roo"
underpass	a passagem subterrânea	"pa**sah**jayng soobte-
		rahneeuh"
to **understand**	compreender	"kompree-en**dehr**"
▷ **I don't understand**	não compreendo	"nowng kompree-**en**doo"
underwear	a roupa interior	"**roh**puh eentere**or**"
United States	os Estados Unidos	"shtahdooz-oo**nee**doosh"
university	a universidade	"oonee-versee**dahd**"
unleaded petrol	a gasolina sem chumbo	"gazoo**lee**nuh sayng
		shoomboo"
to **unpack** (case)	desfazer as malas	"dushfa**zehr** ush **mah**lush"
up	levantado	"luhvan**tah**doo"
	levantada	"luhvan**tah**duh"
▷ **up there**	lá em cima	"**la** ayng **see**muh"
upstairs	lá em cima	"**la** ayng **see**muh"
urgent	urgente	"oor**jent**"
USA	(EUA) os Estados	"shtahdooz- oo**nee**doosh
	Unidos da América	duh a**mer**ikuh"

do you have ...?	tem ...?	"tayng"
is there ...?	há ...?	"ah"
are there ...?	há ...?	"ah"
how much is ...?	quanto custa ...?	"**kwan**too **koosh**tuh"

to **use**	utilizar	"ooteelee**zar**"
	usar	"oo**zar**"
▷ **may I use your phone?**	posso utilizar o seu telefone?	"**pos**soo ooteelee**zar** oo **say**oo tuhluh**fon**"
useful	útil	"**oo**teel"
usual	habitual	"abee**twal**"
usually	geralmente	"juhral**ment**"
vacancies (*rooms*)	os quartos vagos	"**kwar**toosh **vah**goosh"
▷ **do you have any vacancies?** (*campsite*)	tem lugares vagos?	"tayn loo**gah**rush **vah**goosh"
to **vacate:**		
▷ **when do I have to vacate the room?**	quando tenho que deixar o quarto?	"**kwan**doo **ten**yoo kuh day**shar** oo **kwar**too"
vacuum cleaner	o aspirador	"ashpeeruh**dor**"
valid	válido	"**val**idoo"
	válida	"**val**iduh"
valley	o vale	"val"
valuable	valioso	"val**yoh**zoo"
	valiosa	"val**yo**zuh"
valuables	os objectos de valor	"ob**jet**oosh duh va**lor**"
van	a carrinha	"ka**reen**yuh"
vase	o vaso	"**vah**zoo"
VAT	o IVA	"**ee**vuh"
▷ **does the price include VAT?**	o preço já inclui IVA?	"oo **pre**soo **ja een**klwee **ee**vuh"
veal	a carne de vitela	"karn duh vee**tel**uh"
vegan	vegetariano puro	"vejuhtuh-ree**ah**noo **poo**roo"
	vegetariana pura	"vejuhtuh-ree**ah**nuh **poo**ruh"

▷ is this suitable for vegans?	isto serve para vegetarianos puros?	"**eesh**too **serv paruh** vejuhtuh-ree**ah**noosh **poo**roosh"
▷ do you have any vegan dishes?	tem pratos para vegetarianos puros?	"tayng **prah**toosh **paruh** vejuhtuh-ree**ah**noosh **poo**roosh"
vegetables	os legumes	"luh**goom**ush"
▷ are the vegetables included?	inclui legumes?	"een**klwee** luh**goom**ush"
vegetarian	vegetariano vegetariana	"vejuhtuh-ree**ah**noo" "vejuhtuh-ree**ah**nuh"
▷ is this suitable for vegetarians?	isto serve para vegetarianos?	"**eesh**too **serv paruh** vejuhtuh-ree**ah**noosh"
▷ do you have any vegetarian dishes?	tem pratos para vegetarianos?	"tayng **prah**toosh **paruh** vejuhtuh-ree**ah**noosh"
venison	a carne de veado	"**karn** duh vee**ah**doo"
ventilator	o ventilador	"venteeluh**dor**"
vermouth	o vermute	"ver**moot**"
vertigo:		
▷ I suffer from vertigo	tenho vertigens	"**ten**yoo ver**tee**jayngs"
very	muito	"**mween**too"
vest	a camisola interior	"kamee**zol**uh eenteree**or**"
via	via	"**vee**uh"
video	o vídeo	"**vee**deeoo"
Vienna	Viena	"**vienna**"
view	a vista	"**veesh**tuh"
▷ I'd like a room with a view of the sea/the mountains	queria um quarto com vista para o mar/as montanhas	"**kree**uh oom **kwar**too kong **veesh**tuh **paruh** oo **mar**/ush mon**tan**yush"
villa	a casa de campo	"**kah**zuh duh **kam**poo"

village	a aldeia	"al**day**uh"
vinegar	o vinagre	"vee**nah**gruh"
vineyard	a vinha	"**veen**yuh"
visa	o visto	"**veesh**too"
▷ **I have an entry visa**	tenho um visto de entrada	"**ten**yoo oom **veesh**too dayn**trah**duh"
to visit	visitar	"veezee**tar**"
▷ **can we visit the vineyard/church?**	podemos visitar a vinha/igreja	"poo**deh**moosh veezee**tar** uh **veen**yuh/ee**gray**juh"
vitamin	a vitamina	"veetuh**mee**nuh"
vodka	a vodka	"**vod**kuh"
volleyball	o voleibol	"**voh**laybol"
voltage	a voltagem	"vol**tah**jayng"
▷ **what's the voltage?**	qual é a voltagem?	"kwal **e** uh vol**tah**jayng"
waist	a cintura	"seen**too**ruh"
waistcoat	o colete	"koo**leht**"
to wait (for)	esperar (por)	"shpuh**rar** (poor)"
▷ **can you wait here for a few minutes?**	pode esperar aqui uns minutos?	"pod shpuh**rar** a**kee** oonj mee**noo**toosh"
▷ **please wait for me**	por favor, espere por mim	"poor fa**vor** sh**per**uh poor **meeng**"
waiter	o empregado de mesa	"aympruh-**gah**doo duh **may**zuh"
waiting room	a sala de espera	"**sah**luh dush**peh**ruh"
waitress	a empregada de mesa	"aympruh-**gah**duh duh **may**zuh"
to wake:		
▷ **please wake me at 8.00**	por favor, acorde-me às 8	"poor fa**vor** a**kor**duh-muh as **oy**too"

to **wake up**	acordar	"akoor**dar**"
Wales	o País de Gales	"pa**eesh** duh **gah**lush"
walk[1] *n*	o passeio a pé	"pa**say**oo uh **pe**"
▷ to go for a walk	ir dar um passeio a pé	"**eer** dar oom pa**say**oo uh **pe**"
▷ are there any interesting walks nearby?	vale a pena dar alguns passeios por aqui?	"val uh **pay**nuh dar al**goonsh** pa**say**oosh poor a**kee**"
to **walk**[2] *vb*	andar	"an**dar**"
wallet	a carteira	"kar**tay**ruh"
walnut	a noz	"nosh"
to **want**	querer	"kuh**rehr**"
warm	quente	"kent"
warning triangle	o triângulo	"tree**an**gooloo"
to **wash**	lavar	"la**var**"
▷ to wash oneself	lavar-se	"la**var**-suh"
▷ where can I wash my clothes/my hands?	onde posso lavar a roupa/as mãos?	"ond **pos**oo la**var** uh **roh**puh/ush **mownsh**"
washable:		
▷ is it washable?	é lavável?	"e la**vah**vel"
washbasin	o lavatório	"lavuh**tor**yoo"
▷ the washbasin is dirty	o lavatório está sujo	"oo lavuh**tor**yoo sh**ta soo**joo"
▷ do I have to pay extra to use the washbasin?	tenho que pagar extra para usar o lavatório?	"**ten**yoo kuh pa**gar esh**truh **pa**ruh oo**zar** oo lavuh**tor**yoo"
washing:		
▷ where can I do some washing?	onde é que posso lavar a roupa?	"**on**dee e kuh **pos**oo la**var** uh **roh**puh"
washing machine	a máquina de lavar roupa	"**mak**inuh duh la**var roh**puh"

ABSOLUTE ESSENTIALS

do you have ...?	tem ...?	"tayng"
is there ...?	há ...?	"ah"
are there ...?	há ...?	"ah"
how much is ...?	quanto custa ...?	"**kwan**too **koosh**tuh"

▷ how do you work the washing machine?	como se trabalha com a máquina de lavar roupa?	"**koo**moo suh truh**bal**yuh kong uh **ma**kinuh duh la**var roh**puh"
washing powder	o detergente para a roupa	"duhter**jent** pra **roh**puh"
washing-up liquid	o detergente para a louça	"duhter**jent** pra **loh**suh"
wasp	a vespa	"**vesh**puh"
waste bin	o caixote do lixo	"ky**shot** doo **lee**shoo"
watch[1] *n*	o relógio	"ruh**loj**yoo"
▷ I think my watch is slow/fast	acho que o meu relógio está atrasado/ adiantado	"**a**shoo kuh oo **may**oo ruh**loj**yoo shta atruh**zah**doo/ adeean**tah**doo"
▷ my watch has stopped	o meu relógio parou	"oo **may**oo ruh**loj**yoo pa**roh**"
to **watch**[2] *vb (look at)*	ver	"vehr"
▷ could you watch my bag for a minute please?	podia vigiar-me o saco por um minuto, por favor	"poo**dee**uh veegeear-muh oo **sah**koo poor oom mee**noo**too poor fa**vor**"
water	a água	"**ah**gwuh"
▷ there is no hot water	não há água quente	"nowng a **ah**gwuh kent"
▷ a glass of water	um copo de água	"oom **ko**poo duh **ah**gwuh"
waterfall	a queda de água	"**ked**uh **dah**gwuh"
water heater	o esquentador	"shkentuh**dor**"
watermelon	a melância	"melan**see**uh"
waterproof	impermeável	"eempermee**ah**vel"
water-skiing	o esqui-aquático	"shkee-uh**kwa**tikoo"
▷ is it possible to go water-skiing?	é possível ir fazer esquí-aquático?	"e poo**see**vel eer fa**zehr** shkee-uh**kwa**tikoo"
wave *(on sea)*	a onda	"**on**duh"

wax	a cera	"**seh**ruh"
way (*manner*)	a maneira	"ma**nay**ruh"
(*route*)	o caminho	"ka**mee**nyoo"
▷ **which is the way to ...?**	qual é o caminho para ...?	"kwal **e** oo ka**mee**nyoo **pa**ruh"
▷ **this way**	por aqui	"poor a**kee**"
▷ **that way**	por ali	"poor a**lee**"
▷ **what's the best way to get to ...?**	qual é o melhor caminho para ...?	"kwal **e** oo mel**yor** ka**mee**nyoo **pa**ruh"
we	nós	"nosh"
weak (*person*)	fraco	"**frah**koo"
	fraca	"**frah**kuh"
(*coffee*)	aguado	"ag**wah**doo"
to wear	vestir	"vush**teer**"
▷ **what should I wear?**	o que devo vestir?	"oo kuh **deh**voo vush**teer**"
weather	o tempo	"**tem**poo"
▷ **what dreadful weather!**	que tempo horrível!	"kuh **tem**poo oh**rree**vel"
▷ **is the weather going to change?**	o tempo vai mudar?	"oo **tem**poo vy moo**dar**"
weather forecast:		
▷ **what's the weather forecast for tomorrow?**	qual é a previsão do estado do tempo para amanhã?	"kwal **e** uh prevee**sowng** doo sh**tah**doo doo **tem**poo **pa**ruh ahman**yang**"
wedding	o casamento	"kazuh**men**too"
▷ **we are here for a wedding**	estamos aqui para um casamento	"sh**tah**moosh a**kee pa**ruh oom kazuh**men**too"
Wednesday	quarta-feira	"**kwar**tuh-**fai**ruh"
week	a semana	"se**mah**nuh"
▷ **this week**	esta semana	"**esh**tuh se**mah**nuh"
▷ **last week**	na semana passada	"nuh se**mah**nuh pa**sah**duh"

ABSOLUTE ESSENTIALS

I don't understand	não compreendo	"nowng kompree**en**doo"
I don't speak Portuguese	não falo português	"nowng **fah**loo poortoo**gaysh**"
do you speak English?	fala inglês?	"**fah**luh een**glesh**"
could you help me?	podia ajudar-me?	"poo**dee**uh ajoo**dar**muh"

▷ next week	na próxima semana	"nuh **pro**seemuh se**mah**nuh"
▷ for one/2 weeks	por uma/duas semanas	"poor **oom**uh/**doo**ush se**mah**nush"
week day	o dia útil	"**dee**uh **oo**teel"
weekend	o fim-de-semana	"feeng duh se**mah**nuh"
weekly (rate etc)	semanal	"semuh**nal**"
weight	o peso	"**pay**zoo"
welcome	bemvindo	"bayng**veen**doo"
	bemvinda	"bayng**veen**duh"
▷ **you're welcome**	de nada	"duh **nah**duh"
well	bem	"bayng"
▷ **he's not well**	ele não se sente bem	"**ayl** nowng suh **sent** bayng"
well done (steak)	bem passado	"bayng pa**sah**doo"
	bem passada	"bayng pa**sah**duh"
Welsh	galês	"ga**lesh**"
	galesa	"ga**lay**zuh"
▷ **I'm Welsh**	sou galês/galesa	"**soh** ga**lesh**/ga**lay**zuh"
west	o oeste	"**wesht**"
wet	molhado	"mohl**yah**doo"
	molhada	"mohl**yah**duh"
wetsuit	o fato de mergulhador	"**fah**too duh mergool-yuh**dor**"
what	que	"kee"
▷ **what is it?**	o que é?	"oo kee **e**"
wheel	a roda	"**ro**duh"
wheelchair	a cadeira de rodas	"ka**day**ruh duh **ro**dush"
when	quando	"**kwan**doo"

where	onde	"**on**duh"
▷ where are you from?	de onde é?	"**duh** ond **e**"
which:		
▷ which is it?	qual é?	"**kwal** e"
▷ which man?	que homem?	"kuh **o**mayng"
▷ which woman?	que mulher?	"kuh mool**yehr**"
▷ which book?	que livro	"kuh **lee**vroo"
while¹ *n*:		
▷ in a while	dentro de pouco	"**den**troo duh **poh**koo"
while² *conj*	enquanto	"ayn**kwan**too"
▷ can you do it while I wait?	pode fazê-lo enquanto espero?	"pod fa**zeh**-loo ayn**kwan**too shp**ee**roo"
whipped	batido	"ba**tee**doo"
	batida	"ba**tee**duh"
whipped cream	o chantilly	"shantee**lee**"
whisky	o uísque	"oo-**eeshk**"
▷ I'll have a whisky	quero um uísque	"**keh**roo oom oo-**eeshk**"
▷ whisky and soda	uísque com soda	"oo-**eeshk** kong **soh**duh"
white	branco	"**bran**koo"
	branca	"**bran**kuh"
who:		
▷ who is it?	quem é?	"kayng **e**"
whole	inteiro	"een**tay**roo"
	inteira	"een**tay**ruh"
wholemeal	integral	"eentuh**gral**"
whose:		
▷ whose is it?	de quem é?	"duh kayng **e**"
why	porquê	"poor**kay**"
wide	largo	"**lar**goo"
	larga	"**lar**guh"

ABSOLUTE ESSENTIALS

do you have ...?	tem ...?	"tayng"
is there ...?	há ...?	"ah"
are there ...?	há ...?	"ah"
how much is ...?	quanto custa ...?	"**kwan**too **koosh**tuh"

wife	a mulher	"moolyehr"
	a esposa	"shpozuh"
window	a janela	"janeluh"
(*shop*)	a montra	"**mon**truh"
▷ I can't open the window	não consigo abrir a janela	"nowng konseegoo abreer uh janeluh"
▷ I have broken the window	parti a janela	"partee uh janeluh"
▷ may I open the window?	posso abrir a janela?	"**pos**oo abreer uh janeluh"
▷ shop window	a montra	"**mon**truh"
▷ in the window	na montra	"nuh **mon**truh"

window seat:

▷ I'd like a window seat	queria um lugar perto da janela	"kuhreeuh oom loogar pehrtoo duh janeluh"
windscreen	o pára-brisas	"**pah**ruh-**bree**zush"
▷ could you clean the windscreen?	podia limpar o pára-brisas?	"podeeuh leempar oo paruh-**bree**zush"
▷ the windscreen has shattered	o pára-brisas quebrou-se	"oo pahruh-**bree**zush kebroh-suh"

windscreen washers:

▷ top up the windscreen washers	encha o depósito do limpa pára-brisas	"**ayn**shuh oo duh**po**zitoo doo **leem**puh paruh-**bree**zush"
windscreen wiper	o limpa pára-brisas	"**leem**puh-paruh**bree**zush"
windsurfer (*person*)	o/a surfista	"soor**feesh**tuh"
(*board*)	a prancha de surf	"**pran**shuh duh surf"
▷ can I hire a windsurfer?	posso alugar uma prancha de surf?	"**pos**oo aloogar oomuh **pran**shuh duh surf"
windsurfing	o windsurf	"windsurf"
▷ can I go windsurfing?	posso ir fazer windsurf?	"**pos**oo eer fazehr windsurf"

windy:

▷ **it's (too) windy** | está (demasiado) vento | "shta (duhmazee-**ah**doo) **ven**too"

wine | o vinho | "**veen**yoo"

▷ **red/white wine** | vinho tinto/branco | "**veen**yoo **teen**too/**bran**koo"

▷ **rosé/sparkling wine** | vinho rosé/espumoso | "**veen**yoo roh**zay**/ shpoo**moh**zoo"

▷ **sweet/medium-sweet wine** | vinho doce/meio doce | "**veen**yoo **doss**/**may**oo **doss**"

▷ **dry/medium-dry wine** | vinho seco/meio seco | "**veen**yoo **say**koo/**may**oo **say**koo"

▷ **this wine is not chilled** | o vinho não está fresco | "oo **veen**yoo nowng sh**ta fresh**koo"

▷ **can you recommend a good red/white/rosé wine?** | pode recomendar-nos um bom vinho tinto/ branco/rosé? | "pod ruhkoomen**dar**-nooz oom bong **veen**yoo **teen**too/**bran**koo/ roh**zay**"

▷ **a bottle/carafe of house wine** | uma garrafa/um jarro de vinho da casa | "**oom**uh garra**fuh**/oom **jar**roo duh **veen**yoo duh **kah**zuh"

wine list | a lista de vinhos | "**leesh**tuh duh **veen**yoosh"

▷ **may we see the wine list, please?** | pode-nos mostrar a lista de vinhos, por favor? | "**pod**noosh moosh**trar** uh **leesh**tuh duh **veen**yoosh poor fa**vor**"

winter | o inverno | "eem**vehr**noo"

with | com | "kong"

without | sem | "sayng"

woman | a mulher | "mool**yehr**"

wood | a madeira | "ma**day**ruh"
(*forest*) | a floresta | "floo**resh**tuh"

wool | a lã | "lang"

word | a palavra | "pa**lah**vruh"

ABSOLUTE ESSENTIALS

I don't understand	não compreendo	"nowng kompree**een**doo"
I don't speak Portuguese	não falo português	"nowng **fah**loo poortoo**gaysh**"
do you speak English?	fala inglês?	"**fah**luh een**glesh**"
could you help me?	podia ajudar-me?	"poo**dee**uh ajoo**dar**muh"

▷ **what is the word for ...?**	qual é a palavra para ...?	"kwal **e** uh puh**lah**vruh **par**uh"
to work	(*person*) trabalhar	"trabal**yar**"
(*machine, car*)	funcionar	"foonsyoo**nar**"
▷ **this does not work**	isto não funciona	"**eesh**too nowng foons**yon**uh"
▷ **how does this work?**	como é que isto funciona?	"**koo**moo e kuh **eesh**too foons**yon**uh"
▷ **where do you work?**	onde é que trabalha?	"**ond** e kuh tra**bal**yuh"
worried	preocupado	"preeokoo-**pah**doo"
	preocupada	"preeokoo-**pah**duh"
worse	pior	"pee**or**"
worth:		
▷ **it's worth 2000 escudos**	vale dois mil escudos	"vahl doysh meel **shkoo**doosh"
▷ **how much is it worth?**	quanto vale?	"**kwan**too vahl"
to wrap (up)	embrulhar	"aymbrool**yar**"
▷ **could you wrap it up for me, please?**	pode embrulhar, por favor?	"pod aymbrool**yar** poor fa**vor**"
wrapping paper	o papel de embrulho	"pa**pel** daymb**rool**yoo"
to write	escrever	"shkruh**vehr**"
▷ **could you write that down please?**	podia escrever isso, por favor?	"poo**dee**uh shkruh**vehr ees**oo poor fa**vor**"
writing paper	o papel de carta	"pa**pel** duh **kar**tuh"
wrong	errado	"**errah**doo"
	errada	"**errah**duh"
▷ **sorry, wrong number**	desculpe, enganei-me no número	"dush**koolp** aynga**nay**-muh noo **noo**mero"
▷ **there is something wrong with the brakes/the electrics**	há qualquer problema com os travões/o sistema eléctrico	"a kwal**ker** proo**blay**muh kong oosh tra**voynsh**/oo seesh**tay**muh ee**le**trikoo"
▷ **I think you've given me the wrong change**	acho que me deu o troco errado	"**a**shoo kuh muh **day**oo oo **troh**koo ee**rrah**doo"

ABSOLUTE ESSENTIALS

I would like ...	queria ...	"**kree**uh"
I need ...	preciso de ...	"pre**see**zoo duh"
where is ...?	onde fica ...?	"ond **fee**kuh"
I'm looking for ...	procuro ...	"pro**koo**roo"

▷ **what's wrong?**	o que se passa?	"**oo** kuh suh **pas**uh"
yacht	o iate	"yat"
year	o ano	"**ah**noo"
▷ **this year**	este ano	"esht**ah**noo"
▷ **last year**	no ano passado	"noo **ah**noo pa**sah**doo"
▷ **next year**	no próximo ano	"noo **proh**seemoo **ah**noo"
▷ **every year**	todos os anos	"**to**doozoo-**zahn**oosh"
yellow	amarelo	"amuh**rel**oo"
	amarela	"amuh**rel**uh"
yes	sim	"seeng"
▷ **yes please**	sim, por favor	"seeng poor fa**vor**"
yesterday	ontem	"**on**tayng"
yet:		
▷ **not yet**	ainda não	"uh**een**duh nowng"
yoghurt	o iogurte	"yoo**goort**"
you (*informal singular*)	tu	"too"
(*informal plural*)	vós	"vohsh"
(*formal singular*)	você	"vo**seh**"
(*formal plural*)	vocês	"vo**sehsh**"
young	novo	"**noh**voo"
	nova	"**noh**vuh"
yours (*informal singular*)	teu	"**te**oo"
	tua	"**too**uh"
	teus	"**te**oosh"
	tuas	"**too**ush"
(*informal plural*)	vosso	"**vo**so"
	vossa	"**vo**suh"
	vossos	"**vo**soosh"
	vossas	"**vo**sush"
(*formal singular*)	seu	"**se**oo"
	sua	"**soo**uh"
(*formal plural*)	seus	"**se**oosh"
	suas	"**soo**ush"

ABSOLUTE ESSENTIALS

do you have ...?	tem ...?	"tayng"
is there ...?	há ...?	"ah"
are there ...?	há ...?	"ah"
how much is ...?	quanto custa ...?	"**kwan**too **koosh**tuh"

youth hostel	a pousada de juventude	"poh**zah**da duh jooven**tood**"
▷ **is there a youth hostel?**	há alguma pousada de juventude?	"a al**goo**muh poh**zah**da duh jooven**tood**"
zebra crossing	a passadeira	"puhsuh**day**ruh"
zero	o zero	"**zeh**roo"
zip	o fecho éclair	"**fay**shoo ay**klehr**"
zoo	o jardim zoológico	"jar**deeng** zoh- oo**lo**jikoo"

In the pronunciation system used in this book, Portuguese sounds
are represented by spellings of the nearest possible sounds in
English. Hence, when you read out the pronunciation – shown in
the third column, after the translation – sound the letters as if
you were reading an English word. Whenever we think it is not
sufficiently clear where to stress a word or phrase, we have used
bold to highlight the syllable to be stressed. The following notes
should help you:

	REMARKS	EXAMPLE	PRONUNCIATION
a, e, o	As in *pat, pet, pot*	**pá, pé, pó**	*pa, pe, po*
ah, oh	As in *ma, so*	**maço, dou**	**mah***soo*, *doh*
ee, oo	As in *tree, too*	**triste, tudo**	*treesht*, **too***doo*
ay	As in *may*	**medo**	**may***doo*
eh	As in *air*	**aéreo**	*uh***ehr***yoo*
uh	As in *mother*	**que**	*kuh*
j	Like *s* in *leisure*	**jejum**	*juh***joong**

There are a number of nasal sounds in Portuguese which, as with
similar sounds in French, are pronounced by letting air out through
the nose as well as the mouth:

ang	As in *angry*	**maçã**	*ma***sang**
yng	Like *mine*	**mãe**	*myng*
ayng	Like *main*	**homem**	**o***mayng*
eeng	Midway between *mean* and *Ming*	**mim**	*meeng*
ong	As in *Hong Kong*	**com**	*kong*
oong	Midway between *goon* and *gong*	**algum**	*al***goong**
owng	Like *town*	**tão**	*towng*
oyng	Like *oi* in *point*	**põe**	*poyng*

Pronouncing Portuguese words from their spelling is not easy as
it is a 'flowing' language in which the sounds change depending on
the way in which words are joined together. The following rules
will help:

ç	As in *facile*	**faço**	**fah***soo*
ch	As in *shampoo*	**champô**	*sham***poh**
h	Always silent	**homem**	**o***mayng*
lh	Like *lli* in *million*	**milhão**	*meel***yowng**
nh	Like *ni* in *opinion*	**pinha**	**peen***yuh*

In the weight and length charts the middle figure can be either metric or imperial. Thus 3.3 feet = 1 metre, 1 foot = 0.3 metres, and so on.

feet		metres	inches		cm	lbs		kg
3.3	1	0.3	0.39	1	2.54	2.2	1	0.45
6.6	2	0.61	0.79	2	5.08	4.4	2	0.91
9.9	3	0.91	1.18	3	7.62	6.6	3	1.4
13.1	4	1.22	1.57	4	10.6	8.8	4	1.8
16.4	5	1.52	1.97	5	12.7	11.0	5	2.2
19.7	6	1.83	2.36	6	15.2	13.2	6	2.7
23.0	7	2.13	2.76	7	17.8	15.4	7	3.2
26.2	8	2.44	3.15	8	20.3	17.6	8	3.6
29.5	9	2.74	3.54	9	22.9	19.8	9	4.1
32.9	10	3.05	3.9	10	25.4	22.0	10	4.5
			4.3	11	27.9			
			4.7	12	30.1			

°C	0	5	10	15	17	20	22	24	26	28	30	35	37	38	40	50	100
°F	32	41	50	59	63	68	72	75	79	82	86	95	98.4	100	104	122	212

Km	10	20	30	40	50	60	70	80	90	100	110	120
Miles	6.2	12.4	18.6	24.9	31.0	37.3	43.5	49.7	56.0	62.0	68.3	74.6

Tyre pressures

lb/sq in	15	18	20	22	24	26	28	30	33	35
kg/sq cm	1.1	1.3	1.4	1.5	1.7	1.8	2.0	2.1	2.3	2.5

Liquids

gallons	1.1	2.2	3.3	4.4	5.5		pints	0.44	0.88	1.76
litres	5	10	15	20	25		litres	0.25	0.5	1

CAR PARTS

air conditioning	o ar condicionado	"ar kondees-yoonahdoo"
antifreeze	o anticongelante	"antee-konjelant"
automatic	automático	"owtoomatikoo"
	automática	"owtoomatikuh"
battery	a bateria	"batuh-reeuh"
boot	a mala do carro	"maluh doo karroo"
brake fluid	o óleo dos travões	"olyoo doosh travoynsh"
brakes	os travões	"travoynsh"
car	o carro	"karroo"
carburettor	o carburador	"karboooruhdor"
car (registration) number	a matrícula do carro	"matreekooluh doo karroo"
chain	a corrente	"koorrent"
de-ice	descongelar	"dushkonjuhlar"
diesel	o gasóleo	"gazolyoo"
engine	o motor	"mootor"
exhaust pipe	o tubo de escape	"tooboo dushkap"
fan belt	a correia da ventoinha	"koo-rrayuy duh ventoo-eenyuh"
fuel pump	a bomba de gasolina	"bombuh duh gazooleenuh"
garage	a garagem	"garah-jayng"
gear	a velocidade	"vuhloo-seedahd"
headlights	os faróis	"faroysh"
indicator	o pisca-pisca	"peeshkuh-peeshkuh"
jack	o macaco	"makahkoo"
jump leads	os cabos de emergência	"kahboosh deemerjensyuh"
leak	a fuga	"fooguh"
luggage rack	o porta-bagagens	"portuh-bagahjaynsh"
oil filter	o filtro do óleo	"feeltroo doo olyoo"
petrol	a gasolina	"gazooleenuh"
points	os platinados	"plateenahdoosh"
radiator	o radiador	"rahdee-uhdor"
roofrack	o tejadilho	"tejuhdeelyoo"
shock absorber	o amortecedor	"amortuh-suhdor"
spare wheel	a roda sobressalente	"roduh sobruhsalent"
spark plug	a vela	"veluh"
speedometer	o velocímetro	"vuhloosee-muhtroo"
suspension	o suspensão	"sooshpensowng"
tyre	o pneu	"pnayoo"
tyre pressure	a pressão dos pneus	"presowng doosh pnayoosh"
warning triangle	o triângulo	"treeangooloo"
windscreen	o pára-brisas	"pahruh-breezush"
windscreen wiper	o limpa pára-brisas	"leempuh paruh-breezush"

COLOURS

black	preto	**"pray**too"
	preta	**"pray**tuh"
blue	azul	"a**zool**"
brown	castanho	"kash**tahn**yoo"
	castanha	"kash**tahn**yuh"
colour	a cor	"kor"
dark	escuro	**"shkoo**roo"
	escura	**"shkoo**ruh"
green	verde	"vehrd"
grey	cinzento	"seen**zen**too"
	cinzenta	"seen**zen**tuh"
light blue/green	luz azul/verde	"loosh a**zool**/vehrd"
navy blue	azul marinho	"a**zool** ma**reen**yoo"
orange	cor de laranja	"kor duh la**ran**juh"
pink	cor-de-rosa	"korduh**roz**uh"
purple	roxo	**"roh**shoo"
	roxa	**"roh**shuh"
red	vermelho	"ver**mel**yoo"
	vermelha	"ver**mel**yuh"
white	branco	**"bran**koo"
	branca	**"bran**kuh"
yellow	amarelo	"amuh**rel**oo"
	amarela	"amuh**rel**uh"

6

COUNTRIES

America	a América	"**am**erikuh"
Australia	a Austrália	"owsh**trah**leeuh"
Austria	a Áustria	"**owsh**-treeuh"
Britain	a Grã-Bretanha	"gram-bruh**tahn**yuh"
Canada	o Canadá	"kanuh**da**"
England	a Inglaterra	"eengluh**terr**uh"
Europe	a Europa	"ayoo-**rop**uh"
France	a França	"**fran**suh"
Germany	a Alemanha	"aluh-**mahn**yuh"
Greece	a Grécia	"**gres**-yuh"
Ireland	a Irlanda	"**eerland**uh"
Italy	a Itália	"**eetal**yuh"
Luxembourg	o Luxemburgo	"**loo**shum-boorgoo"
New Zealand	a Nova Zelândia	"**noh**vuh zuh**land**eeuh"
Northern Ireland	a Irlanda do Norte	"**eerland**uh doo nort"
Portugal	Portugal	"poortoo**gal**"
Scotland	a Escócia	"**shkos**yuh"
Spain	a Espanha	"**shpan**yuh"
Switzerland	a Suíça	"**swees**uh"
United States	os Estados Unidos	"shtahdooz-oo**nee**doosh"
USA	(EUA) os Estados Unidos da América	"shtadooz-oo**nee**doosh duh **am**erikuh"
Wales	o País de Gales	"pa**eesh** duh **gah**lush"

alcohol	o álcool	"**alk**wol"
alcoholic	alcoólico	"alk**wol**ikoo"
	alcoólica	"alk**wol**ikuh"
apéritif	o aperitivo	"apuhree-**tee**voo"
beer	a cerveja	"ser**vay**juh"
brandy	o brandy	"**bran**dee"
champagne	lo champanhe	"sham**pan**yuh"
cider	a sidra	"**see**druh"
cocktail	o cocktail	"cocktail"
cocoa	o cacau	"ka**kow**"
coffee	o café	"kuh**fe**"
Coke®	a coca-cola	"kokuh**kol**uh"
draught beer	o fino	"**fee**noo"
drinking water	a água potável	"**ahg**wuh poo**tah**vel"
fruit juice	o sumo de frutas	"**soo**moo duh **froo**tush"
gin	o gin	"jeen"
gin and tonic	o gin tónico	"jeen **ton**ikoo"
grapefruit juice	o sumo de toranja	"**soo**moo duh too**ran**juh"
juice	o sumo	"**soo**moo"
lager	a cerveja	"ser**vay**juh"
lemonade	a limonada	"leemoo**nah**duh"
lemon tea	o carioca de limão	"karee-**o**kuh duh lee**mowng**"
liqueur	o licor	"lee**kor**"
milk	o leite	"layt"
milkshake	o batido de leite	"ba**tee**doo duh layt"
mineral water	a água mineral	"**ahg**wuh meenuh**ral**"
non-alcoholic	não-alcoólico	"nowng-alk**wol**ikoo"
	não-alcoólica	"nowng-alk**wol**ikuh"
orange juice	o sumo de laranja	"**soo**moo duh la**ran**juh"
rosé (wine)	o vinho rosé	"**veen**yoo ro**zay**"
shandy	a cerveja e limonada	"ser**vay**juh ee leemoo**nah**duh"
sherry	o xerez	"shuh**resh**"
soda	a água bicarbonatada	"**ahg**wuh beekarboo-na**tah**duh"
soft drink	a bebida não alcoólica	"buh**bee**duh nowng alk**wol**ikuh"
spirits	a bebida alcoólica	"buh**bee**duh alk**wol**ikuh"
squash	o sumo	"**soo**moo"
tea	o chá	"sha"
tomato juice	o sumo de tomate	"**soo**moo duh too**mat**"
tonic water	a água tónica	"**ahg**wuh **ton**ikuh"
vermouth	o vermute	"ver**moot**"
vodka	a vodka	"**vod**kuh"
whisky	o uísque	"oo-**eeshk**"
wine	o vinho	"**veen**yoo"

anchovy	a anchova	"an**shov**uh"
caviar	o caviar	"kuh**viar**"
cod	o bacalhau	"bakuh**lyow**"
crab	o caranguejo	"karan-**gej**oo"
fish	o peixe	"**paysh**"
haddock	o eglefim	"**eg**luhfeeng"
hake	a abrótea	"a**bro**tyuh"
herring	o arenque	"**arenk**"
lobster	a lagosta	"la**gosh**tuh"
mackerel	a cavala	"ka**vah**luh"
mussel	o mexilhão	"musheel-**yowng**"
oyster	a ostra	"**osh**truh"
prawn	o lagostim	"lagoosh**teeng**"
salmon	o salmão	"sal**mowng**"
sardine	a sardinha	"sar**deen**yuh"
scallop	o escalope	"shkuh**lop**"
scampi	os camarões fritos	"kamuh**roynsh free**toosh"
seafood	o marisco	"ma**reesh**koo"
shellfish	o marisco	"ma**reesh**koo"
shrimps	os camarões	"kamuh**roynsh**"
sole	a solha	"**sol**yuh"
trout	a truta	"**troo**tuh"
tuna	o atum	"a**toong**"

FRUIT AND NUTS

almond	a amêndoa	"**amayn**-dwuh"
apple	a maçã	"ma**sang**"
apricot	o damasco	"da**mash**-koo"
banana	a banana	"ba**nah**nuh"
blackcurrant	a groselha	"gro**zel**yuh"
cherry	a cereja	"suh**ray**juh"
chestnut	a castanha	"kash**tahn**yuh"
coconut	o coco	"**koh**koo"
currant	a groselha	"gro**zel**yuh"
date	a tâmara	"**tah**muhruh"
fruit	a fruta	"**froo**tuh"
grapefruit	a toranja	"too**ran**juh"
grapes	as uvas	"**oo**vush"
hazelnut	a avelã	"avuh**lang**"
lemon	o limão	"lee**mowng**"
lime	a lima	"**lee**muh"
melon	o melão	"me**lowng**"
nut	a noz	"nosh"
olive	a azeitona	"azay**ton**uh"
orange	a laranja	"la**ran**juh"
peach	o pêssego	"**pay**suhgoo"
peanut	o amendoim	"amendoo-**eeng**"
pear	a pêra	"**pay**ruh"
pineapple	o ananás	"anuh**nash**"
pistachio	o pistacho	"peesh**tah**shoo"
plum	a ameixa	"a**may**shuh"
prunes	as ameixas secas	"a**may**shush **say**kush"
raisin	a passa	"**pas**uh"
raspberry	a framboesa	"fram**bway**zuh"
strawberry	o morango	"moo**rang**oo"
walnut	a noz	"nosh"
watermelon	a melância	"melan**see**uh"

MEATS

bacon	o toucinho	"toh-**seen**yoo"
beef	o carne de vaca	"karn duh **vah**kuh"
beefburger	o beefburger	"beefboorger"
breast	o peito	"**pay**too"
cheeseburger	o cheeseburger	"cheeseboorger"
chicken	frango	"**fran**goo"
chop	a costeleta	"kooshtuh-**leh**tuh"
cold meat	a carne fria	"**karn free**uh"
duck	o pato	"**pah**too"
goose	o ganso	"**gan**soo"
ham	o presunto	"pruh**zoon**too"
hamburger	o hamburger	"am**boo**rger"
kidneys	os rins	"reensh"
liver	o fígado	"**fee**guhdoo"
meat	a carne	"karn"
mince	a carne picada	"karn pee**kah**duh"
mutton	o carneiro	"karn**ay**roo"
pâté	o paté	"pa**tay**"
pheasant	o faisão	"**fy**zawng"
pork	a carne de porco	"karn duh **por**koo"
rabbit	o coelho	"koo**el**yoo"
sausage	a salsicha	"sal**see**shuh"
steak	o bife	"beef"
stew	o guisado	"ghee**zah**do"
turkey	o peru	"puh**roo**"
veal	a carne de vitela	"karn duh vee**tel**uh"

SHOPS

baker's	a padaria	"paduh-**reeuh**"
barber	o barbeiro	"bar**bay**roo"
bookshop	a livraria	"leevruh-**reeuh**"
butcher's	o talho	"**tal**yoo"
café	o café	"**kuhfe**"
chemist's	a farmácia	"far**mas**yuh"
dry-cleaner's	a limpeza a seco	"leem**payz**uh uh **say**koo"
duty-free shop	a loja franca	"**lo**juh **fran**kuh"
grocer's	a mercearia	"mersee-uh**reeuh**"
hairdresser	o cabeleireiro	"kuhbuh-lay**ray**roo"
	a cabeleireira	"kuhbuh-lay**ray**ruh"
health food shop	a loja de comida natural	"**lo**juh duh koo**mee**duh natoo**ral**"
ironmonger's	a loja de ferragens	"**lo**juh duh fe**rah**jaynsh"
jeweller's	a joalharia	"jwal-yuh**reeuh**"
launderette	a lavandaria automática	"lavanduh**reeuh** owtoo**mat**ikuh"
market	o mercado	"mer**kah**doo"
newsagent	a tabacaria	"tabuh-kuh**reeuh**"
post office	os correios	"koo**ray**oosh"
shop	a loja	"**lo**juh"
stationer's	a papelaria	"papuhluh-**reeuh**"
supermarket	o supermercado	"soopermer**kah**doo"
tobacconist's	a tabacaria	"tabuh-ka**reeuh**"
toy shop	a loja de brinquedos	"**lo**juh duh breen**kay**doosh"

VEGETABLES

artichoke	a alcachofra	"alkuh-**shof**ruh"
asparagus	o espargo	"**shpar**goo"
aubergine	a beringela	"bereen-**je**luh"
avocado	o abacate	"aba**kat**"
bean	o feijão	"fay**jowng**"
beetroot	a beterraba	"betuhr-**rah**buh"
broccoli	os brocolos	"**broh**kooloosh"
Brussels sprouts	as couves de Bruxelas	"**kohv**sh duh broo**she**lush"
cabbage	a couve	"**kohv**"
carrot	a cenoura	"suh**noh**ruh"
cauliflower	a couve-flor	"kohv-**flor**"
celery	o aipo	"**y**poo"
chives	o cebolinho	"suhboo-**leen**yoo"
courgette	a courgette	"koor**jet**"
cucumber	o pepino	"puh**pee**noo"
French beans	o feijão-verde	"fayjowng-**vehrd**"
garlic	o alho	"**al**yoo"
green pepper	a pimenta verde	"pee**men**tuh vehrd"
onion	a cebola	"suh**bo**luh"
parsley	a salsa	"**sal**suh"
peas	as ervilhas	"ehr**veel**yush"
pepper	o pimento	"pee**men**too"
potato	a batata	"ba**tah**tuh"
radish	o rabanete	"rabuh**net**"
spinach	o espinafre	"shpee**na**fruh"
tomato	o tomate	"too**mat**"
turnip	o nabo	"**nah**boo"
vegan	vegetariano puro	"vejuhtuh-ree**ah**noo **poo**roo"
	vegetariana pura	"vejuhtuh-ree**ah**nuh **poo**ruh"
vegetables	os legumes	"luh**goo**mush"
vegetarian	vegetariano	"vejuhtuh-ree**ah**noo"
	vegetariana	"vejuhtuh-ree**ah**nuh"

PORTUGUESE–ENGLISH

A

a to; the; **a dez quilómetros** 10 kilometres away

à to the

abacate *m* avocado

abadia *f* abbey

abafado(a) close (*weather*)

abaixo down

abalar to shake

abanar to fan

abandonar to abandon

abastecer to supply

abater to knock down

abcesso *m* abscess

abelha *f* bee

aberto(a) open; **aberto todo o ano** open all year round; **aberto das ... às ... horas** open from ... to ... o'clock

abertura *f* opening

abóbada *f* arch (*of church*)

abóbora *f* pumpkin

abóbora-menina *f* marrow (*vegetable*)

aborrecer to annoy

aborrecido(a) annoyed; bored

aborrecimento *m*: **é um aborrecimento** it's a nuisance

abraçar to embrace

abraço *m* cuddle

abrande slow down

abre-garrafas *m* bottle-opener

abre-latas *m* tin-opener; can-opener

abrigo *m* shelter

Abril *m* April

abrir to open; to unlock (*door*)

absolutamente definitely

absorventes diários *mpl* mini-pads

absurdo(a) absurd

abundante abundant

acabar to end; to finish; **acabo de chegar** I've just arrived

acalmar to calm

acampar to camp

acaso *m*: **por acaso** by chance

acção *f* action

aceitar to accept

acelerador *m* accelerator

acelerar to accelerate

acenar to wave

acender to switch on; to turn on (*radio etc*); to light (*fire, cigarette*); **acenda as luzes** switch on headlights; **acenda os médios** switch on dipped headlights

acento *m* accent

acepipes *mpl* titbits

aceso(a) on (*light etc*)

acesso *m* access; **acesso para os comboios** to the trains; **com acesso fácil** within easy reach

acetona *f* nail polish remover

achar to think; **acho I** think; **acho que não I** don't think so; **acho que sim I** think so

acidente *m* accident

ácido *m* acid

ácido(a) sour

acima above

aço *m* steel; **aço inoxidável** stainless steel

acolhedor(a) hospitable

acomodações *fpl* accommodation

acompanhar to accompany

acondicionador *m* conditioner

aconselhar to advise

aconselhável advisable; **não aconselhável a menores de ... anos** not recommended for those under ... years of age

acontecer to happen; **o que aconteceu?** what happened?

acontecimento *m* event

açorda *f* bread soup; **açorda à alentejana** bread and fish soup; **açorda de bacalhau** cod in thick bread soup; **açorda de camarão** shrimps in thick bread and egg soup; **açorda de marisco** thick bread soup with shellfish

acordar to awake

acordo *m* agreement; **de acordo** agreed

Açores *mpl* the Azores

açoriano(a) from the Azores

acostumar-se to get

used to
A.C.P. see **automóvel**
acreditar to believe
acrescentar to add
acrílico(a) acrylic
actividades *fpl* activities
actor *m* actor
actriz *f* actress
actual present(-day)
actualizar to modernize
actualmente nowadays
açúcar *m* sugar; **a
cobertura de açúcar**
icing; **açúcar mascavado**
brown sugar
adaptar to adapt
adega *f* wine cellar
adepto(a) *m/f* fan
(*supporter*)
adesivo *m* plaster (*for cut*)
adeus goodbye
adiamento *m*
postponement
adiantado(a) fast (*watch, etc*)
adiantamento *m*
advance
adiar to postpone
adivinhar to guess
administrador *m*
director
administrar to manage
admirar-se to be
amazed; **não admira** no
wonder
admissão *f* admission
admitir to admit
adoecer to fall ill
adolescente *m/f* teenager
adoptar to adopt
adoptivo(a) adopted
(*child*)
adorar to worship
adormecer to fall asleep
adormecido(a) asleep
adquirir to acquire
adubo *m* manure
adulto(a) adult
advertir to warn
advogado *m* lawyer;
solicitor

aéreo(a): a linha aérea
airline; **via aérea** air mail
aeróbica *f* aerobics
aeroporto *m* airport
afastado(a) distant
afastar to keep away
afeição *f* affection
afiar to sharpen
afilhada *f* goddaughter
afilhado *m* godson
afinal in the end
afinar to adjust
afixar to stick
aflição *f* affliction
afligir-se to worry
afluir to flow
afogar-se to drown
africano(a) African
afrouxar to slow down
aftershave *m* aftershave
afundar to sink
agarrar to seize
agência *f* agency; **agência
funerária** undertaker's;
agência imobiliária
estate agent; **agência de
viagens** travel agents
agenda *f* notebook
agente *m/f* agent; **agente
de compra e venda de
propriedades** estate
agent
agir to act
agitar to shake; to stir;
**agitar bem antes de
usar** shake well before
use
agora now
Agosto *m* August
agradar to please
agradável pleasant
agradecer to thank
agradecimento *m* thanks
agrafador *m* stapler
agrafos *mpl* staples
agredir to attack
agressivo(a) aggressive
agrião *m* watercress
agrícola agricultural
agricultor *m* farmer
agricultura *f* agriculture

água *f* water; **água
bicarbonatada** soda
water; **água de colónia**
toilet water; **água
corrente quente e fria**
hot and cold running
water; **água destilada**
distilled water; **água
mineral** mineral water;
água potável drinking
water; **a queda de água**
waterfall; **água quente**
warm water; **água
tónica** tonic water
água-pé *f* diluted wine
aguardar to wait;
**aguardar que se ouça o
sinal de marcar** wait
until you hear the dialling
tone
aguardente *f* spirit
brandy; **aguardente
velha** matured grape
brandy
aguarrás *f* turps
agudo(a) sharp (*pain*)
águia *f* eagle
agulha *f* needle
aí there
ainda still; yet
aipo *m* celery
ajoelhar to kneel
ajudante *m/f* assistant
ajudar to help
ajustar to adjust
alagar to flood
alameda *f* alley
alargar to enlarge
alarme *m* alarm
alastrar to spread
albergue *m* hostel;
albergue da juventude
youth hostel
álbum *m* album (*for
photos*)
alça *f* strap (*of dress*)
alcachofra *f* artichoke
alcatifa *f* carpet (*fitted*)
alcatra *f*: **alcatra à
moda dos Açores** roast
veal in wine sauce

alcomonias *fpl* honey and pine nut cakes
álcool *m* alcohol
alcoólico(a) alcoholic; **bebida alcoólica** alcoholic drink
alcunha *f* nickname
aldeia *f* village; **aldeia de pescadores** fishing village
alegre glad
alegria *f* joy
além over there; **além de** beyond
Alemanha *f* Germany
alemão (alemã) German
alentejano(a) from the Alentejo region
alérgico(a) a allergic to
alface *f* lettuce
alfaiate *m* tailor
alfândega *f* customs
alfinete *m* pin; **alfinete de segurança** safety pin
alforreca *f* jellyfish
algarismo *m* number (*figure*)
algarvio(a) from the Algarve
algas *fpl* seaweed
algodão *m* cotton; **algodão para os ouvidos** earplugs (*for diving*); **algodão em rama** cotton wool
alguém somebody; anybody (*in questions*)
algum(a) some; any; **alguns (algumas)** a few; some; **alguma coisa** something; anything (*in questions*); **alguma pessoa** someone; **mais alguma coisa?** anything else?; **tem algumas maçãs?** do you have any apples?
alheira *f* garlic sausage
alho *m* garlic
alhos-porros *mpl* leeks
ali there
aliás otherwise

alicate *m* pliers
alimentação *f* food
alimentar to feed
alinhamento *m* steering; **alinhamento de direcções** steering alignment
alívio *m* relief
almoçar to have lunch
almoço *m* lunch; **almoço embalado** packed lunch; **pequeno almoço continental** Continental breakfast
almofada *f* pillow; cushion
almôndegas *fpl* meatballs
alojamento *m* accommodation
alojar to lodge
alperche *m* apricot
alpinismo *m* climbing; **as botas de alpinismo** climbing boots
alpinista *m/f* mountaineer
altar *m* altar
alterar to change
alternador *m* alternator
altifalante *m* loudspeaker
altitude *f* altitude
alto! stop!
alto(a) high; tall; loud; **mais alto** higher; **a estação alta** high season; **alta costura** haute couture; **alta fidelidade e estereofonia** hi-fi and stereo equipment; **alta frequência** high frequency
altura *f* height; **a certa altura** then
alugar to hire; to rent; to let (*rent out*); **quarto para alugar** vacancy; **aluga-se** for hire; to rent; **alugam-se quartos** rooms to let
aluguer *m* rental; **aluguer de motorizadas** motorbike hire/rental;

aluguer de vivendas e apartamentos mobilados furnished villas and flats to let
aluno *m* pupil (*learner*)
amador(a) *m/f* amateur
amanhã tomorrow
amar to love
amarelo(a) yellow
amargo(a) bitter
amável gentle; kind
ambiente *m* atmosphere; **ambiente familiar** friendly atmosphere; **ambiente típico** traditional surroundings
ambos(as) both
ambulância *f* ambulance
amêijoa *f* clam; cockle; **amêijoas à Bulhão pato** clams with coriander, onion and garlic; **amêijoas na cataplana** layers of pork, clams, ham and onion
ameixa *f* plum; **ameixa cláudia** greengage; **ameixa pequena** damson; **ameixa seca** prune
amêndoa *f* almond; **amêndoa amarga** bitter almond liqueur; **petitfour de amêndoa** almond petit four
amendoeira *f* almond tree
amendoim *m* peanut
América *f* America
americano(a) American
amido *m* starch
amigdalite *f* tonsillitis
amigo(a) *m/f* friend
amolgado(a) dented
amontoar to pile up
amor *m* love
amora *f* blackberry; mulberry
amortecedor *m* shock absorber
amostra *f* sample

ampliações *mpl* enlargements

amplificador *m* amplifier

analgésico *m* painkiller

ananás *m* pineapple

anão (anã) *m/f* dwarf

anca *f* hip

anchovas *fpl* anchovies

âncora *f* anchor

ancorar to anchor

andar¹ to walk

andar² *m* floor; storey; **andares de luxo** luxury flats

andebol *m* handball

andorinha *f* swallow

anedota *f* joke

anel *m* ring

anestésico *m* anaesthetic

anfitriã *f* hostess

anfitrião *m* host

angina *f* sore throat

animado(a) lively

animal *m* animal; **animal doméstico** pet

anis *m* aniseed

aniversário *m* anniversary; birthday

ano *m* year; **Ano Novo** New Year

anorak *m* anorak

antena *f* aerial

antepassados *mpl* ancestors

antes de before

anti-aderente non-stick

antibiótico *m* antibiotic

anticonceptivo *m* contraceptive

anticongelante *m* antifreeze

antigamente in the past

antigo(a) ancient

antiguidades *fpl* antiques

antipático(a) unpleasant

antiséptico *m* antiseptic

antitranspirante *m* antiperspirant

anual yearly

anunciar to advertise

anúncio *m* advertisement

(*in paper*); commercial (*on TV*)

anzol *m* hook (*fishing*)

ao = **a** + **o**

apagado(a) off (*radio etc*); out (*light etc*)

apagar to switch off (*light etc*); to turn off (*radio etc*)

apalpar to feel (*with hand etc*)

apanhar to pick (up) (*object*); to catch

aparador *m* cupboard

apara-lápis *m* pencil sharpener

aparar to trim (*hair*)

aparecer to appear

aparelhagem de som *f* audio equipment

aparelho *m* gadget; machine; **aparelho para a surdez** hearing aid

aparência *f* appearance

apartamento *m* apartment; flat; **apartamento com cozinha** self-catering flat; **apartamento modelo** show flat; **cinquenta apartamentos com dois quartos** 50 double-roomed apartments

apeadeiro *m* halt

apelido *m* surname; **apelido de solteira** maiden name

apenas only; **apenas dois** just two

apendicite *f* appendicitis

aperitivo *m* aperitif

apertado(a) tight

apertar to fasten; to squeeze; **apertar a mão** to shake hands; **apertar o cinto de segurança** fasten your seat belt

apesar de in spite of

apetecer to desire; to fancy; **não me apetece** I don't fancy it

apetite *m* appetite; **bom apetite!** enjoy your meal!

apontamento *m* note

A positivo/negativo A positive/negative

apreciar to appreciate

aprender to learn

apresentar to introduce

apressado(a) hurried

apressar-se to hurry

aprontar-se to get ready

apropriado(a) suitable

aprovar to approve

aproveitar-se de to take advantage of; to make good use of

aquário *m* aquarium

aquecedor *m* heater; electric fire

aquecer to heat; to warm; **aquecer excessivamente** to overheat

aquecimento *m* heating; **aquecimento central** central heating

aquele (aquela) that; **aquele livro** that book; **aquela mesa** that table; **aquele ali** that one; **aqueles (aquelas)** those; **aqueles livros** those books

àquele = **a** + **aquele**

aqui here

ar *m* air; choke (*car*); **ar e água** air and water (*at garage*); **ar condicionado** air conditioning; **a corrente de ar** draught (*in room*); **o filtro de ar** air filter; **ao ar livre** outdoor; **o tubo de ar** snorkel

árabe Arabian

arado *m* plough

aranha *f* spider

árbitro *m* referee

arbusto *m* bush

arco *m* arch (*of bridge*)

arco-íris *m* rainbow

arder to burn

área f area
areia f sand
arenoso(a) sandy
arenque m herring
argolas fpl doughnut rings
árido(a) arid
arma f: **arma de fogo** gun
armações fpl frames (spectacles)
armário m cupboard; closet; **armário para a bagagem** locker; **armário de quarto de banho** bathroom cabinet
armazém m: **grande armazém** department store
aroma f scent
arquitecto m architect
arquitectura f architecture
arquivo m archives
arraial m open air festival
arrancar to pull; to start (engine)
arranjar to arrange
arranjos mpl repairs
arrefecer to cool down (weather); to grow cold (food)
arrendar to let
arrependido(a) sorry
arroz m rice; **arroz de atum** rice and tuna in mayonnaise, egg and tomato; **arroz branco** boiled rice; **arroz doce** sweet rice dessert; **arroz de ervilhas** rice with peas; **arroz de frango** chicken rissotto; **arroz de marisco** shrimps and clams with rice; **arroz à valenciana** a type of paella
arruinar to ruin
arrumado(a) tidy
arrumar to tidy
arte f art
artéria f artery

artesanato m handicrafts
articulação f joint
artificial artificial
artigo m item; **artigos fotográficos** photographic equipment; **artigos de menage** household goods; **artigos de praia** beachwear; **artigos regionals** regional handicrafts; **artigos de viagem** travel goods; **artigos de vime** wickerwork
artista m/f artist
artrite f arthritis
árvore f tree
as the
às = **a** + **as**
ás m ace
asa f wing; handle (of bucket, basket)
ascensor m lift; elevator
asma f asthma
áspero(a) rough (surface)
aspersor m lawn sprinkler
aspirador m vacuum cleaner
aspirar to hoover
aspirina f aspirin
assado(a) roast
assaltar to attack
assalto m assault
assassínio m murder
asseado(a) clean
assembleia f assembly
assim like this; so; **assim como** just as; like; **mesmo assim** even so
assinante m/f subscriber
assinar to sign
assinatura f signature
assistência f audience; assistance; **assistência ao domicílio** home repairs; **assistência técnica** servicing (machines)
assistente de bordo f air hostess
assistir to attend; to

assist
assoar-se to blow one's nose
assobio m whistle
associação f society
assustar to frighten
atacadores mpl laces
atalho m short-cut
ataque m attack
atar to tie
até till; until; even; **até mesmo você** even you; **até a** as far as; **até já** see you in a moment; **até logo** see you later; **até que** until
atenção f attention; caution; **atenção!** pay attention!; **atenção ao comboio** beware of trains; **atenção aos degraus** mind the step; **atenção porta automática** attention automatic door; **atenção zona escolar – seja prudente** school ahead – drive carefully
attendedor de chamadas m answering machine
atender to answer (door, telephone)
atendimento m: **atendimento preferencial** preferential service
Atentamente Yours faithfully
aterragem f landing (of plane)
aterrar to land
atingir to hit; to reach
atirar to throw; **atirar a** to shoot at
Atlântico m the Atlantic
atleta m/f athlete
atletismo m athletics
atmosfera f atmosphere
atómico(a) atomic
atordoar to stun

atrair to attract
atrás behind
atrasado(a) late (for appointment); **o comboio está atrasado dez minutos** the train is 10 minutes late
atrasar to delay
através de across (to the other side); through
atravessar to cross; **atravesse pela passadeira** use the zebra crossing
atrelado m trailer
atropelar to run over
atum m tuna; tunny fish
aula f lesson
aumentar to increase
aumento m rise; increase
au pair f au pair
auscultadores mpl earphones
ausente away (not here)
Austrália f Australia
australiano(a) Australian
autobrilhante m polish
autocarro m bus; coach; **de autocarro** by bus; **a excursão de autocarro** bus tour; **a paragem de autocarro** bus stop
autoclismo m: **o autoclismo não funciona** the toilet won't flush
autocolante self-adhesive
autoestrada f motorway; **autoestrada com portagem** toll motorway
automático(a) automatic
automatizada f bus using ticket machine
automercado m autoshop
automobilismo m motor-racing
automobilista m/f driver
automóvel m car; **Automóvel Clube de Portugal (A.C.P.)**

Portuguese RAC; **automóveis de aluguer** car hire
autor m author
auto-rádio m car radio
autorização f licence; permit
auxiliar to help
avance go ahead
avarento(a) mean
avaria f breakdown
avariado(a) broken down; out of order
avarias fpl breakdown service
ave f bird
aveia f oats
avelã f hazelnut
avenida f avenue
avental m apron
aventura f adventure
avião m plane; **de avião** by plane
avisar to warn
aviso m warning; **aviso prévio** notice (time)
avô m grandfather
avó f grandmother
azar m bad luck
azedo(a) bitter
azeite m olive oil
azeitona f olive; **azeitona preta** black olive; **azeitona verde** green olive
azerias fpl potato and almond fritters
azevinho m holly
azinhaga f lane (in country)
azul blue; **azul marinho** navy blue
azulejo m ornamental tile

B

babete m bib
bacalhau m cod; **bacalhau à Brás** cod with eggs, onion and potatoes; **bacalhau à Gomes de Sá** cod with onions and potatoes; **bacalhau à lagareiro** mashed potato and oven-roasted cod; **bacalhau à portuguesa** baked cod with potato and onions; **bacalhau com todos** cod with potatoes, onion, vegetables and coriander; **bacalhau à Zé do Pipo** cod in egg sauce
bacia f washbasin
bacio m potty (child's)
bacon m bacon
baga f berry
bagaço m wine brandy
bagagem f luggage; baggage; **o carrinho para a bagagem** luggage trolley; **bagagem de mão** hand luggage
baía f bay
bailado m dance
bailarino(a) m/f dancer
baile m ball (dance)
bainha f hem
bairro m quarter; district
baixa-mar f low tide
baixar to lower; **baixar os máximos** to dip one's headlights
baixo: em baixo below; **para baixo** down; **por baixo** below
baixo(a) low; short
bala f bullet
balança f scales
balcão m balcony; counter (in bank, shop);

bife

circle (*in theatre*); bar (*in restaurant, pub*); **balcão do check-in** check-in desk

balde *m* bucket; pail

baleia *f* whale

baliza *f* goalposts

ballet *m* ballet

balneário *m* changing room

baloiço *m* swing (*in park*)

banana *f* banana

bancada *f* stall

banco *m* bank; seat (*in car etc*)

banda *f* band; **banda desenhada** comic; **banda musical** (musical) band

bandeira *f* flag

bandido *m* bandit

bando *m* gang

banha *f* lard

banheira *f* bath (*tub*)

banheiro *m* lifeguard

banhista *m* bather

banho *m* bath; **com banho privativo** with private bathroom; **a casa de banho** bathroom; toilet; **o fato de banho** bathing costume; **a touca de banho** bathing cap; **tomar banho** to bathe; to take a bath

baptizado *m* christening

bar *m* bar

baralho *m*: **baralho de cartas** pack of cards

barato(a) cheap; **mais barato** cheaper

barba *f* beard; **fazer a barba** to shave

barbatanas *fpl* flippers

barbeiro *m* barber

barco *m* boat; ship; **barco a motor** motor boat; **barco pneumático** rubber dinghy; **barco a remos** rowing boat; **barco à vela** sailing boat; **barcos de aluguer** boats

for hire; **barcos para pesca e recreio** fishing and pleasure boats

barman *m* barman

barraca *f* hut (*shed*); sunshade

barragem *f* dam; reservoir

barreira *f* fence; gate (*in field*)

barriga *f* stomach

barros *mpl* clay pottery

barulhento(a) noisy

barulho *m* noise

base *f* basis

basquetebol *m* basketball

bastante enough

bastar to be enough; **basta** that's enough

batalha *f* battle

batata *f* potato; **o puré de batata** mashed potato; **batatas assadas** baked potatoes; **batatas cozidas** boiled potatoes; **batatas fritas** chips; crisps

bate-chapas *m* panel-beater; body repairs

bater to knock (*on door*); **ele bateu-me** he hit me; **bata à porta** please knock

bateria *f* battery (*for car*)

batido de leite *m* milkshake

bâton *m* lipstick; **bâton para o cieiro** lip salve

baunilha *f* vanilla

bêbado(a) drunk

bebé *m* baby

beber to drink; **não beber** do not drink

bebida *f* drink; **tomar uma bebida** to have a drink; **bebida alcoólica** spirits; **bebida não alcoólica** soft drink

beco *m* alley; lane; **beco sem saída** dead end

bege beige

beijar to kiss

beijo *m* kiss

beira *f* edge

beirão (beirã) from the Beiras region

beleza *f* beauty

beliche *m* berth (*bed*)

belo(a) beautiful; **belos panoramas** fabulous views

bem well; **está bem** O.K.; **muito bem!** fine!; **bem mobilado(a)** well furnished; **bem passado** well done (*steak*)

bemvindo(a) welcome

beneficiar to benefit

bengala *f* walking stick

bengaleiro *m* cloakroom

beringela *f* aubergine

berma *f* hard shoulder; **bermas baixas** steep verge – no hard shoulder

berço *m* cot; cradle

bestial terrific

besugo *m* sea bream; **besugo na grelha** charcoal-grilled sea bream

beterraba *f* beetroot

bexiga *f* bladder

biberão *m* feeding bottle

Bíblia *f* the Bible

biblioteca *f* library

bica *f* small strong black coffee

bicha *f* queue; **fazer bicha** to queue

bicho *m* animal

bicicleta *f* bicycle; cycle; **bicicleta de corrida** racing bike

bico *m* nappy-liner

bidé *m* bidet

bifanas *fpl* pork fillets in garlic and wine sauce

bife *m* steak; **bife de alcatra** rump steak; **bife com batatas fritas** steak and chips; **bife de carne picada** hamburger; **bife**

grelhado grilled steak

bifurcação f junction

bigode m moustache

bilhar m billiards

bilhete m ticket; fare; **bilhete de entrada** admission charge; **bilhete de ida e volta** return ticket; **bilhete postal** postcard; **bilhete turístico** tourist ticket; **bilhetes de portagem** toll tickets; **bilhetes à venda** tickets on sale

bilheteira f booking office; ticket office; box office

binóculos mpl binoculars

biografia f biography

biquini m bikini

biscoito m flat biscuit

bispo m bishop

bitoque m steak, fried eggs and chips

bloco m: **bloco de apontamentos** note pad

bloqueado(a) blocked; stuck; jammed

blusa f blouse

blusão m short jacket

boa see **bom**

boca f mouth

bocadinho m: **um bocadinho** a little bit

bocadito m: **um bocadito** a little bit

bocado m piece; **um bocado de** a bit of

bocejar to yawn

boi m ox

bóia f buoy

boite f night club

bola f ball; **bola de Berlim** doughnut

bolacha f thick biscuit

boleia f: **andar à boleia** to hitchhike; **dar boleia** to give a lift; **pessoa que anda à boleia** hitchhiker

boletim meteorológico m weather report

bolha f blister

bolinhos mpl dainty cakes

bolo m small cake; **bolo de chocolate** chocolate cake; **bolo inglês** fruit cake; **bolo de nozes** walnut cake; **bolo rei** cake eaten at Christmas

bolorento(a) mouldy

bolsa f purse; **bolsa de toilete** sponge bag

Bolsa f stock exchange

bolso m pocket

bom (boa) good; fine (weather); well; **bom dia** good morning; **boa noite** good evening; good night; **boa tarde** good afternoon

bomba f bomb; pump

bombazina f corduroy

bombeiros mpl fire brigade

bombom m chocolate sweet

bombordo m port side

boné m cap

boneca f doll (girl's)

boneco m doll; puppet toy

bonito(a) pretty

borboleta f butterfly

borbulha f heat rash; spots (on skin)

borda f edge; border

bordado(a) embroidered

bordados mpl embroidered items

borracha f rubber; **borrachas** rubber connections (in car)

borrachinhos mpl cakes soaked in liqueur

borracho m drunk (person)

borrego m lamb; **borrego assado no forno** roast lamb; **borrego à jardineira** lamb stew

bosque m forest

bota f boot (to wear); **botas de futebol** football boots

botão m button; knob

bote m boat

botins mpl wellingtons

boutique f fashion shop

boxe m boxing

B positivo/negativo B positive/negative

braçadeiras fpl armbands

bracelete f strap; bracelet

braço m arm

bradar to cry

branco(a) white

brasão m coat-of-arms

bravo(a) rough (sea)

breve: em breve soon

brigada de trânsito f traffic police

brigar to fight

brilhante bright; shiny

brincadeira f joke

brincar to play (children)

brincos mpl earrings

brindes mpl presents; gifts

brinquedo m toy

brisa f breeze

britânico(a) British

broa f corn cake

broche m brooch

brochura f brochure; paperback

bronquite f bronchitis

bronzeado m suntan

bronzeador m suntan oil

brushing m blow-dry

bufete m buffet

bugigangas fpl bric-à-brac

bule m teapot

bungalow m: **bungalows com cozinha, casa de banho e varanda independente** bungalows with kitchen, bathroom and private balcony

buraco m hole

burro m donkey

busca f search
buscar: ir buscar to fetch; **mandar buscar** to send for
bússola f compass
buzina f horn (car)
buzinar: buzine só quando necessário use your horn only when necessary

C

cá here
cabana f hut
cabeça f head; **tenho dores de cabeça** I have a headache
cabedais mpl leather goods
cabeleira postiça f hair piece; wig
cabeleireiro m hairdresser; **cabeleireiro de senhoras e cavalheiros** unisex hairdressers
cabelo m hair; **o corte de cabelo** haircut; **a escova de cabelo** hairbrush; **o gancho de cabelo** hairgrip; **o secador de cabelo** hairdryer; **o spray para o cabelo** hair spray
caber to fit (in)
cabide m coat hanger; hook (for coats); peg (for clothes)
cabine f: **cabine telefónica** telephone box; phone box; **a cabine número quatro** phone booth number four
cabo m handle (of knife); lead (electric); **cabos de emergência** jump leads; **cabo de reboque** tow

rope
cabra f goat
cabrito m kid goat; **cabrito assado** roast kid
caça f game (to eat); hunting; **caça submarina** spear fishing
caçar to hunt
caçarola f saucepan; casserole dish
cacau m cocoa
cachecol m scarf (long)
cachimbo m pipe; **o tabaco para o cachimbo** pipe tobacco
cacholeira f smoked sausage
cachorro m hot dog
cada each; every; **cada um(a)** each one; **cada vez mais** more and more; **100 escudos cada um** 100 escudos each
cadáver m corpse
cadeado m padlock
cadeia f prison
cadeira f chair; **cadeira de bebé** high chair; push chair; **cadeira de lona** deck chair; **cadeira de rodas** wheelchair
cadela f dog (bitch)
caderneta de bilhetes f book of tickets
caderno m exercise book
café m (black) coffee; café; **café instantâneo** instant coffee; **café com leite** white coffee; **café torrado** roast coffee
cafeteira f coffee pot
cair to fall; to come off (button)
cais m quay
caixa f box (container); cashier; cash desk; till; **caixa automática** cash machine/dispenser; **caixa do correio** letterbox; **caixa fechada** till closed; **caixa de papelão**

cardboard box; **caixa de primeiros socorros** first aid box; **caixa de velocidades** gear box
caixote m bin; **caixote do lixo** waste bin
calçada f slope
calçado m footwear; **calçado desportivo** sports shoes; **calçado para senhoras e crianças** ladies' and children's footwear
calcanhar m heel
calçar to put on (shoes etc)
calças fpl trousers; **calças de ganga** jeans
calções mpl shorts; **calções de banho** trunks
calços para travões mpl brake pads
calculadora f calculator
cálculo m calculation
caldeirada f fish stew
caldo m stock (for soup); **caldo verde** cabbage soup
calendário m calendar
calhar to happen; **se calhar** perhaps; probably
calibragem f wheel alignment
calmante m tranquillizer
calmo(a) calm
calo m corn (on foot)
calor m heat; **está calor** it's hot (weather); **tenho calor** I'm hot
calorífero m heater
calvo(a) bald (person)
cama f bed; **cama de campismo** campbed; **cama de casal** double bed; **cama de criança** cot; **a roupa de cama** bedding
camada f layer
câmara f: **câmara de ar** inner tube; **câmara municipal** town hall

camarão m shrimp; **camarões cozidos** boiled shrimps; **camarões fritos** shrimps fried in garlic and lemon sauce; **camarões grelhados** grilled shrimps

camarote m cabin

cambalear to stagger

cambiar to exchange; to change (money)

câmbio m exchange rate

camião m lorry; **o motorista de camião** lorry driver

caminho m track (path); way; path; **qual é o caminho para ...?** which is the way to ...?; **caminho de ferro** railway; **Caminhos de Ferro Portugueses (C.P.)** Portuguese Railways

camioneta f bus; delivery van; **camioneta de passageiros** coach

camisa f shirt; **camisa de noite** nightdress

camisaria f men's shop

camisetes fpl T-shirts

camisola f jersey; **camisola de gola alta** poloneck; **camisola interior** vest

campainha f bell (on door); **a campainha está a tocar** there's someone at the door

campanário m steeple

campanha promocional f publicity campaign

campeonato m championship

campião m champion

campismo m camping

campista m/f camper

campo m field; country (not town); **campo de futebol** football pitch; **campo de golfe de 18**

buracos 18 hole golf course; **campo de tiro** shooting range

camponês (camponesa) m/f peasant

camurça f suede

Canadá m Canada

canadiano(a) Canadian

canal m: **o Canal da Mancha** the Channel; **canal de televisão** TV channel

canalizador m plumber

canção f song

cancela f gate (of iron)

cancelado(a) cancelled

cancelar to cancel

cancro m cancer

candeeiro m lamp

candeia f lamp; torch

caneca f mug; mug of beer

canela¹ f cinnamon

canela² f shin

caneta f pen; **caneta de ponta de feltro** felt-tip pen

canhão m cannon

canhoto(a) left-handed

canivete m penknife

canja f chicken soup

cano de esgoto m drain

canoa f canoe

canoagem f canoeing

cansado(a) tired

cansar-se to become tired

cansativo(a) tiresome; tiring

cantar to sing

canteiro m flowerbed

cantina f canteen

canto m corner (inside); corner shot (in football)

cão m dog; **cão de guarda** guard dog

capa f cape; book cover; **capa impermeável de nylon** cagoule

capacete m crash helmet

capaz capable

capela f chapel

capital f capital (town)

capitão m captain

capot m bonnet (of car); hood (of car)

capuz m hood

caqui m sharon fruit

cara f face

carabina f rifle

caraça f mask (for carnival)

caracóis mpl snails

caramelos mpl sweets

caranguejo m crab

carapau m mackerel; **carapaus assados** roast mackerel

caravana f caravan

caravanismo m caravanning

carburador m carburettor

careca bald (tyre)

carecer de to be in need of; to need

carga f refill; load; **carga para a caneta** ink cartridge; **carga para o isqueiro** gas refill; **carga máxima** maximum load

caril m curry

carimbo m rubber stamp

carinhoso(a) affectionate

carioca m weak coffee; **carioca de limão** lemon tea

carmesim crimson

carnaval m carnival

carne f meat; **carne de borrego** lamb; **carne picada** mince; **carne de porco** pork; **carne de porco à alentejana** pork, cockles and chips; **carne de vaca** beef; **carne de vaca assada** roast beef; **carne de veado** venison; **carne de vitela** veal; **carnes frias** cold meats; **carnes**

fumadas smoked meats
carneiro m mutton
carniceiro m butcher
caro(a) dear; expensive;
Cara Maria Dear Mary
carpinteiro m carpenter
carregador m porter
carregue: carregue no botão press the button
carreiras regulares fpl regular service (bus etc)
carril m rail
carrinha f van
carrinho m: **carrinho para a bagagem** luggage trolley; **carrinho de bebé** pram; carry cot
carro m car; **carros de aluguer** car hire/rental
carroça f cart
carroçaria f bodywork
carrocel m roundabout (at fair)
carruagem f carriage (railway); coach (on train); **carruagem-cama** sleeper (railway)
carruagem-restaurante f restaurant car
carta f letter; **carta verde** green card
cartão m card; business card; cardboard; **cartão de aniversário** birthday card; **cartão bancário** cheque card; **cartão de crédito** credit card; **cartão de embarque** boarding card; **cartão de felicitações** greetings card; **cartão garantia** cheque card; **cartão jovem** youth pass
cartaz m notice (poster); list of films now showing
carteira f wallet
carteirista m pickpocket
carteiro m postman
cartucho m cartridge (for pen)
carvalho m oak

carvão m coal
casa f home; house; **em casa** at home; **em minha casa** at my home; **ir para casa** to go home; **casa de banho** toilet; bathroom; **casa de campo** villa; **casa de fados** restaurant where 'fados' are sung; **casa de jantar** dining room; **casa de pasto** cheap eating house; **casa de saúde** nursing home; **casa da sorte** lottery office; **a dona da casa** housewife; **o vinho da casa** house wine
casaco m jacket; coat; **casaco de desporto** sports jacket; **casaco de lã** cardigan; **casaco rústico** hunting jacket
casado(a) married
casal m couple
casamento m wedding
casar com to marry
casar-se to get married
casca f shell (of egg, nut)
casino m casino
caso m: **em caso de acidente marque 115** in case of accident ring 115; **em caso de dificuldade nas ligações, marque 099** if you have any problems with dialling, ring 099; **em caso de emergência** in case of emergency; **em caso de incêndio** in case of fire
cassette f cassette
castanha f chestnut; **castanhas assadas** roast chestnuts; **castanhas piladas** dried chestnuts
castanheiro m chestnut tree
castanho(a) brown; **castanho claro** fawn
castelo m castle

catálogo m catalogue
catarata f waterfall
catedral f cathedral
categoria f category
católico(a) Catholic
catorze fourteen
cauda f tail
caule m stalk
causa f cause; **causa judicial** case (legal); **por causa de** because of
causar to cause
cautela take care
cavala f mackerel
cavaleiro m horseman; rider
cavalheiro m gentleman; **cavalheiros** Gentlemen; Gents
cavalo m horse
cavar to dig
cave (c/v) f cellar; basement
caverna f cave
cebola f onion
cedo early; **mais cedo** earlier; sooner
cego(a) blind
ceia f supper
ceifa f harvest
célebre famous
célula f cell
cem hundred
cemitério m cemetery
cena f scene
cenário m scenery
cenoura f carrot
centeio m rye
centígrado m centigrade
centímetro m centimetre
cento: por cento per cent; **cento e cinquenta** a hundred and fifty
central central; **aquecimento central** central heating
centrifugador de roupa m spin-drier
centro m centre; **centro da cidade** city/town

centre; **centro comercial** shopping centre; **centro de enfermagem** clinic; **centros de reserva** car hire centres; **centro de saúde** health centre

cera f wax

cerâmica f pottery; **cerâmica árabe** traditional Arab pottery

cerca: cerca de 50 about 50

cereal m cereal

cérebro m brain

cereja f cherry

cerejeira f cherry tree

certeza f: **ter a certeza** to be sure; **com certeza** of course

certificado m certificate

certo(a) right (*correct, accurate*); certain

cerveja f beer; lager; **cerveja e limonada** shandy; **cerveja preta** bitter (*beer*)

cervejaria f pub

cesto m basket; **cesto dos papéis** wastepaper basket

cetim m satin

céu m sky

cevada f barley

chá f tea; **chá de limão** lemon tea; **chá de tília** linden blossom tea; **saquinho de chá** teabag

chaleira f kettle

chamada f telephone call; **chamada gratuita** free call; **chamada internacional** international call; **chamada interurbana** long distance call; **chamada local** local call; **chamada à cobrança** reverse charge call

chamar to call

chamar-se to be called;

chamo-me ... my name is ...

chaminé f chimney

champanhe m champagne

champô m shampoo

chanfana f lamb casserole; **chanfana à Bairrada** veal in red wine

chão m floor

chapa f: **chapa de aquecimento eléctrico** hotplate; **chapa de matrícula** license plate

chapéu m hat; **chapéu de sol** sunhat

charcada f caramel and egg yolk dessert

charcutaria f delicatessen

charuto m cigar

chatear to annoy; to bore

chatice f: **que chatice!** what a nuisance!

chato m: **que chato!** how boring!

chave f key; **não tenho a chave para entrar** I'm locked out; **chave inglesa** adjustable spanner; **chave de parafusos** screwdriver; **chave de porcas** wrench; **chave de roda** wheel brace

chávena f cup

check-in m: **fazer o check-in** to check in

chefe m boss; **chefe de cozinha** chef; **chefe de estação** station master

chegadas fpl arrivals

chegar to arrive

cheia f flood

cheio(a) full; **o hotel está cheio** the hotel is fully booked; **cheio de gente** crowded

cheirar to smell

cheiro m smell

cheque m cheque; **cheque de viagem** traveller's cheque; **o livro de cheques** cheque book; **levantar um cheque** to cash a cheque

cherne m black jewfish

chicotear to whip

chifre m horn

chinelo m slipper

chispe no forno m roast pig's trotters

chocar contra to crash into

chocolate m chocolate; **leite com chocolate** drinking chocolate

chocos mpl cuttlefish; **chocos com tinta** cuttlefish cooked in their ink

choque m shock

chorar to cry

chouriço m spicy sausage

chover: está a chover it's raining

chucha f dummy

chumbo m lead (*metal*); filling (*in tooth*)

chupa-chupa m lollipop

chupar to suck

chupeta f dummy

churrascaria f barbecue restaurant

churrasco m barbecue; **no churrasco** barbecued

chuva f rain; **chuva fraca** drizzle

chuveiro m shower

chuvoso(a) wet (*weather*)

Cia. see **companhia**

cicatriz f scar

ciclismo m cycling

ciclista m/f cyclist

ciclomotor m motorbike

cidadão (cidadã) m/f citizen; **cidadãos nacionais** Portuguese nationals (*at passport control*)

cidade f town; city; **o centro da cidade** town centre; **o mapa da cidade** town plan
cidra f cider
ciência f science
científico(a) scientific
cientista m/f scientist
cigarro m cigarette
cima: em cima de on (top of); **lá em cima** upstairs; **para cima** upwards; **por cima de** above; **por cima da casa** above the house; **ainda por cima** besides
cimbalino m small strong black coffee
cimo m top (of mountain)
cinco five
cinema m cinema
cine-teatro m cinema theatre
cinquenta fifty
cinta f corset
cinto m belt; **cinto de salvação** lifebelt; **cinto de segurança** seat belt
cintura f waist
cinza f ash (from burning)
cinzeiro m ashtray
cinzento(a) grey
circo m circus
circuito m: **circuito turístico** round trip; **com circuitos fechados de televisão** with closed-circuit television
circular f roundabout (for traffic)
circule: circule pela direita/esquerda keep right/left; **circule com velocidade reduzida** slow; drive slowly
círculo m circle
cirurgia f surgery
cirurgião m surgeon
ciumento(a) jealous
clarete m claret
claridade f brightness

claro(a) light (colour); clear (transparent); bright (room, weather)
classe f class; **de 2a classe** second class
clássico(a) classic(al)
cliente m/f client
clima m climate
clínica f clinic; **clínica dentária** dental clinic; **clínica geral** general practitioner's
clipe m paperclip
clube m club; **clube náutico** sailing club; **clube nocturno** night club; **clube de saúde** health club
coador m colander
coberta f cover
cobertor m blanket; **cobertor eléctrico** electric blanket
cobra f snake
cobrador m conductor (in bus)
cobrança f: cobrança pelo guarda-freio pay the brakeman (on tram); **cobrança pelo motorista** pay the driver
cobrar: cobrar demais to overcharge
cobre m copper
cobrir to cover
cocktail m cocktail; **cocktail de camarão** prawn cocktail
coco m coconut
côdea f crust
código m code; dialling code; **código postal** postcode
codorniz f quail; **codornizes fritas** fried quail
coelho m rabbit; **coelho de fricassé** rabbit fricassee
coentro m coriander
cofre m safe

cofre-forte m safe
cofre-nocturno m nightsafe
cogumelo m mushroom
coisa f thing
cola f glue; **cola branca** clear adhesive
colar¹ m necklace
colar² to stick
colcha f bedspread
colchão m mattress; **colchão de molas** spring mattress; **colchão pneumático** air mattress; rubber dinghy
colecção f collection (of stamps etc)
coleccionar to collect (as hobby)
colega m/f colleague
colégio m school
colete m waistcoat; **colete de salvação** life jacket
colheita f harvest (of corn)
colher f spoon; **colher de chá** teaspoon; **colher de sobremesa** dessertspoon; **colher de sopa** tablespoon
cólica f colic
colina f hill
collants mpl tights
colocar to place
colorau m paprika
colorido(a) tinted
coluna f pillar; **coluna vertebral** spine
com with
comandar to lead
comandos mpl controls
combate m fight
combinação f petticoat
combinado agreed
comboio m train; **de comboio** by train; **comboio directo** direct train; **comboio intercidades** intercity train; **comboio inter-**

regional inter-region train; **comboio rápido** express train; **comboio regional** regional train
combustão f combustion
combustível m fuel
começar to begin; to start
começo m start; beginning
comédia f comedy
comer to eat
comercial commercial
comerciante m dealer
comércio m trade; business
comichão f itch
cómico(a) comical
comida f food; **comida de bebé** baby food; **comida para levar** take-away food
comigo with me
comissão f commission
comissário de bordo m steward; purser
como as; how; **tão grande como** as big as; **assim como** as well as; **como disse?** I beg your pardon?; **como está?** how are you?
comoção cerebral f concussion
cómoda f chest of drawers
comodidade f convenience; **para comodidade do público os lugares são marcados** all seats are numbered for the convenience of the public
cómodo(a) comfortable
companhia (Cia.) f company; **companhias de aviação** airline companies
comparar to compare
compartimento m compartment

competente competent
competição f competition
competir to compete
complemento m compliment
completamente completely; quite; **completamente renovado** newly decorated
completar to complete
completo(a) full; no vacancies
complicado(a) complicated
compota f jam
compra f purchase
comprar to buy
compras fpl shopping; **ir às compras** to go shopping
compreender to understand
compreensão f understanding
compreensivo(a) receptive
comprido(a) long
comprimento m length
comprimido m pill; tablet; **comprimido para dormir** sleeping pill
computador m computer
comunhão f communion
comunicação f communication
comunicar to communicate
comunidade f community
comunista m/f Communist
concelho m council
concentrado de tomate m tomato purée
concerto m concert
concha f ladle; shell (of shellfish)
concordar to agree

concorrente m/f candidate
concurso m: **concurso de elegância** beauty competition; **concurso hípico** horse race
conde m count (nobleman)
condição f condition
condução f driving; **a carta de condução** driving licence
condutor m driver; chauffeur; **com e sem condutor** with driver or self-drive
conduza: conduza com cuidado drive carefully; **conduza pela direita/ esquerda** drive on the right/left
conduzir to drive
cone m ice-cream cone
confecções fpl: **confecções para senhora** ladies wear
conferência f conference
conferir to check
confessar to confess
confiança f confidence; trust; **de confiança** reliable
confidencial confidential
confirmar to confirm
confissão f confession
conforme: é conforme it depends
confortável comfortable
conforto m comfort
confusão f confusion
congelado(a) frozen (food)
congelador m freezer; **congelador vertical** upright freezer
congelar to freeze; **não congelar** do not freeze
congestão f congestion
congratular-se to rejoice
conhaque m cognac
conhecer to know

(person, place)
conhecido(a) known
conhecimento m knowledge
conjuntivite f conjunctivitis
conjunto m set (of objects); group (musical)
consciente conscious
conseguir to obtain
conselho m advice
consentir to permit
consertar to repair
consertos mpl repairs
conserva f tinned food
conservar to preserve; **conservar no frio** store in a cold place; **conservar este bilhete até ao fim da viagem** keep your ticket until you arrive
consigo with you
constipação f cold
constipar-se to catch a cold
construção f construction
construir to build
construtor m builder
consul m consul
consulado m consulate
consulta f consultation; appointment (at dentist etc)
consultório m surgery; **consultório dentário** dental surgery
consumidor(a) m/f consumer
consumir: consumir dentro de ... best before ...
conta f account; bill
contabilista m/f accountant
contactar to contact
contacto m contact
contador m meter
contagioso(a) infectious (person)

contar to tell; to count
contente pleased
conter to contain; **não contem ...** does not contain ...
contigo with you
continente m continent
continuar to go on
conto¹ m tale
conto² m = one thousand escudos
contra against
contrabandista m smuggler
contrário m opposite; **ao contrário** upside down
contratar to make a contract
contratempo m drawback
contrato m contract
contribuição f contribution
controlar to control
controlo m control; **controlo de passaportes** passport control
convalescença f convalescence
convencer to persuade
conveniente convenient
convento m convent
conversa f talk; conversation
conversar to talk
convés m deck
convidado(a) m/f guest
convidar to invite; to ask (invite)
convite m invitation
convosco with you
cooperar to cooperate
cooperativa f cooperative
cópia f copy
copiar to copy
copo m glass (container)
cor f colour; **de cor** by heart
coração m heart; **o ataque de coração** heart

attack; **coração de vitela recheado** stuffed veal's heart
corajoso(a) brave
corda f rope
cordeiro m lamb
cordel m string
cor de laranja orange (colour)
cor-de-rosa pink
coroa f crown
corpo m body
correctamente properly
correcto(a) correct
corredor m corridor
correia f strap; **correia da ventoinha** fan belt
correio m: **o marco do correio** postbox
correios mpl post office; **correios e telecomunicações (C.T.T.)** post office
corrente f chain; current; **corrente alterna** alternating current (A.C.); **corrente contínua** direct current (D.C.)
correr to flow; to run (person)
corrida f bullfight; **corridas de cavalos** races
corrigir to correct
corrimão m handrail
cortante sharp (knife)
cortar to cut; to cut off; **cortar e fazer brushing** cut and blow dry
corte m cut
cortejo m procession
cortiça f cork
cortina f curtain
cortinados mpl curtains
cortisona f cortisone
coscorões mpl orange fritters
coser to sew
cosméticos mpl cosmetics
costa f shore; coast

costas fpl back (of person)
costela f rib
costeleta f chop (meat); cutlet
costumar: eu costumava (fazer isso) I used to (do it)
costume m custom
costura f sewing
cotonetes mpl cotton swabs
cotovelo m elbow
couchette f couchette
courgette f courgette
couro m leather
court m court; **court de squash** squash court; **court de ténis de piso rápido** hard court (tennis)
couve f cabbage; **couves de Bruxelas** Brussels sprouts
couve-flor f cauliflower
coxa f thigh
coxear to limp
coxia f aisle
coxo(a) lame
cozer to boil
cozido(a) boiled; **mal cozido** underdone; **cozido à portuguesa** beef stew, with beans, vegetables, and spicy sausages
cozinha f kitchen; **cozinha internacional** international cuisine; **cozinha seleccionada** select cuisine
cozinhar to cook
cozinheiro(a) m/f cook; **cozinheiro chefe** chef
C.P. see **caminho**
crânio m skull
cravinhos mpl cloves
cravo m carnation
creche f crèche
crédito m credit
creio I think
creme f cream; foundation cream; **creme**

amaciador conditioner; **creme de barbear** shaving cream; **creme para bronzear** suntan cream; **creme para a cara** face cream; **creme hidratante** moisturizer; **creme de limpeza** cleansing cream; **creme de marisco** cream of shellfish soup; **cremes e pomadas** creams and ointments
crepe de carne m meat crêpe
crer to believe
crescer to grow
criação f poultry
criado(a) m/f servant
criança f child; **crianças** children crossing; **crianças até 12 anos 10% de desconto nas refeições** discount of 10% on meals for children under 12
crime m crime
criminoso(a) criminal
crise f crisis
cristal m crystal; **cristais e porcelana** crystal and porcelain ware
cristão (cristã) Christian
critério m standard
critério m standard
crochet: de crochet crocheted
croissant m croissant
croquete m croquette; **croquetes de batata** potato croquettes
cru(a) raw
crucifixo m crucifix
cruz f cross; **a Cruz Vermelha** the Red Cross
cruzamento m junction (crossroads)
cruzar to cross
cruzeiro m cruise
C.T.T. see **correios**

cubo m cube
cuecas fpl briefs; pants
cuidado m care (caution); **tenha cuidado** be careful; **tome cuidado** take care; **cuidado com o cão** beware of the dog
cuidadoso(a) careful
cuidar de to look after
culpa f: **a culpa não foi minha** it was not my fault
cultura f culture
cumprimento m greeting
cunhada f sister-in-law
cunhado m son-in-law
cupão m reply coupon
cúpula f dome
curar to cure
curioso(a) curious
curso m course; **cursos de língua portuguesa** Portuguese language courses
curto(a) short
curva f bend; turning; curve; **curva perigosa** dangerous bend
curvar to bend
cuspir to spit
custar to cost; **quanto custa?** how much does it cost?
custo m charge; cost; **ao preço de custo** at cost price
cutelaria f cutlery
c/v see **cave**

D

da = de + a
dactilógrafa f typist
dádiva f gift
dados mpl dice
daltónico(a) colour-blind
damas fpl Ladies; draughts (game)

damasco m apricot
dança f dance; **danças folclóricas** folk dancing
dançar to dance
dano m damage
dantes before
daquele = de + aquele
dar to give; **dá-mo** give it to me; **dar boleia a** to give a lift to; **dar de mamar** to feed (*baby*); **dar prioridade** to give way; **dar uma volta de carro** to go for a drive
das = de + as
data f date; **data de nascimento** date of birth
de of; from; **de luxo** de luxe
dê: dê prioridade give way
debaixo de under
débito m debit balance
decepção f disappointment
decepcionar to disappoint
decidir to decide
decimal decimal
décimo(a) tenth
décimo(a) primeiro(a) eleventh
decisão f decision
declaração f declaration
declarar to declare
declive m slope
decorativo(a) decorative
decote m: **decote em V** V-neck
decrescer to decrease; to go down (*pressure etc*)
decreto m decree; law
dedal m thimble
dedicar to dedicate
dedo m finger; **dedo do pé** toe
defeito m flaw
defeituoso(a) faulty
defender to defend
defesa f defence
deficiente disabled;

handicapped
definitivo(a) definite
degelo m thaw
degradé: em degradé layered (*hair*)
degrau m step (*stair*)
deitar to throw; **deite o lixo no lixo** put your rubbish in the bin
deitar-se to lie down
deixar to let (*allow*)
delegado m delegate
deles (delas) their
delicadeza f kindness
delicado(a) delicate
delicioso(a) delicious
delito m crime
demais too much; too many; **é bom demais** it's too good
demasia f change (*money*)
demasiado too much; too many
demonstração f demonstration (*of product etc*)
demonstrar to demonstrate
demora f delay
demorado(a) late
demorar to delay
dentadura postiça f dentures
dente m tooth; **dentes** teeth; **dentes postiços** false teeth; **a dor de dentes** toothache; **a escova de dentes** toothbrush
dentista m dentist
dentro: dentro de in; **dentro do carro** inside the car; **está lá dentro** it's inside
dependência f branch (*of company etc*)
depender de to depend on; **depende** it depends
depilações a cera mpl wax hair removal; waxing
depois after(wards);

depois de after
depositante m/f depositor
depositar to deposit; **deposite moedas na ranhura** place coins in the slot
depósito m deposit (*in bank*); **depósito de bagagens** left-luggage (office)
depressa quickly
deputado m deputy; M.P.
derramar to pour
derrapar to skid
derreter: está a derreter it's thawing
derrota f defeat
derrubar to knock down
desabitado(a) uninhabited
desacordo m disagreement
desafiar to challenge
desafio m match; game (*sport*)
desagradável unpleasant
desajeitado(a) clumsy
desanimado(a) discouraged
desânimo m depression
desaparafusar to unscrew
desaparecer to disappear
desaparecido(a) missing
desapertado(a) undone
desapertar to loosen
desaprovar to disapprove
desarrumação f mess (*in room etc*)
desassossego m restlessness
desastre m disaster; accident
desastroso(a) disastrous
descafeinado m decaffeinated coffee
descansar to rest
descanso m rest

descapotável convertible (*car*)

descarregar to unload

descartável throw-away; disposable

descascar to peel

descendente *m* descendant

descer to go down; **descer do autocarro** to get off the bus; **descer a estrada** to go down the road

descida perigosa *f* steep hill

descoberta *f* discovery

descobrir to discover

descomunal unusual (*size*)

desconfiado(a) suspicious

descongelar to defrost (*food*); to de-ice (*windscreen*)

desconhecido *m* stranger

descontar to discount

desconto *m* discount; reduction

descontrair-se to relax

descrever to describe

descrição *f* description

descuidado(a) careless

desculpar to excuse

desculpe excuse me; sorry (*apology*); **desculpe?** pardon?

desde since

desdobrar to unfold

desejar to desire; to wish

desejo *m* desire; wish

desembarcar to disembark

desempregado(a) unemployed

desemprego *m* unemployment

desenhar to draw (*picture*)

desenho *m* design (*pattern, decoration*); drawing

desenvolver to develop

desenvolvido(a) developed

desenvolvimento *m* development

deserto *m* desert

desfalecer to faint

desfazer to unpack (*case*)

desfile *m* procession

desígnio *m* design

desiludido(a) disappointed

desinchar to go down (*swelling*)

desinfectante *m* disinfectant

desinfectar to disinfect

desistir to give up

desligado(a) off (*engine, gas*)

desligar to hang up (*phone*); to switch off (*engine*); to turn off (*radio*); **desligue o motor** switch off your engine; **não desligue** do not hang up (*phone*)

deslocar to dislocate

desmaiado(a) faint

desmaiar to faint

desmontar to dismantle; to dismount

desodorizante *m* deodorant; **desodorizante de ambiente** air freshener

desordem *f* disorder

desorientar to confuse

despachante *m* shipper; transport agent

despachar-se to hurry (up)

despedir to dismiss; **despedir-se** to say goodbye

despejar to empty (*bottle etc*)

despensa *f* pantry

desperdiçar to waste

despertador *m* alarm clock

despesa *f* expense

despir to undress

desportivo(a) sports; sporty

desporto *m* sport; **desportos náuticos** sailing; water sports

desse = de + esse

deste = de + este

destilar to distil

destinatário *m* addressee

destino *m* destiny; destination; **com destino a Paris** leaving for Paris

destruir to destroy

desvalorização *f* devaluation

desviar to hijack

desviar-se to swerve; to turn off (*on journey*)

desvio *m* bypass; detour; diversion; **desvio para estacionamento** layby

detective *m* detective

deter to detain

detergente *m* detergent; **detergente líquido** liquid detergent; washing-up liquid; **detergente para a louça** washing-up liquid; **detergente para a roupa** washing powder

deteriorar to damage

determinado(a) determined; certain

determinar to settle

detestar to hate

Deus *m* God

devagar slow down (*on road sign*); drive slowly

dever: eu devo I must; **você deve** you must; **ele deve** he must; **eu devia** I should; **você devia** you should; **ele devia** he should; **deve-me ...** you owe me ...

devolver to give back; to return (*give back*)

devorar to devour

dez ten

dezanove nineteen

dezasseis sixteen

dezassete seventeen

Dezembro *m* December

dezoito eighteen

dia *m* day; **um dia** one day; **no outra dia** the other day; **dia útil** weekday; **dias de semana** weekdays

diabético(a) diabetic

diabo *m* devil

diálogo *m* dialogue

diamante *m* diamond

diante de before (*place*)

diária *f* daily cost

diariamente daily

diário *m* diary

diário(a) daily

diarreia *f* diarrhoea

dicionário *m* dictionary

dieta *f* diet

diferença *f* difference

diferente different

difícil difficult

dificuldade *f* difficulty

digerir to digest

digestão *f* digestion

diluir: diluir num pouco de água dissolve in a little water

dimensão *f* dimension

diminuir to reduce

dínamo *m* dynamo

dinheiro *m* money; cash

diploma *m* degree (*university*)

diplomata *m/f* diplomat

dique *m* dam

direcção *f* steering; **a coluna da direcção** steering column

directo(a) direct

director *m* director

director-geral *m* managing director

direita *f* right(-hand side); **à direita** on the right; **para a direita** to the right

direito *m* law

direito(a) straight; right(-hand); **Dto.** on the right-hand side (*in addresses*)

direitos *mpl* duty (*tax*); rights; **isento de direitos** duty-free

dirigir to run (*business etc*); to manage

disco *m* record (*music etc*); **discos e cassettes** records and cassettes

discordar to disagree

discoteca *f* disco; record shop

discreto(a) discreet

discurso *m* speech

discussão *f* discussion; argument

discutir to discuss

disfarce *m* fancy dress

disparar to fire (*gun etc*)

disponível available

dispor to arrange

disposição *f* arrangement; mood

disputar to dispute

dissolver to dissolve

distância *f* distance; **a que distância fica ...?** how far is it to ...?

distrair-se to entertain

distribuição *f* distribution

distribuidor *m* distributor

distribuir to distribute

distrito *m* district

ditadura *f* dictatorship

divã-cama *f* bed-settee

diversões *fpl* entertainment

divertido(a) funny

divertimento *m* treat; **divertimentos** entertainment

divertir-se to enjoy oneself; to have fun

dívida *f* debt

dividir to divide

divisão *f* division

divisas *fpl* foreign currency

divorciado(a) divorced

divorciar-se to get divorced

divórcio *m* divorce

dizer to say; **quer dizer** that is (i.e.)

do = de + o

dobrada *f* tripe with chickpeas; **dobrada à moda do Porto** tripe and chicken

dobrado(a) bent

dobrar to fold; **ao dobrar a esquina** round the corner

dobro *m* double

doçaria caseira *f* home-made desserts

doce[1] sweet (*taste*)

doce[2] *m* dessert; **doce de abóbora** marrow preserve/jam; **doce de amêndoa** almond spread; **doce de ovos** custard-like dessert made with eggs and sugar; **doces regionais** regional desserts

documentos *mpl* documents

doença *f* illness

doente[1] ill; sick

doente[2] *m/f* patient

doer to ache; to hurt; **isso dói** that hurts

dois (duas) two

dólar *m* dollar

doloroso(a) sore; painful

doméstico(a) domestic

domicílio *m* residence

domingo *m* Sunday; **domingos e dias feriados** Sundays and holidays

dominó *m* dominoes

dono(a) *m/f* owner

do que than

dor *f* ache; pain; **tenho**

dores de ouvidos I have earache
dormente numb
dormida f: **dormida e pequeno almoço** bed and breakfast; **dormida, pequeno almoço e banho** bed and breakfast with bath included
dormir to sleep
dos = de + os
dose f dose
dourado(a) golden
doutor m doctor
doutro(a) = de + outro(a)
doze twelve
drama m drama
dramático(a) dramatic
droga f drug
drogaria f drugstore; hardware store
drops mpl sweet drops
Dto. see **direito(a)**
duas two
duche m shower
dum(a) = de + um(a)
duna f dune
duplo(a) double
duração f duration
duradouro(a) lasting
durante during
durar to last
duro(a) hard; stiff; tough (*meat*)
dúvida f doubt
duvidar to doubt
duzentos(as) two hundred
dúzia f dozen

E

e and
economia f economy
económico(a) economical
economizar to save
écran m screen

eczema m eczema
edição f publication
edifício m building
editar to publish
editor m publisher
edredão m duvet; quilt
educação f education; politeness
educado(a) polite; **mal educado** naughty
efectivamente in fact
efervescente sparkling
eficaz effective
eficiente efficient (*method*)
egoísta selfish
égua f mare
eixo de roda m axle
ela she; her; it; **para ela** for her; **o pai dela** her father; **a mãe dela** her mother; **os livros dela** her books; **é dela** it's hers; **onde está o dela?** where is hers?; **onde estão os dela?** where are hers?
elástico m rubber band; elastic band
elástico(a) elastic; rubbery
ele he; him; it; **para ele** for him; **é dele** it's his; **onde está o dele?** where is his?; **onde estão os dele?** where are his?
electricidade f electricity; **o contador de electricidade** electricity meter; **o quadro de electricidade** mains
electricista m electrician
eléctrico m tram
eléctrico(a) electric; **o cobertor eléctrico** electric blanket
electrodomésticos mpl household electrical appliances
electrónico(a) electronic

elefante m elephant
elegante neat (*person*)
eleição f election
elemento m component
eles (elas) they; **a eles/a elas** them
elevador m lift; **elevador para a praia** lift down to the beach
em at; in (*with towns, countries*); into
emagrecer to grow thin
emalar to pack up
embaixada f embassy
embaixador m ambassador
embalagem f: **embalagem económica** economy pack; **embalagem familiar** family pack
embalar to parcel up
embaraçado(a) embarrassed
embaraçoso(a) embarrassing
embarcar to board (*ship, plane*)
embarque m embarkation; time of sailing
embebedar-se to get drunk
emblema m badge
embora although
embraiagem f clutch
embriagado(a) drunk
embrulhar to wrap (up)
embrulho m package
ementa f menu
emergência f: **é uma emergência** it's an emergency
em fim at last
emigrante m/f emigrant
emissor m transmitter
emitir to issue
empadão m: **empadão de bacalhau** cod, potato, onion and egg baked in a mould; **empadão de**

carne meat pie; **empadão de peixe** fish pie

empate m draw (football, etc)

empregada f: **empregada de bar** barmaid; **empregada de mesa** waitress; **empregada de quarto** chambermaid

empregado m waiter

empregado(a) m/f attendant (at petrol station); assistant (in shop); employee (in office)

empregar to employ; to use

emprego m job

empresa f firm

emprestar to lend

empréstimo m loan

empurrar to push

empurre push

E.N. see **estrada**

encaixar to fit (in)

encantador(a) lovely

encaracolado(a) curly

encarnado(a) red

encerrado(a) closed; **encerrado às segundas-feiras** closed on Mondays

encher to fill (up); to pump up (tyre etc); **encha o depósito** fill it up (petrol tank)

enchidos mpl processed meats

enciclopédia f encyclopedia

encolher to shrink

encomenda f parcel

encomendar to order

encontrar to meet

encontro m appointment; meeting; game (match)

encorajar to encourage

encosta f hill (slope)

encostar to lean

encruzilhada f crossroads

endereço m address

energia f: **o corte de energia** power cut

enérgico(a) energetic

enervar-se to become nervous

enevoado(a) hazy; misty

enfeitar to decorate

enfermaria f ward

enfermeiro(a) m/f nurse

enfermidade f illness

enfermo(a) infirm; ill

enferrujado(a) rusty

enfraquecer to weaken

enfrentar to face

enganado(a): estás enganado you're wrong

enganar-se to make a mistake

engano m mistake

engarrafado(a) jammed; stuck; bottled

engarrafamento m hold-up; traffic jam

engenharia f engineering

engenheiro m engineer

engolir to swallow; **não engolir** do not swallow

engordar to fatten

engraçado(a) funny

engraxar to polish (shoes)

enguia f eel; **enguias fritas** fried eels

enjoado(a) (sea)sick

enjoar to be sick

enorme huge

enquanto while

ensaio m trial; test

ensinar to teach

ensino m education; instruction

ensopado m stew; **ensopado de borrego** lamb stew; **ensopado de enguias** eel stew; **ensopado de lulas** fried squid in onion, garlic and herb sauce

então then

enteada f stepdaughter

enteado m stepson

entender to understand

enterrar to bury

enterro m burial

entornar to spill; to pour

entorse m sprain

entrada f entrance; starter (in meal); hors d'œuvre; **entrada livre** admission free; **entrada proibida** no entry

entrar to go in; to come in; to get in (to car etc)

entre among; between

entrecosto m entrecôte; **entrecosto com amêijoas** entrecôte with clams; **entrecosto frito** fried entrecôte

entrega f: **entrega ao domicílio** home delivery service

entregar to deliver

entretanto meanwhile

entreter to entertain

entrevista f interview

entrevistar to interview

entroncamento m T-junction

entusiástico(a) enthusiastic

envelhecer to grow old

envelope m envelope

envergonhado(a) ashamed

enviar to send

enxada f spade

enxaqueca f migraine

enxugar to dry

epilepsia f epilepsy

época f period; **época balnear** holiday period (in the summer)

equilibrar to balance

equilíbrio m balance; **equilíbrio de rodas** wheels balanced

equipa f team

equipamento m equipment

equipar to equip
equitação f riding
equivalente equivalent
equivocado(a) mistaken
ermida f hermitage
errado(a) wrong
errar to wander
erro m mistake; **salvo erro** unless I am mistaken
erva f grass; herb
ervanário f herbalist
ervilhas fpl peas
esc. see **escudo**
escada f ladder; stairs; **escada rolante** escalator
escafandrismo m diving
escala f stopover (in air travel)
escaldar to burn
escalfado(a) poached
escalope m escalope; **escalope de carneiro** mutton escalope; **escalope panado** breaded escalope; **escalope de porco** pork escalope; **escalopes de vitela ao Madeira** veal escalopes in Madeira wine
escanção m wine waiter
escândalo m scandal
escapar to escape
escape m exhaust
esclarecer to explain
esclarecimento m explanation
escocês (escocesa) Scottish
Escócia f Scotland
escola f school; **escola de condução** driving school; **escola primária** primary school; **escola secundária** secondary school
escolha f choice
escolher to choose
esconder to hide
escorrega m slide (in playground)
escorregadio(a) slippery
escorregar to slide; to slip
escorrer to drain (vegetables)
escova f brush; **escova de dentes** toothbrush; **escova de unhas** nailbrush
escovar to brush
escrever to write; **escrever à máquina** to type; **a máquina de escrever** typewriter; **como se escreve?** how do you spell it?
escrita f handwriting
escrito: por escrito in writing
escritor(a) m/f writer
escritório m office
escritura f deed
escrivaninha f desk (for writing)
escudo (esc.) m escudo; **dois mil escudos de gasolina** 2000 escudos worth of petrol; **vale dois mil escudos** it's worth 2000 escudos
escultor m sculptor
escultura f sculpture
escurecer to get dark
escuridão f darkness
escuro(a) dark (colour); **está escuro** it's dark
escuta listen
escutar to listen to
esferográfica f ballpoint
esfomeado(a) starving
esforço m effort
esfregão m cleaning pad
esfregar to rub
esfregona f mop
esgotado(a) sold out (tickets); exhausted (person)
esgoto m drain
esmagar to squash; to crush

esmalte m enamel
esmeralda f emerald
espaço m space; room (space)
espaçoso(a) roomy
espadarte m swordfish; **espadarte fumado** smoked swordfish
espalhar to scatter
Espanha f Spain
espanhol(a) Spanish
espantar to amaze
espantoso(a) astonishing; terrific
espargo m asparagus
esparguete m spaghetti; **esparguete à bolonhesa** spaghetti Bolognese
esparregado m puréed spinach
especial special
especialidade f speciality; **especialidades regionais** regional dishes our speciality
especialista m/f expert
especialmente especially
especiarias fpl spices
espécie f kind (sort)
espectáculo m show (in theatre etc); **espectáculo de variedades** cabaret
espectador(a) m/f onlooker; spectator
espelho m mirror; **espelho retrovisor** driving mirror
esperar to expect; to hope; **esperar por** to wait for; **à espera** waiting; **espere** wait; **espere pelo sinal** wait for the tone
esperguiçadeira f sunbed
esperto(a) clever
espetada f kebab; **espetadas à Beiroa** kebabs of pork liver, bacon, kidney and peppers; **espetada de**

leitão suckling pig kebab; **espetadas de lulas** squid and bacon kebabs; **espetada mista** mixed kebab; **espetada de rins** kidney kebab; **espetada de vitela** veal kebab

espeto m skewer

espinafre m spinach; **espinafres gratinados** spinach au gratin; **espinafres salteados** spinach with butter sauce

espingarda f gun (*rifle*); speargun (*diving*)

espinha f fish bone

espirrar to sneeze

esplanada f terrace

esplêndido(a) excellent

esponja f sponge

esposa f wife

espremedor de limões m lemon-squeezer

espuma f foam

espumante m sparkling wine

espumoso(a) sparkling (*wine*)

Esq. see **esquerda**

esquadra f police station

esquecer-se de to forget

esquentador m water heater; **esquentadores e fogões** gas heaters and stoves

esquerda f left(-hand side); **à esquerda** on the left; **para a esquerda** to the left; **Esq.** on the left(-hand) side (*in addresses*)

esquerdo(a) left

esqui m ski; **esqui aquático** water-skiing

esquiar to ski

esquina f corner (*outside*)

esquisito(a) strange; **que esquisito!** how strange!

esse (essa) that one

essencial essential

estabelecer to fix

(*arrange*)

estabelecimento m shop

estaca f tent peg

estação f station; **estação alta** high season; **estação do ano** season; **estação dos autocarros** bus depot; bus station; **estação baixa** low season; **Estação de Caminho de Ferro (Esta. C.F.)** railway station; **estação do comboio** railway station; **estação final** terminus; **estação fluvial** river ferry port; **estação rodoviária** bus station; **estação de serviço** service station

Esta. C.F. see **estação**

estacionamento m parking; **o disco de estacionamento** parking disk; **a multa de estacionamento** parking ticket; **estacionamento privado** private parking; **estacionamento proibido** no parking; **estacionamento reservado aos hóspedes** private car park − guests only

estacionar to park (*car*)

estadia f stay

estádio m stadium; **estádio polidesportivo** sports complex

estado m state

Estados Unidos (EUA) mpl United States

estalagem f inn

estância f timber yard; **estância termal** spa; medicinal springs

estanque watertight

estante f bookcase

estar to be; **está bem, já vou** all right, I'm coming; **estou constipado** I have

a cold; **estás bem?** are you all right?; **está a falar** the line is engaged

estatística f statistics

estátua f statue

estável stable

este (esta) this; **este livro** this book; **esta mesa** this table; **este mesmo** this one; **estes (estas)** these; **estes livros** these books

estereofónico(a) stereo

esterilizar to sterilize

esterlino(a) sterling

estilhaço m splinter

estilo m style

estômago m stomach; **o mal-estar de estômago** stomach upset

estores mpl blinds

estrada f road; **estrada encerrada ao tráfego** road closed; **estrada em mau estado** uneven road surface; **estrada florestal** forestry track; **estrada nacional (E.N.)** major road; national highway; **estrada principal** main road; **estrada com prioridade** priority; **estrada sem saída** no through road; **estrada secundária** minor road; **estrada de via dupla** dual carriageway

estrado m platform

estragado(a) bad (*food*); off (*milk*, etc)

estragar to spoil

estrangeiro: no estrangeiro abroad

estrangeiro(a) m/f foreigner; **estrangeiros** non-nationals this way (*at airport*, etc)

estranho(a) strange

estreia f first showing; **estreia hoje** first showing today

estreito(a) narrow
estrela f star
estuário m estuary
estudante m/f student
estudar to study
estufado(a) braised; stewed
estufa fria f glasshouse (in botanical gardens)
estúpido(a) stupid
etiqueta f ticket; label
eu I
EUA see **Estados Unidos**
eucalipto m eucalyptus tree
Europa f Europe
europeu (europeia) European
evaporação f evaporation
evidente obvious; clear (obvious)
evidentemente of course
evitar to avoid
exactamente exactly
exacto(a) exact
exagerar to exaggerate
exagero m exaggeration
exame m examination
exaustor m extractor fan
exceder to exceed; **não exceder a dose indicada** do not exceed the prescribed dose
excelente excellent
excepção f exception
excepcional exceptional; unusual
excepto except; **excepto aos bombeiros** access for fire engines only; **excepto cargas e descargas das 8h às 13 horas** loading and unloading only 8 am till 1 pm; **excepto aos domingos** Sundays excepted; **excepto veículos públicos** public service vehicles only

excesso m: **excesso de bagagem** excess luggage
excitado(a) excited
excitante exciting
excursão f excursion; tour; **excursão guiada** guided tour
excursões fpl trips; excursions
exemplar m copy (of book)
exemplo m example; **dar um exemplo** to give an example; **por exemplo** for example
exercício m exercise
exigente hard to please; demanding
exigir to demand
existir to exist
experiência f experience
experimentar to try
expirar to expire
explicação f explanation
explicar to explain
explodir to explode
exploração f exploitation; exploration
explosão f explosion
expor to exhibit; to expose
exportação f exportation
exportar to export
exposição f exhibition; **exposição de arte** art exhibition; **exposição de flores** flower show
exterior external
extintor m fire extinguisher
extracção f extraction (of tooth)
extraordinário(a) extraordinary; unusual; super
extravagante strange
extremidade f edge
extremo m end
extremo(a) extreme
eye liner m eye liner

F

fábrica f factory
fabricado(a) em ... made in ...
fabricante m manufacturer
fabricar to produce
fabuloso(a) fabulous
faca f knife
face f cheek
fachada f front
fácil easy
facilidade f facility; **facilidades de pagamento** easy payments
facilitar to make easy
facto m fact; **de facto** in fact
factura f invoice; **factura com os artigos discriminados** itemized bill
fadiga f fatigue
fadista m/f fado singer
fado m traditional Portuguese song
faiança f pottery
faisão m pheasant
faixa f lane (in road); **faixa da esquerda** outside lane; **faixa lateral** hard shoulder
falador(a) talkative
falar to speak
falecer to die
falésias fpl cliffs
falha f flaw
falhar: está a falhar the engine's misfiring
falsificação f fake; counterfeit
falso(a) false
falta f lack; **falta de corrente** power cut
faltar to be lacking; **faltam dois** there are

two missing
fama *f* fame
família *f* family
famoso(a) famous
fantástico(a) fantastic
farda *f* uniform
farinha *f* flour
farinheira *f* type of black pudding
farmacêutico(a) *m/f* chemist
farmácia *f* chemist's; **farmácia permanente** duty chemist; **farmácias de serviço** emergency chemists
farófias *fpl* egg whites in milk dessert
faróis *mpl* headlights
farol *m* headlight; lighthouse
farolim *m* sidelight
farto(a): estar farto to be fed up
farturas *fpl* long tube-like fritters
fatias douradas *fpl* egg and cinnamon bread pudding
fatigante tiring
fato *m* suit (*man's*); **fato de banho** swimsuit; bathing costume; **fato de ginástica** track suit; **fato de mergulhador** wetsuit; **fato de treino** track suit
favas *fpl* broad beans
favor *m* favour; **por favor** please; **é favor conferir o troco no acto de pagamento** please check if you have received the right change; **é favor fechar a porta** please close the door; **é favor não incomodar** do not disturb; **é favor pedirem a brochura** please ask for our brochure
favorito(a) favourite

fax *m* fax
fazenda *f* material
fazer to do; to make; **fazer a barba** to shave; **fazer contrabando** to smuggle; **fazer falta** to be needed; **fazer a ligação** to get through (*on phone*); **fazer as malas** to pack up; **fazer malha** to knit; **fazer-se sócio** to become a member; **eu faço** I do; I make; **você faz** you do; you make; **ele faz** he does; he makes; **não o fiz** I didn't do it; **ela fará isso** she will do it; **eu farei isso** I will do it; **fazem-se chaves** keys cut here; **faz favor** please
fé *f* faith
febras de porco *fpl* thin slices of pork
febre *f* fever; **febre dos fenos** hay fever
fechado(a) shut; closed; **fechado para balanço** closed for stocktaking; **fechado para férias** closed for holidays
fechadura *f* lock
fechar to shut; to close
fecho *m* clasp; **fecho éclair** zip
feijão *m* beans
feijão-verde *m* French beans
feijoada *f* bean stew; **feijoada à alentejana** beans and mixed meat dish; **feijoada à algarvia** bean stew with pig's ear, black pudding and cabbage; **feijoada à transmontana** red beans and pork
feio(a) awful; ugly
feira *f* fair (*commercial*); market; **feira popular**

fairground
feito(a) à mão handmade
felicidade *f* happiness
feliz happy
felizmente fortunately
fêmea *f* female (*animals*)
feminino(a) feminine
fenda *f* split; crack
feno *m* hay
feriado *m* holiday; public holiday; **feriado nacional** bank holiday
férias *fpl*: **em férias** on holiday
ferida *f* wound
ferido(a) injured
ferir to hurt
fermento *m* yeast
ferragens *fpl* ironware
ferramenta *f* tool
ferro *m* iron; **ferro de engomar** iron (*for clothes*)
ferro-velho *m* scrap merchant
ferrugento(a) rusty
ferry-boat *m* ferry
ferver to boil
festa *f* party (*celebration*); **festas dos santos populares** saints' feast days
festival *m* festival; **festival da canção** song festival
feto *m* fern
Fevereiro *m* February
fiação *f*: **fiação e tecelagem** spinning and weaving
fiambre *m* ham
ficar to stay; to be; to remain; **não me fica bem** it doesn't fit; **fiquei sem gasolina** I've run out of petrol; **ficar como convidado** to stay (*as guest*)
ficha *f* plug (*electrical*); **ficha dupla/tripla** adaptor (*electrical*)

fígado *m* liver; **fígado de porco à portuguesa** pig's liver in wine

figo *m* fig; **figos com amêndoas** figs with almonds; **figos secos** dried figs

figueira *f* fig tree

fila *f* row (*line*)

filarmónica *f* brass band

fileira *f* file; row

filete *m* fillet steak; tenderloin; **filete de bife com foie gras** beef fillet steak with foie gras; **filetes de pescada** hake steaks

filha *f* daughter

filho *m* son

filhozes *fpl* sugared buns; **filhozes de forma** orange and port fritters

filial *f* branch (*of bank etc*)

filigranas *fpl* filigree work

filmar to film

filme *m* film

filtro *m* filter; **com filtro** filter-tipped; tipped

fim *m* end; **ao fim de** at the end of; **ao fim e ao cabo** in the end; **fim de autoestrada** end of motorway; **fim de estação** end of season; **fim da proibição de estacionamento** end of parking restrictions; **fim de semana** weekend; **fim de traço de obras** end of roadworks

fino(a) fine

fio *m* wire; **fios de ovos** sugared filaments of egg yolk

firma *f* firm

firme steady

fiscal *m* inspector

fita *f* tape; ribbon; **fita adesiva** adhesive tape; **fita gomada** sticky paper; **fita métrica** tape-measure

fita-cola *f* sellotape ®

fixar to fix

fixo(a) steady

flanela *f* flannel

flash *m* flash; **o cubo flash** flash cube; **a lâmpada de flash** flash bulb

flauta *f* flute

flipper *m* pinball machine

flor *f* flower

floresta *f* forest

florista *f* florist

fluentemente fluently

flutuar to float

focagem de faróis headlight focus aligned

fofo(a) soft

fogão *m* cooker; **fogão eléctrico** electric cooker

fogareiro a gás *m* gas stove

fogo *m* fire; **fogo!** fire!; **fogo de artifício** fireworks

folga *f*: **dia de folga** free day; day off

folha *f* leaf; **folha de alumínio** foil (*for cooking*); **folha de estanho** tinfoil

folhados *mpl* puff pastries

folheto *m* leaflet

fome *f*: **tenho fome** I'm hungry

fondue *m*: **fondue de carne** meat fondue; **fondue de chocolate** chocolate fondue; **fondue de queijo** cheese fondue

fonte *f* fountain; source

fora: fora de out of; **de fora** from outside; **lá fora** outside; **para fora** out; **fora de moda** out of fashion

força *f* power (*strength*); force; **à força** by force

forma *f* shape; **de forma que** in such a way that

formalidade *f* formality;

formalidades alfandegárias customs formalities

formar to form; to shape

formidável amazing

formiga *f* ant

fornecedor(a) *m/f* supplier

fornecer to supply

forno *m* oven; **forno de micro-ondas** microwave oven; **no forno** in the oven

fortaleza *f* fortress

forte strong

fortuna *f* wealth

fósforo *m* match

fotocine *m* cine photography

fotocópia *f* photocopy

fotografia *f* photograph; print (*photograph*)

fotógrafo *m* photographer

fotómetro *m* exposure meter

fraco(a) weak

fractura *f* fracture

frágil breakable

fralda *f* nappy; **fraldas descartáveis** disposable nappies; **fralda-calças** nappy pants

framboesa *f* raspberry

França *f* France

francês (francesa) French

franco *m* franc

frango *m* chicken; **frango à açoriana** chicken in onion sauce; **frango assado** roast chicken; **frango no churrasco** barbecued chicken; **frango no espeto** spit roast chicken; **frango frito/grelhado** fried/ grilled chicken; **frango na púcara** chicken boiled in the pot; **frango no tacho** chicken casserole

franja f fringe
frasco m flask
frase f sentence
freguês (freguesa) m/f customer
frente f front; **em frente de** in front of; opposite; **sempre em frente** straight on
frequentar to attend
frequente frequent
fresco(a) fresh; cool; crisp
frieira f chilblain
frigideira f frying pan
frigorífico m fridge; **com frigorífico e kitchenet** with fridge and cooking facilities
frio(a) cold
fritadeira f frying pan
fritar to fry
frito(a) fried
fronha f pillow case
fronteira f border (*frontier*)
frota f fleet
frouxo(a) slack
fruta f fruit; **fruta da época** seasonal fruit
frutaria f fruit shop
fruto m fruit; **frutos secos e verdes** dried fruits and nuts
fuga f leak; **fuga de gás** gas leak
fugir to run away
fulano m so-and-so
fumado(a) smoked
fumador(a) m/f smoker; **para não fumadores** non-smoking (*compartment etc*)
fumar to smoke; **não fumar** no smoking; **não fume e desligue o motor** no smoking and switch off engine
fumo m smoke
funcionar to work (*machine*); **não funciona** out of order
funcionário(a) m/f civil servant; **funcionário aduaneiro** customs officer
fundir to melt
fundo m bottom
fundo(a) deep
funeral m funeral
furar to pierce; **furam-se orelhas sem dor** ear-piercing
furnas fpl caverns
furo m puncture
furtar to steal
furto m theft
fusível m fuse
futebol m football; **futebol de mesa** table football; **futebol de salão** indoor football
futuro m future

G

gabinete de provas m changing room
gado m cattle; **gado bravo** beware – unfenced cattle
gaivota f seagull; pedal boat
gajo m guy; type
galantine f: **galantine de coelho** cold rabbit roll; **galantine de galinha** cold chicken roll; **galantine de vegetais** cold vegetable roll
galão m large white coffee
galeria f: **galeria de arte** art gallery; **galeria comercial** shopping arcade
Gales m: **o País de Gales** Wales
galês (galesa) Welsh
galinha f hen; chicken;

galinha de fricassé chicken fricassee
galo m cockerel
GALP m national petrol station
gamba f prawn; **gambas com alhinho** prawns fried in garlic; **gambas grelhadas** grilled prawns
ganga f denim
ganhar to earn; to win
ganso m goose
garagem m garage
garantia f guarantee; **garantia de cheques** cheque guarantee
gare f quay; platform
garfo m fork
garganta f throat
garoto m little boy; half black, half white coffee
garrafa f bottle
garrafão m 5 litre bottle
gás m gas; **gás butano** butane gas; **gás campismo** camping gas; **a botija de gás** gas cylinder
gasóleo m diesel; **a gasóleo** diesel-driven
gasolina f petrol; **gasolina normal** 2 star petrol; **gasolina super** 4 star petrol; **a bomba de gasolina** fuel pump; petrol pump; petrol station; **o depósito da gasolina** petrol tank; **o indicador do nível da gasolina** fuel gauge; petrol gauge; **a lata de gasolina** petrol can
gasosa f fizzy mineral water
gasoso(a) fizzy
gaspacho m chilled soup of tomato, cucumber and peppers
gastar to spend
gato m cat
gaveta f drawer

geada f frost

gelado m ice-cream; icelolly; **gelado de baunilha** vanilla ice-cream; **gelado de frutas** fruit ice-cream

gelado(a) frozen (water); iced

gelar to freeze

gelataria f ice-cream parlour

geleia f jelly

gelo m ice; **gelo invisível** black ice; **o ringue de gelo** ice rink

gelosia f shutter

gémeo(a) twin

general m general

género m kind; type

generoso(a) generous

gengibre m ginger

gengivas fpl gums

genro m son-in-law

gente f people; **toda a gente** everybody

gentil handsome; courteous

gentileza f kindness

genuíno(a) genuine

geografia f geography

geral[1] f gallery (in theatre)

geral[2] general; **em geral** generally; **de uma maneira geral** generally

geralmente usually

gerência f management

gerente m manager

gerir to manage

gesso m plaster (for broken limb)

gestão f management

gesto m gesture

gestor m manager

gigante m giant

gin m gin

ginásio m gymnasium; gym hall

ginástica f gymnastics

gininha f bitter cherry liqueur

ginja f cherry liqueur;

ginjas bitter cherries

gin-tónico m gin and tonic

gira-discos m record-player

girar to spin

girassol m sunflower

gíria f slang

giro(a) very nice

giz m chalk

G.N.R. see **guarda**

gola f collar

golfe m golf; **o campo de golfe** golf course; **o clube de golfe** golf club (place); **o taco de golfe** golf club (stick)

golfo m gulf

golo m goal

golpe m blow

gordo(a) fat

gordura f fat

gorjeta f tip (to waiter etc)

gostar: gostar de to like; **gosta?** do you like it?; **eu gostaria de** I would like

gosto m taste

gostoso(a) savoury

gotas fpl drops

governanta f nanny

governar to rule

governo m government

gozar to enjoy; **está a gozar** you're joking

Grã-Bretanha f Britain

graça f charm; joke

graças a thanks to

gracejo m joke

grama m gramme

gramática f grammar

grande big; large; great; **o Grande Prémio** Grand Prix

granizo m hail (weather)

grão m chickpeas

gratificação f tip

gratificar to tip

grátis free (costing nothing)

grato(a) grateful

grau m degree (on scale)

gravador m tape-

recorder; **gravador de cassettes** cassette recorder; **gravador de mensagens** telephone recorder; **gravador de video-tape** video recorder

gravata f tie

grave serious

grávida pregnant

gravidez f pregnancy

gravura f print (picture)

graxa f polish

grelha f grill

grelhado(a) grilled

grelhador de placa m grill; hotplate

grelhados mpl grilled dishes

grelos mpl sprouts

greve f strike (industrial); **em greve** on strike

gripe f flu

gritar to shout

grito m scream; shout; cry

groselha f currant; redcurrant; blackcurrant; gooseberry

grosseiro(a) rude (person)

grosso(a) thick

grupo m group; party (group); **grupo sanguíneo** blood group

grutas fpl caves

guarda m: **guarda fiscal** coastguard; customs officer; **Guarda Nacional Republicana (G.N.R.)** National Guard

guarda-chuva m umbrella

guarda-lamas m mudguard

guardanapo m napkin

guarda-nocturno m night watchman

guardar to keep; to watch (sb's luggage etc)

guarda-redes m

goalkeeper
guarda-roupa m
wardrobe
guarda-sol m sunshade
guerra f war
guia m/f guide; **guia intérprete** interpreter and guide; **gula turístico(a)** courier (for tourists); tourist guide
guiar to drive
guiché m window (at post office, bank)
guisado m stew
guitarra f guitar
guloso(a) greedy

H

há there is; there are; **há vagas** vacancies; **há uma semana/um ano** a week/year ago
hábil skilful
habilidade f skill
hábito m custom
habituado(a) accustomed; **estou habituado a isso** I'm used to it
habitual usual
habituar-se a to get used to
hall m hall (in house)
hamburguer m hamburger; **hamburguer com batatas fritas** hamburger and chips; **hamburguer com ovo** hamburger with an egg; **hamburguer no pão** hamburger roll
helicóptero m helicopter
hemorragia f haemorrhage
hemorróidas fpl haemorrhoids
herdade f farm
herói m hero

hidroplanador m hydroplane
higiene f hygiene
hino m hymn; **hino nacional** national anthem
hipismo m horse racing; riding
hipoteca f mortgage
hipotecar to mortgage
história f history; story
hoje today; **hoje em dia** nowadays
homem m man
homens mpl Gents'; men's room
homossexual homosexual
honestidade f honesty
honesto(a) honest
honra f honour
hóquei m hockey
hora f hour; time (by the clock); **hora de chegada** time of arrival; **hora de partida** time of departure; **hora de ponta** rush hour; **que horas são?** what time is it?
horário m timetable; **horário de funcionamento** opening times; **horários dos ferry-boats** ferry timetable
horizonte m horizon
horrível dreadful; horrible
horta f garden (for vegetables, fruit etc)
hortaliça f vegetables
hortelã f mint (herb)
hortelã-pimenta f peppermint (herb)
hospedar to give accommodation to
hóspede m/f guest
hospedeira f hostess; **hospedeira de bordo** stewardess; air hostess
hospital m hospital

hospitalidade f hospitality
hotel m hotel
hovercraft m hovercraft
humano(a) human
humidade f humidity
húmido(a) damp
humor m humour; mood
humorístico(a) comical

I

iate m yacht
icterícia f jaundice
idade f age; **que idade tem?** how old are you?
ideia f idea
idem the same
idêntico(a) identical
identidade f identity
identificação f identification
idioma m idiom
idoso(a) aged
idosos mpl the elderly; old people
ignição f ignition; starter (in car); **a chave de ignição** ignition key
igreja f church
igual equal
igualar to make equal
ilha f island
iluminação f lighting
iluminado(a) floodlit (building)
iluminar to light up
imaginação f imagination
imaginar to imagine
imediatamente immediately
imenso(a) vast; **gostei imenso** I really enjoyed it
imigrante m/f immigrant
imitação f imitation
imóvel still (immobile)
impaciente impatient
ímpar odd (number)

impedir to prevent
imperfeito(a) imperfect
imperial m draught beer
impermeável m
raincoat; waterproof
importação f
importation
importância f
importance; **não tem
importância** it doesn't
matter
importante important
**importar: importa-se
que...?** do you mind if...?;
não me importo I don't
care; I don't mind
impossível impossible
imposto m tax; duty;
impostos duty; tax;
**imposto de selo não
incluido** stamp duty not
included; **imposto de
valor acrescentado
(IVA)** VAT
imprensa f the Press
impressão f: **tenho a
impressão que...** I've got
a feeling that...
impresso m form (to fill
in)
impressora f printer
imprevisto(a)
unexpected
impulso m unit of charge
(for phone); **impulsos**
dialled units
inauguração f opening
inaugurar to open
incapaz unable
incêndio m fire
incerteza f uncertainty
inchaço m lump (swelling)
inchado(a) swollen
inchar to swell
incluído(a) included;
**incluído jantar e uma
bebida** a drink and a
meal included in the
price
incluir to include
inclusivamente inclusive

incomodar to disturb;
não incomodar do not
disturb
incómodo(a)
uncomfortable
incomparável
incomparable
inconsciente
unconscious
incrível incredible
indeciso(a) undecided
indemnizar to
compensate
independente
independent
indicações fpl
instructions for use
indicativo m dialling
code; **indicativo
europeu** dialling prefix
for Europe; **indicativo
intercontinental** dialling
prefix for long-distance
calls; **indicativo do país**
dialling prefix for the
country; **indicativo de
zona** dialling prefix for
the town
indigestão f indigestion
indispensável essential
indivíduo m person
indústria f industry
inesperado(a)
unexpected
infantário m kindergarten
infecção f infection
infeccioso(a) infectious
(illness)
infeliz unhappy
infelizmente
unfortunately
inflação f inflation
inflamação f
inflammation
inflamado(a) inflamed
inflamável inflammable
informação f
information; **informação
turística** tourist
information
informações fpl

information office;
**informações/secção de
informações** enquiry
desk/office; **para
informações e
reclamações marcar ...**
for information or
complaints dial ...
informado(a) well-
informed
informal informal (dance,
dinner etc)
informar to inform
infracção f offence
Inglaterra f England
inglês (inglesa) English
íngreme steep
iniciais fpl initials
iniciar to begin
início m beginning; **início
de autoestrada** start of
motorway
injecção f injection
injusto(a) unfair
inquilino m tenant
inscrever to register
insecticida f fly-killer
insecto m insect
insistir to insist
insolação f heatstroke;
sunstroke
insolente cheeky
insónia f insomnia
inspecção f inspection
inspector m inspector
instalações fpl facilities;
**instalações de tradução
simultânea** simultaneous
translating facilities
instalar to install
instituto m institute
instrução f instruction
instrumento m
instrument;
instrumentos musicais
musical instruments
instrutor m instructor
insucesso m failure
(mechanical)
insuflável inflatable
insulina f insulin

insulto *m* insult
insuportável intolerable
inteiro(a) whole
inteligente intelligent; clever
intenção *f* intention
intercidades see **comboio**
interdito(a) forbidden; **interdito m/18 anos** under 18s strictly not admitted; **interdito a menores de ... anos** no admission to those under ... years of age
interessado(a) interested; **estou interessado em ...** I'm interested in ...
interessante interesting
interessar to interest
interesse *m* interest
interior inside
intermediário *m* middleman
internacional international
interno(a) internal
interpretar to interpret
intérprete *m/f* interpreter
interromper to interrupt
interrupção de viagem *f* stopover
interruptor *m* switch
intervalo *m* interval (*in theatre*)
intestinos *mpl* bowels
intoxicação *f* food poisoning
introdução *f* introduction
introduzir to introduce; **introduza a moeda na ranhura** insert coin in slot
inundação *f* flood
inútil useless
inválido(a) invalid
inverno *m* winter

inversão de marcha *f* U-turn
investigação *f* investigation
invulgar unusual (*strange*)
ioga *m* yoga
iogurte *m* yoghurt
iogurteira *f* yoghurt maker
IP see **itinerário**
ir to go; **eu vou I go, I am going; você vai** you go, you are going; **ele vai** he goes, he is going; **ir dar uma volta de carro** to go for a ride (*in car*)
Irlanda *f* Ireland; **a Irlanda do Norte** Northern Ireland
irlandês (irlandesa) Irish
irmã *f* sister
irmão *m* brother
iscas *fpl*: **iscas fritas com batatas** fried liver and French fries; **iscas de porco** marinated pig's liver; **iscas à portuguesa** beef liver
isolar to isolate
isqueiro *m* lighter
isso that; **por isso** therefore
isto this
Itália *f* Italy
italiana *f* small expresso coffee
italiano(a) Italian
itinerário *m* route; **itinerário principal** main route
IVA *m* VAT

J

já already
jacto *m* jet
Janeiro *m* January
janela *f* window; **o lugar à janela** window seat
jantar *m* dinner; evening meal; **jantares e ceias** evening meals and dinners served
jardim *m* garden; **jardim botânico** botanical garden; **jardim infantil/ de infância** kindergarten; **jardim zoológico** zoo
jardineira *f* vegetable stew
jarra *f* vase
jarro *m* jar; carafe; jug
jazz *m* jazz
jeans *fpl* jeans
jeito *m* skill
joalharia *f* jeweller's; jewellery
joelho *m* knee
jogador(a) *m/f* player
jogar to play
jogging *m*: **ir fazer jogging** to go jogging
jogo *m* game; gambling; play; **jogo de dardos** darts; **jogos de vídeo** video-games
jóia *f* jewel; **jóias** jewellery
jornal *m* newspaper
jornalista *m/f* journalist
jovem young
judaico(a) Jewish
juiz *m* judge
julgamento *m* trial
julgar to think
Julho *m* July
Jumbo *m* jumbo jet
Junho *m* June
junta de culatra *f* head gasket

juntar to join
junto near; **junto ao aeroporto** close to the airport
juntos together
jurar to swear
justo(a) fair
juventude f youth

K L

kg see **quilo(grama)**
kispo m nylon anorak; child's jumpsuit
lá there; **lá em baixo** downstairs
lã f wool; **lã de vidro** fibreglass
-la her; it; **vimo-la** we saw her/it
lábio m lip
laboratório m laboratory
laca f lacquer; hair spray
laço m bow (ribbon, string)
lacticínios mpl dairy products
ladeira f slope
lado m side; **ao lado de** beside; **por outro lado** on the other hand
ladrão m thief
ladrar to bark
lagarto m lizard
lago m lake; **pequeno lago** pond
lagosta f lobster; **lagosta à americana** lobster with tomato and onions; **lagosta thermidor** lobster thermidor
lagostim m crayfish
lágrima f tear
lama f mud
lamber to lick
lamento I'm sorry
lâminas de barbear fpl razor blades
lâmpada f light bulb; **lâmpada eléctrica** torch;

lâmpada piloto pilot light
lampreia f lamprey eel; **lampreia à moda do Minho** whole lamprey in a thick sauce; **lampreia de ovos** dessert made of eggs and sugar
lançar to throw
lanchar to go for something to eat
lanche m luncheon; light afternoon meal
lanterna f torch
lápis m pencil; **lápis de cera** crayons
lar m home
laranja f orange; **o doce de laranja** marmalade; **cor de laranja** orange (colour)
laranjeira f orange tree
lareira f fireside
largar to let go
largo m small square
largo(a) broad; loose (clothes); wide
largura f width
lasanha f lasagne
lata f tin; can (of food)
latão m brass
lavabo m lavatory; toilet; **lavabos** toilets
lavagante m a kind of lobster
lavagem f: **lavagem e mise** shampoo and set; a **lavagem automática** car wash
lava-louça m sink
lavandaria f laundry; **lavandaria automática** launderette; **lavandaria a seco** dry cleaner's; **lavandaria e tinturaria** laundry and dyers; **com lavandaria** with laundry facilities; **o serviço de lavandaria** laundry service
lava pára-brisas m

windscreen washer
lavar to wash (clothes etc); **lavar-se** to wash (oneself); **lavar a louça** to wash up; **lavar à mão** to handwash; **lavar as mãos** to wash one's hands
lavatório m washbasin
lavável washable
lavoura f farming
lavrador m farmer
lavrar to plough
laxativo m laxative
leão m lion
lebre f hare
legal legal
legendas fpl subtitles
legumes mpl vegetables
lei f law
leilão m auction
leitão m sucking pig; **leitão assado** roast sucking pig; **leitão da Bairrada** sucking pig from Bairrada
leitaria f dairy
leite m milk; **com leite** white (coffee); **leite achocolatado** chocolate-flavoured milk drink; **leite condensado** condensed milk; **leite creme** egg custard; **leite desnatado** skimmed milk; **leite evaporado** evaporated milk; **leite gordo** full cream milk; **leite de limpeza** cleansing cream; **leite magro/meio gordo** skimmed/semi-skimmed milk; **leite pasteurizado** pasteurized milk; **leite em pó** powdered milk; **leite ultrapasteurizado** UHT milk; **o batido de leite** milkshake
leiteiro m milkman
leitor m reader (gen); **leitor de cassetes** cassette player

lembranças *fpl* souvenirs

lembrar-se de to remember

leme *m* rudder

lenço *m* handkerchief; tissue; **lenço de papel** paper tissue; **lenço de pescoço** scarf (*square*)

lençol *m* sheet

lenho *m* log

lente *f* lens; **lentes de contacto** contact lenses

lentilhas *fpl* lentils

lento(a) slow

leque *m* fan

ler to read

leste *m* east

letra *f* letter

letreiro *m* sign

leucemia *f* leukemia

levantado(a) up (*out of bed*)

levantar to draw (*money*); to lift; **levante o auscultador** lift the receiver

levantar-se to stand up; to get up

levar to take

leve light (*not heavy*)

lhe to him; to her; **lhes** to them

lho(a) = lhe + o(a)

libra *f* pound; **libras esterlinas** pounds sterling

lição *f* lesson

licença *f* permit; **com licença** excuse me

liceu *m* secondary school

licor *m* liqueur; **licores** wines and spirits; **licor de medronho** strawberry liqueur; **licor de ovo** advocaat; **licor de peras** pear liqueur; **licor de whisky** Drambuie ®

ligação *f* connection (*trains etc*); **ligação com ... connects with ...**;

ligações intercontinentais international connections; **ligações para outros destinos** connections for other destinations

ligado(a) on (*engine, gas etc*)

ligadura *f* bandage; **ligadura adesiva** elastoplast ®

ligeiro(a) light; **ligeiros** light vehicles

lilás mauve

lima[1] *f* lime (*fruit*)

lima[2] *f* file; **lima das unhas** nailfile

limão *m* lemon

limitar to limit

limite *m* limit; **limite de peso autorizado** luggage allowance; **limite de velocidade** speed limit

limoeiro *m* lemon tree

limonada *f* lemonade

limpa-cachimbos *m* pipe cleaner

limpa-móveis *m* furniture cleaner

limpa pára-brisas *m* windscreen wiper

limpar to wipe; to clean

limpa-vidros *m* window-cleaning liquid

limpeza *f* cleaning; **limpeza a seco** dry cleaning; **a mulher da limpeza** cleaner (*person*)

limpo(a) clean

lindo(a) lovely

língua *f* language; tongue; **língua de porco** tongue of pork; **língua de fricassé** tongue, **língua de vaca** tongue of beef

linguado *m* sole (*fish*); **linguado no forno** baked sole; **linguado frito** fried sole; **linguado grelhado** grilled sole; **linguado à meunière** sole meunière

linguiça *f* spicy pork sausage

linha *f* line; thread; platform (*railway*); **linha aérea** airline; **linha jovem** young people's fashions

linho *m* linen

liquidação *f* (clearance) sale

líquido *m* liquid; **líquido para a louça** washing-up liquid

lírio *m* lily

Lisboa (Lx) Lisbon

liso(a) smooth

lista *f* list; **lista de preços** price list; **lista telefónica** telephone directory

listagens *fpl*: **listagens de nomes e endereços** mailing list

literatura *f* literature

litoral *m* seaboard

litro *m* litre

livrar to set free

livraria *f* bookshop

livre free; vacant

livrete *m* car documents

livro *m* book; **livro de cheques** cheque book; **livro de frases** phrase book; **livro de textos** textbook

lixa *f* sandpaper

lixívia *f* bleach

lixo *m* rubbish

-lo/-los him/them

lobo *m* wolf

local[1] local

local[2] *m* site; **local de interesse turístico** place of interest to tourists; **local sossegado** quietly situated

localidade *f* place; town

loção *f* lotion

locutor(a) *m/f* presenter (*TV, radio*)

logo: logo que possível

as soon as possible
loja f shop; **loja de antiguidades** antique shop; **loja de artesanato** handicrafts shop; **loja de desportos** sports shop; **loja de ferragens** ironmonger's; **loja de fotografia** photography shop; **loja franca** duty-free shop; **loja de malas** handbag shop; **com lojas e cabeleireiro** with shopping arcade and hairdressing salon
lombo m: **lombo de porco** pork loin; **lombo de vaca** sirloin
lona f canvas
Londres London
longa metragem f full length feature film
longe far; **longe de** far from; **é longe?** is it far? **mais longe** farther
longo: ao longo da rua along the street
long-playing m album (record)
lotação f: **lotação esgotada** sold out (tickets)
lotaria f lottery; **lotaria nacional** state lottery
louça f dishes; crockery; **esfregão para lavar a louça** dishcloth; **a máquina de lavar louça** dishwasher
louco(a) mad; crazy
louro(a) fair (hair)
lua f moon
lua-de-mel m honeymoon
luar m moonlight
lubrificantes mpl lubricants
lucro m profit
lugar m seat (in theatre); space (room); place; **lugares marcados em**

todas as sessões all seats numbered in every session; **lugares em pé** standing room; **lugares reservados a acompanhantes de crianças com menos de 4 anos** seats reserved for those with children under 4; **lugares reservados a cegos e inválidos** seats reserved for blind people and disabled; **lugares reservados a grávidas** seats reserved for expectant mothers
lulas fpl squid; **lulas de caldeirada** squid in onion, potato, nutmeg and wine sauce; **lulas fritas** fried squid; **lulas com natas** stewed squid in cream; **lulas recheadas** squid stuffed with bacon and onion; **lulas à sevilhana** fried squid in batter
luta f fight
lutar to fight
luvas fpl gloves; **luvas de borracha** rubber gloves
luxo m luxury; **de luxo** de luxe
luxuoso(a) sumptuous
luz f light; **luzes de presença** sidelights; **luzes de perigo** hazard lights
Lx see **Lisboa**

M

M. underground (railway)
ma = **me** + **a**; **dê-ma** give me it
má see **mau**
maçã f apple; **maçã assada** baked apple

maca f stretcher
macaco m jack; monkey
maçapão m marzipan
maçaroca f corn on the cob
macarrão m macaroni
macedónia de frutas f fruit cocktail
machado m axe
macho m male (animal)
maciço(a) solid (strong)
macieira f apple tree
macio(a) soft
maço[1] m mallet
maço[2] m: **maço de cigarros** packet of cigarettes
madeira f wood
madrasta f stepmother
madrinha f godmother
madrugada f early morning
maduro(a) ripe
mãe f mother
maestro m conductor
magnético(a) magnetic
magnífico(a) magnificent; splendid
magoar: magoar alguém to hurt someone; **magoar-se** to hurt oneself
magro(a) thin
Maio m May
maionese f mayonnaise; **maionaise de alho** garlic mayonnaise
maior larger; **a maior parte de** the majority of; **para maiores de 16 anos** for over-16's only
maioria f majority
maiôts mpl knitwear
mais more; **o/a mais** the most; **mais pão** more bread; **mais ou menos** more or less; **mais tempo/dinheiro** extra time/money; **cada vez mais** more and more; **custa mais** it costs extra

mal wrong; evil; **mal disposto** in a bad mood
mala f suitcase; bag; trunk
malagueta f chilli
mal-entendido m misunderstanding
mal-estar m discomfort
malhas fpl knitwear
mal-humorado(a) in a bad mood
malmequer m marigold
malta f: **a malta** us lot; we
mancha f stain
manchar to stain
mandar to send; **mandar uma carta expresso** to send a letter express
maneira f way (method); **de uma maneira geral** generally; **de maneira nenhuma** in no way; **de maneira que** in such a way that
manequim m model
manga f sleeve
manhã f morning
manicura f manicure; **manicura e pedicura** manicurist and chiropodist
manifestação f demonstration (political)
manso(a) tame
manta f heavy blanket
manteiga f butter; **manteiga de anchova** anchovy butter; **manteiga meio sal** slightly salted butter; **manteiga queimada** butter sauce for fish
manter to keep
manter-se: mantenha-se à direita, caminhe pela esquerda keep to the right, walk on the left
mantimentos mpl provisions

manutenção f keep-fit; maintenance
mão f hand; **o creme para as mãos** hand cream; **feito à mão** handmade; **mão de obra** labour force; **o saco de mão** handbag; **o travão de mão** handbrake
mapa m map; **mapa das estradas** road map; **mapa das ruas** street plan
maquilhagem f make-up
máquina f machine; **máquina de calcular** calculator; **máquina de filmar** movie camera; cine camera; **máquina fotográfica** camera; **máquina de lavar louça** dishwasher; **máquina de lavar roupa** washing machine
mar m sea; **mar de pequena vaga** choppy sea
maracujá m tropical fruit
maravilhoso(a) wonderful
marca f brand; **marca registada** registered trade mark
marcação f booking; dialling
marcar to dial (phone number); to book (hotel etc); **marcar o número** to dial the number
marcha-atrás f reverse (gear)
Março m March
marco do correio m pillar box
maré f tide
maré-baixa f low tide
maré-cheia f high tide
marfim m ivory
margarina f margarine
margem f bank; edge
marido m husband

marinada f marinade
marinha f navy
marinheiro m sailor
marisco m seafood; shellfish
marisqueira f shellfish restaurant
marmelada f quince preserve
marmelo m quince; **marmelos assados** baked quince
mármore m marble (substance)
mármores mpl articles made from marble
marque: marque o número desejado dial the number you want
Marrocos Morocco
marroquinaria f leather goods
martelo m hammer
martini m Martini
mas but
máscara f mascara
masculino m male
massa f dough; **massas** pasta; **massa folhada** puff pastry
massagista m masseur; **massagista e manicura** massage and manicure
mastro m mast
mata f forest
matar to kill
matéria f material; substance
material material
maternidade f maternity hospital
mato m bush
matraquilhos mpl table football
matrícula f number plate; **matrícula do carro** car number
matrimónio m marriage
mau (má) bad
maxila f jaw
máximo(a) maximum

mazagran m iced coffee and lemon

me me

mecânica geral f general repairs

mecânico m mechanic

mecanismo m mechanism

média f average

medicamento m medicine

médico(a) m/f doctor

medida f measure; size; **feito por medida** made-to-measure; **na medida em que** as far as

medieval medieval

médio(a) medium

medir to measure

Mediterrâneo m the Mediterranean

medo m fear

medusa f jellyfish

meia f sock

meia-hora f half an hour

meia-idade: de meia-idade middle-aged

meia-noite f midnight

meias fpl stockings; **meias de vidro** hosiery

meigo(a) gentle; tender

meio m middle; **no meio de** in the middle of

meio(a) half; **meio bilhete** half fare; **meia desfeita** cod and chickpeas; **meia garrafa** a half bottle; **meia de leite** glass of milk; **meia pensão** half board; **duas e meia** half past two

meio-dia m midday; noon

meio-seco medium sweet (wine)

mel m honey; **a lua-de-mel** honeymoon

melancia f watermelon

melão m melon; **melão com presunto** melon and ham

melhor best; better

melhorar to get better

meloa f small melon; **meloa com vinho do Porto/da Madeira** small melon with Port or Madeira wine

melocoton m peach melba

melodia f tune

membro m member

memória f memory

mencionar to mention

menina f Miss; girl

menino m boy

menor smaller

menos least; less; **menos leite** less milk; **pelo menos** at least; **mais ou menos** more or less; **o menos importante** the least important

mensageiro(a) m/f messenger

mensagem f message

menstruação f period (menstruation)

mercado m market; **mercado municipal** town market; **o dia de mercado** market day

mercearia f grocer's

merceeiro m grocer

merengue m meringue

mergulhador(a) m/f diver

mergulho m dive

mês m month

mesa f table; **na mesa** on the table

mesmo(a) same; even; **mesmo assim** even so; **mesmo que** even though; **dá na mesma** it's all the same

mesquita f mosque

mestre m master

metade f half; **metade do preço** half price

metal m metal

meter to put; to place

método m method

metro m metre; underground (railway)

metropolitano m underground (railway); tube (underground); **a estação do metropolitano** underground station

meu (minha) my; **o meu é ...** mine is ...; **os meus são ...** mine are ...; **o meu pai** my father; **os meus pais** my parents; **é meu** it is mine; **a minha mãe** my mother

mexer to move; **não mexer** do not touch

mexilhão m mussel

micróbio m germ

migas fpl: **migas à alentejana** thick bread soup

mil thousand; **mil folhas** sweet flaky pastry

milha f mile

milhão m million

milho m maize; **milho doce** corn (sweet corn); **a farinha de milho** cornflour

milímetro m millimetre

mim me

minha see **meu**

mini-autocarro m minibus

mini-golf m mini-golf

mini-mercado m small supermarket

mínimo(a) minimum

ministério m ministry

ministro m minister

minoria f minority

minúsculo(a) tiny

minuto m minute

miolos mpl (sheep's) brains; **miolos com ovos** brains with eggs

mirar to look at

missa f mass

mistério m mystery

mistura f mixture;

petrol/oil mix (*2-stroke*)

misturadora *f* mixer tap

misturar to mix

miúdo(a) *m/f* child

miúdos *mpl*: **miúdos de cabrito** offals of kid in garlic sauce

mo = me + o; dê-mo give me it

mobília *f* furniture

mochila *f* backpack; rucksack

moço *m* youth; boy

moda *f* fashion; **na moda** popular (*fashionable*); **moda jovem** young people's fashions; **modas** fashion wear; **modas para senhora** ladies' fashions

modelo *m* model

moderno(a) modern

modo *m* manner; way; **de modo que** so that

moeda *f* coin; currency

moído(a) ground (*coffee etc*)

moinha *f* dull pain

moinho *m* windmill; **moinho de café** coffee grinder

mola *f* peg; spring (*coiled metal etc*)

mole soft

moleja *f* soup made with pig's blood

molhado(a) wet

molhar to soak

molho *m* sauce; gravy; **molho bearnaise** sauce made from egg yolk, lemon juice and herbs; **molho bechamel** béchamel sauce; **molho branco** white sauce; **molho de cogumelos** creamed mushroom sauce; **molho cor-de-rosa** creamy tomato sauce; **molho à espanhola** spicy onion

and garlic sauce; **molho holandês** hollandaise sauce; **molho ao Madeira** Madeira wine sauce; **molho mornay** béchamel sauce with cheese; **molho mousseline** hollandaise sauce with cream; **molho tártaro** tartar sauce; **molho de tomate** tomato and onion purée; **molho veloutée** white sauce with egg yolks and cream; **molho vinagrete** vinaigrette

momento *m* moment; **(só) um momento** just a moment

monge *m* monk

monótono(a) boring

montanha *f* mountain

montanhismo *m* hill-walking

montante *m* amount (*total*)

montar to ride (*on horse*)

monte *m* hill; pile

montra *f* shop window

monumento *m* monument

morada *f* address

moradia *f* villa

morango *m* strawberry; **morangos com chantilly** strawberries and whipped cream

morar to live; to stay

morcela *f* black pudding

mordedura de insecto *f* insect bite

morder to bite; **ele foi mordido** he has been bitten

morgados *mpl* almond sweets

moroso(a) slow

morrer to die

mortadela *f* spicy sausage

morto(a) dead; killed

mosaicos *mpl* mosaic tiles

mosca *f* fly (*insect*)

moscatel *m* muscatel wine

mosquito *m* mosquito

mostarda *f* mustard

mosteiro *m* monastery

mostrador *m* dial; glass counter

mostrar to show

mota *f* motorbike; **mota aquática** wet bike; jet ski

motel *m* motel

motivo *m* pattern (*design*); cause

motocicleta *f* motorbike

motociclismo *m* motorbike racing

motor *m* engine; motor; **motor de arranque** starter motor; **motor fora de borda** outboard motor

motorista *m* driver

motorizada *f* motorbike

Mouraria *f* Moorish quarter

Mouros *mpl* Moors (*people*)

mousse *f* mousse; styling mousse; **mousse de chocolate** chocolate mousse; **mousse de fiambre** ham soufflé; **mousse de leite condensado** condensed milk mousse

móveis *mpl* furniture; **móveis de cozinha** kitchen furniture

móvel *m* piece of furniture

mover to move

muçulmano(a) Muslim

mudança *f* change (*money*)

mudar to change (*clothes*)

mudo(a) dumb (*unable to speak*)

muito very; much; quite (*rather*); very much; **Muito atentamente** Yours sincerely; **muito mais quente** much hotter; **muito obrigado** thank you very much; **muito prazer em conhecê-lo** pleased to meet you

muitos(as) a lot (of); many; plenty (of); **muitas pessoas** many people; **muitas vezes** often

muleta *f* crutch

mulher *f* female; woman; wife

mulher-polícia *f* policewoman

multa *f* fine

multidão *f* crowd

multar to fine

mundial world

mundo *m* world

municipal municipal

muralhas *fpl* ramparts

murmurar to whisper

muro *m* wall

músculo *m* muscle

museu *m* museum; **museu de arte** art gallery

música *f* music

músico(a) *m/f* musician

N

na = em + a

nabo *m* turnip

nacional national

nacionalidade *f* nationality

nada nothing; **nada a declarar** nothing to declare

nadador salvador *m* lifeguard

nadar to swim

namorada *f* girlfriend

namorado *m* boyfriend

não no; not; **não é?** isn't it?; **não é verdade?** isn't it?; **a não ser que** unless; **não só** not only

não-alcoólico(a) non-alcoholic

napolitanas *fpl* long biscuits

narinas *fpl* nostrils

nariz *m* nose

nas = em + as

nascer to be born; **nasci em mil novecentos e sessenta** I was born in 1960

nata *f* cream; custard

natação *f* swimming

Natal *m* Christmas

nativo(a) native

natural natural

naturalidade *f* place of birth

naturalmente of course

natureza *f* nature

navalha de barbear *f* razor

navio *m* ship

neblina *f* mist

necessário(a) necessary

necessidade *f* need

necrologia *f* obituary column

negar to refuse

negativo(a) negative

negócio *m* bargain (*transaction*)

negócios *mpl* business; **o homem/a mulher de negócios** businessman/woman; **a viagem de negócios** business trip

negro(a) black

nela = em + ela

nele = em + ele

nem: nem ... nem ... neither ... nor ...

nenhum(a) none; **não tenho nenhum** I haven't any; **não o encontro em lado nenhum** I can't find

it anywhere; **em parte nenhuma** nowhere

nenhumas see **nenhum(a)**

nenhuns see **nenhum(a)**

nervoso(a) nervous

nêspera *f* loquat

nessa = em + essa

nesse = em + esse

nestas = em + estas

nestes = em + estes

neta *f* granddaughter

neto *m* grandson

netos *mpl* grandchildren

nevar to snow; **está a nevar** it's snowing

neve *f* snow; **coberto de neve** snowed-up

névoa *f* mist

nevoeiro *m* fog

ninguém nobody; **não vejo ninguém** I can't see anybody

ninho *m* nest

nível *m* level; **nível de vida** standard of living

no = em + o

nó *m* knot; **nó rodoviário** motorway interchange

No. see **número**

nocivo(a) harmful

nódoa *f* stain; **nódoa negra** bruise

noite *f* evening; night; **à noite** in the evening; **esta noite** this evening; tonight; **a noite de Santo António** festival on the 13th June; **a noite de São João** festival on the 24th June; **a noite de São Pedro** festival on the 29th June; **noites de gala** gala evenings; **o vestido de noite** evening dress

noiva *f* bride; fiancée

noivo *m* bridegroom; fiancé

no-lo = nos + o

nome *m* name; **nome de**

baptismo Christian name; **nome próprio** first name

nono(a) ninth

nora *f* daughter-in-law

nordeste *m* north-east

normal normal

normalmente usually

noroeste *m* north-west

norte *m* north

nos[1] us

nos[2] = **em** + **os**

nós we

nosso(a) our; **é nosso** it's ours; **o nosso carro** our car; **os nossos carros** our cars; **Nosso Senhor** Our Lord; **Nossa Senhora** Our Lady

nota *f* note; banknote

notar to notice

notário *m* notary public

notícia *f* piece of news

noticiário *m* news (*on TV, radio*)

noutra = **em** + **outra**

noutro = **em** + **outro**

novamente again

Nova Zelândia *f* New Zealand

nove nine

novecentos(as) nine hundred

Novembro *m* November

noventa ninety

novo(a) new; young

noz *f* nut; walnut

noz-moscada *f* nutmeg

nu(a) naked

nublado(a) dull (*weather*); cloudy

nuclear nuclear

numerar to number

número (No.) *m* number; size (*of clothes, shoes*); **número de telefone** phone number

numismática *f*: **numismática e selos para colecção** coin and stamp collecting items

nunca never; **nunca mais** never again

nuvens *fpl* clouds

nylon *m* nylon

O

o the; him

objectivo *m* goal

objecto *m* object; **objectos perdidos** lost property; lost and found

obra-prima *f* masterpiece

obras *fpl* roadworks

obrigado thank you

obrigatório(a) compulsory

obter to get

obviamente obviously

óbvio(a) obvious

ocasião *f* opportunity

ocaso *m* sunset

oceano *m* ocean

ocidental western

ócio *m* leisure time

oco(a) hollow

oculista *m* optician

óculos *mpl* glasses; **óculos de protecção** goggles (*for swimming*); **óculos de sol** sunglasses

ocupado(a) busy; engaged (*telephone, toilet*); occupied

odiar to hate

oeste *m* west

ofender to insult

oferecer to offer

oferta *f* offer; **oferta especial** special offer

oficial official; **oficial de bordo** *m* air steward

oficina *f* workshop

ofício *m* occupation

oitavo(a) eighth

oitenta eighty

oito eight

oitocentos(as) eight hundred

olá hello

olaria *f* pottery

óleo *m* oil; **óleo dos travões** brake fluid; **o filtro do óleo** oil filter

oleoso(a) greasy

olhar: olhar (para) to look (at); **olhe** look

olho *m* eye

oliveira *f* olive tree

ombro *m* shoulder

omeleta *f* omelette; **omeleta de camarão** shrimp omelette; **omeleta de cogumelos** mushroom omelette; **omeleta com ervas** vegetable omelette; **omeleta de fiambre** ham omelette; **omeleta de presunto** gammon omelette; **omeleta de queijo** cheese omelette

onça *f* ounce

onda *f* wave (*on sea*)

onde where

O negativo/positivo O negative/positive

ontem yesterday

onze eleven

ópera *f* opera; **o teatro de ópera** opera house

operação *f* operation

operador(a) *m/f* operator

operar to operate

operário *m* workman

opinião *f* opinion; **na minha opinião** in my opinion

oportunidade *f* opportunity

oportuno(a) convenient

optar to choose

optimista optimistic

óptimo(a) excellent

ora now; well now

oração *f* prayer

orçamento *m* budget;

orçamentos grátis free estimates

ordenado m wage

ordenar to command; to put in order

ordinário(a) coarse

orelha f ear; **orelha de porco assada** roast pig's ear; **orelha de porco de vinagrete** pig's ear in vinaigrette

organização f organization

organizado(a) organized

organizar to organize

órgão m organ

orgulhoso(a) proud

original original

ornamento m ornament

orquestra f orchestra

orquídea f orchid

os the; them

osso m bone

ostra f oyster; **ostras ao natural** oysters; **ostras recheadas** oysters stuffed with a sauce made with egg yolks

otorrinolaringólogo m ear, nose and throat specialist

ou or

ourivesaria f gold and silver goods and watches; **ourivesaria e joalharia** goldsmith's and jeweller's

ouro m gold; **de ouro** gold (*made of gold*)

outono m autumn

outro(a) other; **um outro** another (*a different one*); **outras localidades** other places; **outra vez** again; **outras vezes** other times

Outubro m October

ouvido m ear

ouvinte m/f listener

ouvir to hear; to listen (to)

oval oval

ovelha f sheep

ovo m egg; **ovo bem cozido** hard-boiled egg; **ovo cozido** boiled egg; **ovo escalfado** poached egg; **ovo escalfado sobre tostas** poached egg on toast; **ovo em geleia** jellied egg; **ovo com maionaise** egg mayonnaise; **ovo pouco cozido** soft-boiled egg; **ovo quente** soft-boiled egg; **o suporte para ovos** eggcup; **ovos egg dishes; **ovos escalfados** poached eggs; **ovos estrelados** fried eggs; **ovos mexidos** scrambled eggs; **ovos mexidos à portuguesa** scrambled eggs with peppers, tomato and garlic; **ovos moles** egg dessert; **ovos verdes** fried stuffed eggs

oxalá let's hope

oxigénio m oxygen

P

pá f shovel

paciente patient

paço m palace; **paço ducal** duke's palace

pacote m packet

padaria f baker's

padeiro m baker

padrasto m stepfather

padre m priest

padrinho m godfather; best man

pagamento m payment; **pagamento a prestações** hire purchase; **pagamento a pronto** cash payment

pagar to pay

página f page; **páginas amarelas** Yellow Pages

pago(a) paid

pai m father; parent

paio m type of salami

país m country

pais mpl parents

paisagem f scenery

palácio m palace; **Palácio Episcopal** bishop's palace

palavra f word; **palavras cruzadas** crossword puzzle

palco m stage

palestra f talk (*lecture*)

palha f straw; drinking straw

pálido(a) pale

palito m toothpick

palmeira f palm tree

panadinhos de pescada mpl fish cakes

panado(a) fried in breadcrumbs

pancada f bump; crash

panela f pan; pot; **panela de pressão** pressure cooker

panfleto m pamphlet

pânico: em pânico in panic

pano m cloth; **pano de chão de tenda** groundsheet; **pano de louça** dishcloth; **panos e mantas de tear de algodão e lãs** materials woven from cotton and wool

panqueca f pancake

pão m bread; loaf; **pão de centeio** rye bread; **pão integral** wholemeal bread; **pão de ló** sponge cake; **pão de milho** maize bread; **pão torrado** croutons; **pão de trigo** wheat bread

Papa m Pope

papeira f mumps

papéis mpl wastepaper; papers

papel m paper; **papel de**

carta writing paper; **papel de embrulho** wrapping paper; brown paper; **papel gomado** sticky paper; **papel higiénico** toilet paper; **papel de parede** wallpaper; **o lenço de papel** paper handkerchief; **o saco de papel** paper bag

papelaria f stationer's; **papelaria e livraria** bookshop and stationer's

papos de anjo mpl eggs baked in kirsch

papo-seco m roll (of bread)

par m pair

para for; towards; to; **para que** so that

parabéns mpl congratulations; happy birthday

pára-brisas f windscreen; **pára-brisas de emergência** emergency windscreen

pára-choques m bumper

parafina f paraffin

parafuso m screw

paragem f stop (for bus etc); **paragem proibida** no waiting; **paragem zona** fare stage

paralisado(a) paralysed

parar to stop

pardal m sparrow

pare: pare, escute e olhe stop, look and listen; **pare ao sinal vermelho** stop when lights are red

parecer to seem; **parece** it looks; it seems; it sounds

parede f wall

parente m relation (family)

pargo m sea bream; **pargo assado** roast

bream; **pargo cozido** boiled bream

parlamento m parliament

parque m park; **parque de campismo** campsite; **parque de campismo para caravanas** caravan site; **parque de estacionamento** car park; **parque de estacionamento subterrâneo** underground car park; **parque florestal** forestry park; **parque infantil** play group; **parque de merendas** picnic park; **parque privativo** private parking; **parque recreativo** amusement park

parquímetro m parking meter

parrilhada f grilled fish

parte f part; **em parte** partly; **a maior parte de** the majority of; **parte de trás** back (of head, of house)

particular private

partida f departure; start; **partidas** departures

partidário(a) m/f supporter

partido m party

partido(a) broken

partir to break; to leave; **a partir de ...** from ...

Páscoa f Easter

passa f raisin

passadeira f zebra crossing; **na passadeira dê prioridade aos peões** give way to pedestrians on the crossing

passado m the past

passado(a): mal passado underdone (steak); **bem passado** well done

(steak)

passageiro m passenger; **passageiros** passengers this way

passagem f: **passagem de nível** level-crossing; **passagem de peões** pedestrian crossing; **passagem proibida** no right of way; **passagem subterrânea** underpass

passajar to darn

passaporte m passport; **o controle de passaportes** passport control; **temos um passaporte familiar** we have a joint passport

passar to pass; **passar a ferro** to iron

pássaro m bird

passatempo m hobby; **passatempos** entertainment; hobbies

passe[1] m season ticket; **passe social** travel pass

passe[2] go (when crossing road); walk

passear to go for a walk

passeio m walk; pavement; **passeio de barco** boat trip; **passeio a cavalo** pony-trekking

passo m step

pasta[1] f briefcase

pasta[2] f paste; **pasta dentífrica** toothpaste

pastéis mpl cakes; croquettes; **pastéis de bacalhau** cod croquettes; **pastéis de tentugal** custard tart with almonds

pastel m pie; pastry (cake); **pastel folhado** puff pastry cake

pastelaria f pastry; café; cake shop; **pastelaria e confeitaria** baker's and confectioner's

pastilha f pastille;

pastilha elástica chewing gum; pastilhas para a garganta throat lozenges; pastilha de mentol mint (sweet)

pastor m minister (church); shepherd

pataniscas fpl salted cod fritters

paté m pâté; paté de aves chicken pâté; paté de coelho rabbit pâté; paté de fígado liver pâté; paté de galinha chicken pâté; paté de lebre hare pâté

patim m skate

patinagem f skating (ice); rollerskating

patinar to skate

pátio m courtyard

pato m duck; pato com arroz duck and rice with Port and white wine sauce; pato assado roast duck; pato com laranja duck in orange sauce

patrão m boss

pátria f home (country)

pau m stick

pavimento m: pavimento escorregadio slippery (road) surface

pé m foot; a pé on foot; ao pé de near

peão m pedestrian

peça[1] f part; play; peças e acessórios spares and accessories

peça[2]: peça folhetos ask for a leaflet; peça informações ask for information

pechincha f bargain (good buy)

pedal m pedal

pediatra m/f pediatrician

pedir to ask; pedir alguma coisa to ask for something; pedir a alguém para fazer to

ask someone to do; pedir emprestado to borrow

peditório m collection (for charity)

pedra f stone; pedra na vesícula biliar gallstone

pega f handle

pegajoso(a) sticky

pegar to stick; to grab

peito m breast; chest

peixaria f fish shop

peixe m fish; peixe congelado frozen fish

peixe-espada m swordfish; peixe-espada de escabeche marinated swordfish; peixe-espada de fricassé swordfish fricassee

pela = por + a

pelas = por + as

pele f fur; skin

película f film (for camera)

pelo = por + o

pelos = por + os

pena[1] f feather

pena[2] f pity; é pena! it's a pity!; que pena what a pity

penalidade f penalty

pendurar to hang up (clothes)

peneira f sieve

penhasco m cliff

penicilina f penicillin

pensão m boarding house; guesthouse; pensão completa full board; pensão residencial boarding house

pensar to think

penso m sticking plaster; penso higiénico sanitary towel

pente m comb

penteado m hairstyle

pentear-se to do one's hair

Pentecostes m Whitsun

peões mpl pedestrians

pepino m cucumber; pepino de conserva gherkin

pequenino(a) tiny

pequeno(a) little; small; mais pequeno smaller; pequeno almoço breakfast; pequeno almoço continental Continental breakfast

pera f pear; pera abacate avocado pear

perceber to understand; percebe? do you understand?

percebes mpl edible barnacles

percurso m route

perda f loss

perdão I beg your pardon; I'm sorry

perder to lose; to miss (train etc)

perdido(a) lost; perdidos e achados lost and found; lost property

perdiz f partridge; perdizes assadas no forno roast partridges; perdizes de escabeche marinated partridges; perdizes estufadas partridges rolled in ham and cooked with onion and carrot; perdizes fritas fried partridges; perdizes na púcara casseroled partridges

pereira f pear tree

perfeitamente of course

perfeito(a) perfect

perfumaria f perfume shop

perfume m perfume

pergunta f question

perguntar to ask

perigo m danger; perigo de incêndio fire hazard; perigo de morte extreme danger

perigoso(a) dangerous
perito(a) m/f expert
permanecer to stay
permanente f perm
permissão f permission
permitir to allow
perna f leg; **perna de carneiro assada** roast leg of lamb; **perna de carneiro entremeada** stuffed leg of lamb; **pernas de rã** frogs' legs
pernoitar to spend the night
pérola f pearl
persiana f shutter-blind
perto: perto de near; close to; **mais perto** nearer; **o mais perto** nearest; **perto do banco** near the bank
peru m turkey; **peru assado** roast turkey; **peru de fricassé** turkey fricassee; **peru recheado** stuffed turkey
pesadelo m nightmare
pesado(a) heavy; **pesados** heavy vehicles
pesar to weigh
pesca f fishing; **a cana de pesca** fishing rod; **pesca desportiva** competition fishing; **pesca à linha** line fishing; **pesca submarina** spear fishing
pescada f hake; **pescada cozida** boiled hake
pescadinhas fpl whiting; **pescadinhas de rabo na boca** whiting with their tail in their mouth
pescador m fisherman
pescar to fish
pescoço m neck
peso m weight; **peso líquido** net weight
pêssego m peach
pessegueiro m peach tree
pessimista m pessimist

péssimo(a) very bad
pessoa f person; **pessoas** people
pessoal¹ m staff
pessoal² personal
pestana f eyelash
petiscos mpl snacks
petróleo m oil
peugas fpl socks
pezinhos de coentrada mpl pig's trotters in coriander sauce
piada f joke
piano m piano
picada f sting
picado(a) stung
picante spicy
pijama m pyjamas
pilha f pile; battery (for torch)
pilotar to pilot
piloto m pilot; racing driver
pílula f the pill
pimenta f pepper
pimento m pepper (vegetable); **pimentos assados** roast peppers
pinça f tweezers
pincel m brush
pingar to drip
pingue-pongue m table tennis
pinha dourada f meringue dessert
pinhal m pine wood
pinheiro m pine tree
pintado: pintado à mão hand-painted; **pintado de fresco** wet paint
pintar to paint
pintor(a) m/f painter
pintura f painting; **pintura, cerâmica, escultura, gravura** painting, ceramics, sculpture, engravings
pionés m drawing pin
pior worse; worst
pipi m cooked sparrow
piquenique m picnic

pirata do ar m hijacker
pires m saucer
Pirinéus mpl the Pyrenees
piripiri m hot chilli dressing
piscadela de olhos f wink
pisca-pisca m indicator (on car)
piscina f swimming pool; **piscina aberta** outdoor swimming pool; **piscina aquecida** heated swimming pool; **piscina coberta** indoor swimming pool; **piscina coberta climatizada** heated indoor swimming pool; **piscina para crianças** paddling pool; **piscina exterior para crianças** children's outdoor paddling pool; **piscina de mar aquecida** heated sea-water swimming pool
piso m road surface; **piso escorregadio** slippery road surface; **piso irregular** uneven road surface
pista f track; runway
pistão m piston
planear to plan
planetário m planetarium
plano m plan
plano(a) flat; level
planta f plant
planta de Lisboa f street map of Lisbon
planta do pé f sole (of foot)
plástico m plastic; **o saco de plástico** plastic bag
plataforma f platform
plateia f stalls (in theatre)
platinados fpl points (in car)
pneu m tyre; **a pressão dos pneus** tyre pressure

pneumonia f pneumonia

pó m dust; powder; **pó de limpeza** cleaning powder; **pó de talco** talcum powder

pobre poor

poço m well

poder to be able; can; **eu posso** I can; **tu podes** you can; **ele pode** he can

poderoso(a) powerful

pôdre rotten

poeira f dust

pois yes, of course; **pois é** yes, of course; fine

polainas fpl knee socks

polegada f inch

polegar m thumb

polícia[1] f police; **o carro da polícia** police car; **Polícia de Segurança Pública (P.S.P.)** the Portuguese police

polícia[2] m policeman; police officer

policial thriller; **o filme policial** thriller; **o romance policial** thriller (*novel*)

polidesportivo m sports centre

poliéster m polyester

poliomielite f polio

polistireno m polystyrene

política f politics; policy

político(a) political

poltrona f armchair

poluição f pollution

poluído(a) polluted

polvo m octopus

pomada f ointment; **pomada para o calçado** shoe polish

pomar m orchard

pombo m pigeon

ponta f end; tip

pontapé m kick

ponte f bridge

ponteagudo(a) pointed

ponto de encontro m meeting point

popa f stern (*of boat*)

população f population

popular popular

por by (*through*); **por aqui/por ali** this/that way; **por conseguinte** therefore; **por hora** per hour; **por pessoa** per person

pôr to put; **pôr no correio** to post (*a letter*); **pôr a mesa** to lay the table

porca f nut (*for bolt*)

porção f portion

porcelana f porcelain; china

porco m pig; pork

por favor please

pormenores mpl details

porque because

porquê why

porta f door; **porta telecomandada** automatic door; **a porta No. ...** gate number ...

porta-bagagens m boot (*of car*); luggage rack

porta-biberões m babies' bottle holder

porta-chaves m key ring

portagem f toll; **portagem a 6 kilómetros** 6 kilometres to pay toll

porta-moedas m purse

portanto therefore

portão m gate (*of garden*)

portátil portable

porteiro m porter

porto[1] m harbour; **porto de pesca** fishing port

porto[2] m port (*drink*)

Porto m: **o Porto** Oporto; **o vinho do Porto** Port wine

português (portuguesa) Portuguese

posição f position

positivo(a) positive

posologia f dose

possibilidade f possibility

possível possible; **é possível que eu venha** I might come

postal f postcard; **postal de aniversário** birthday card; **postal de natal** Christmas card

posta-restante f poste-restante

poster m poster

posto m post; job; **posto clínico** first aid post; **posto de socorros** first aid centre

potente powerful

pouco(a) little; **um pouco** a little; **a pouco e pouco** little by little

poupar to save (*money, time*)

pousada f state run hotel

povo m people

povoação f village

praça f square (*in town*); **praça de táxis** taxi rank; **praça de touros** bullring

praia f beach; seaside; **praias de areia fina** fine sandy beaches

prancha f sailboard; **prancha de saltos** diving board; **prancha de surf** surfboard

prata f silver

prateado(a) silver-plated

prateleira f shelf; rack (*for bottles*)

prato m dish; plate; course (*of meal*); **prato da casa** speciality of the house; **prato do dia** today's special; **pratos tradicionais** traditional dishes

prazer m pleasure; **prazer em conhecê-lo** pleased to meet you

preçário m price list

precipício m cliff
precisamente:
  precisamente aí just
  there
precisar to need; **é**
  preciso it is necessary;
  eu preciso ... I need ...
preço m price; **preço**
  por dia price per day;
  preço por mês price per
  month; **preço por**
  pessoa price per person;
  preço por semana price
  per week; **preço de**
  venda por atacado
  wholesale price; **preço**
  de venda a retalho
  retail price; **preços**
  especiais fora de época
  special off-season prices;
  preços especiais para
  longas estadias special
  prices for long stays;
  preços de ocasião
  bargain prices; **preços**
  por pessoa/dia em
  quarto duplo double
  room charges per
  person/per day; **preços**
  reduzidos reduced
  prices; **a lista de preços**
  price list
prédio m building
preencher to fill in
preferência: de
  preferência rather
preferir to prefer
prego[1] m nail
prego[2] m beef cutlet;
  pregos (no pão) beef
  rolls
preguiçoso(a) lazy
preia-mar f high tide
prejudicar to damage
prejuízo m damage
pré-mamã m prenatal
  wear
prémio m prize
prenda f gift
preocupado(a) worried
preocupar-se to worry;

não se preocupe don't
  worry
pré-pagamento pay
  before you eat
preparação f preparation
preparado(a) ready
preparar to prepare;
  prepare pagamento
  have your money ready
presente m gift; present
preservativo m condom
presidente m/f president
pressa f hurry
pressão f pressure;
  pressão dos pneus tyre
  pressure
prestar: preste atenção
  pay attention; **não**
  presta it is no good
presunto m ham
preto(a) black
previsão f forecast
prima f cousin (female)
primário(a) primary
primavera f spring
  (season)
primeiro(a) first;
  primeiro andar first
  floor; **primeira classe**
  first class (seat etc);
  primeiros socorros first
  aid
primeiro-ministro m
  prime minister
primo m cousin (male)
princesa f princess
principal main
príncipe m prince
principiante m/f beginner
princípio m beginning; **ao**
  princípio in the
  beginning
prioridade f priority;
  prioridade à direita give
  way to the right
prisão f prison; **com**
  prisão de ventre
  constipated
privado(a) private
proa f bow (of ship)
problema m problem;

problemas trouble
processo m process; trial
procissão f procession
procuração f power of
  attorney
procurar to look for
produção f production
produto m product;
  proceeds; **produtos**
  alimentares foodstuffs;
  produtos de beleza
  beauty products;
  produtos para
  diabéticos products for
  diabetics; **produtos**
  expostos são para
  consumo da casa items
  on display are for
  consumption on the
  premises only; **produtos**
  de limpeza cleaning
  products; **produtos**
  naturais health foods
produzir to produce
professor(a) m/f teacher
profissão f profession;
  profissão, idade, nome
  profession, age and name
profissional professional
profundidade f depth
profundo(a): pouco
  profundo shallow
prognóstico do tempo
  m weather forecast
programa m programme
proibido(a) forbidden;
  proibido acampar no
  camping; **proibido afixar**
  cartazes stick no bills;
  proibida a entrada keep
  out; no entry; **proibida a**
  entrada a cães no dogs;
  proibida a entrada a
  menores de ... anos no
  admittance to those
  under ... years of age;
  proibida a entrada a
  pessoas estranhas ao
  serviço staff only;
  proibido estacionar no
  parking; **proibido fumar**

no smoking; **proibida a paragem** no stopping; **proibida a passagem** no access; **proibido pisar a relva** do not walk on the grass; **proibido tirar fotografias** no photographs; **proibido tomar banho** no bathing

projecção f: **projecção de filmes** film show; **projecção de gravilha** loose chippings

projectar to plan

projecto m plan; project

promessa f promise

prometer to promise

promoção f special offer

pronto(a) ready

pronto-a-comer take away

pronto-a-vestir ready-to-wear

pronto-socorro m breakdown van

pronunciar to pronounce

propina f fee

proporção f rate

propósito m intention; **a propósito** by the way; **de propósito** on purpose

propriedade f estate (property); **propriedade privada** private property

proprietário m owner

protecção f protection

protector da pele m skin protection cream

proteger to shelter; **proteger do calor e da humidade** store in a cool dry place

prótese dentária m dental fittings

protestante Protestant

prova f proof; **prova (de vinho)** sampling (of wine)

provar to taste; to try on

provável likely

provavelmente probably

província f province

provisório(a) temporary

próximo(a) near; next; **próxima sessão às ... horas** next performance at ...

prudente careful (prudent)

psiquiatra m/f psychiatrist

P.S.P. see **polícia**[1]

publicidade f advertising

público m audience

público(a) public

pudim m pudding; **pudim de amêndoa** almond pudding; **pudim flan** crème caramel; **pudim de frutas** fruit pudding; **pudim de laranja** orange pudding; **pudim de leite** milk pudding; **pudim molotov** caramel and whipped egg white; **pudim de ovos** egg pudding; **pudim de peixe** fish baked in a mould

pulga f flea

pulmão m lung

pulover m sweater; pullover

pulsação f pulse

pulseira f bracelet; wrist strap; **pulseira de relógio** watchstrap

pulso m wrist

punho m cuff

pupila f pupil (of eye)

pura lã f pure wool

puré m: **puré de batata** mashed potato; **puré de castanhas** chestnut purée

purificador do ar m air freshener

puro(a) pure

puxador m handle (of door, suitcase)

puxar to pull; **puxar a**

alavanca em caso de emergência pull lever in case of emergency; **puxar o autoclismo** to flush (toilet)

puxe pull

Q

quadrado(a) square (shape)

quadril m hip

quadro m picture; painting; **quadro de instrumentos** dashboard

qual which; **qual é?** which is it?

qualidade f quality

qualquer: de qualquer maneira anyway; **em qualquer parte** anywhere; somewhere; **qualquer medicamento deve estar fora do alcance das crianças** keep all medicines out of the reach of children

quando when; **quando tenho que fazer o pagamento?** when is it due? (money)

quantia f amount

quantidade f quantity

quanto how much; **quantos(as)?** how many?; **quanto custa?** how much does it cost?; **quanto tempo?** how long? (time); **quantos são hoje?** what's the date? **quanto a ...** as far as ...

quarenta forty

quarentena f quarantine

quarta-feira f Wednesday

quartel m barracks

quarto[1] m room; bedroom; **quartos alcatifados** carpets in all rooms; **quarto de banho** bathroom; **quarto com duas camas** twin-bedded room; **quarto de casal** double room; **quarto para duas pessoas** double room

quarto[2] fourth; quarter; **um quarto de hora** a quarter of an hour; **um quarto para as duas** quarter to 2; **duas e um quarto** quarter past 2; **quarto andar** fourth floor

quase almost

quatro four

quatrocentos(as) four hundred

que what; **o que é?** what is it?; **que livro?** what book?; **o quê?** what?

quebra-cabeças *m* jigsaw puzzle

quebra-luz *m* lampshade

quebra-mar *m* pier

quebrar to crack; to break; **quebrar em caso de emergência** break in case of emergency

queda *f* fall; **queda de pedras** falling rocks

queijada *f* cheesecake; **queijadas de Tomar** almond cup cakes

queijo *m* cheese; **queijo de Azeitão** soft, smooth cheese; **queijo de cabra** goat's milk cheese; **queijo de Castelo Branco** sheep's milk cheese; **queijos e doces** cheeses and desserts; **queijo fresco** mild goat's milk cheese; **queijo da Ilha** peppery cheese from the Azores; **queijo de ovelha** sheep's milk cheese; **queijo do Pico** cow's milk cheese; **queijo Rabaçal** sheep's

milk cheese; **queijo saloio** sheep's milk cheese; **queijo de São Jorge** cow's milk cheese; **queijo de Serpa** cheese with a strong smell and taste; **queijo da Serra** sheep's milk cheese; **queijo da Serra da Gardunha** goat's milk cheese

queimado(a) burnt

queimadura *f* burn; **queimadura do sol** sunburn (*painful*)

queimar to burn

queixa *f* complaint (*about goods etc*)

queixar-se de to complain about

queixo *m* chin

quem who; **de quem é?** whose is it?

quente hot; warm; **água quente** hot water; **a botija de água quente** hot-water bottle

quer ... quer ... either ... or ...

querer to want; to wish; **quero** I want; **eu quero fazer** I want to do; **quer dizer** that is to say; **quería** I would like

querido(a) *m/f* darling

questão *f* question

queito(a) quiet

quilo(grama) (kg) *m* kilo

quilómetro *m* kilometre

quinhentos(as) five hundred

quinquilharias *fpl*: **quinquilharias e velharias** bric-à-brac and curios

quinta *f* farm

quinta-feira *f* Thursday

quintal *m* garden; yard

quinto fifth; **quinto andar** fifth floor

quinze fifteen

quinzena *f* fortnight

quiosque *m* kiosk; newsstand

quota *f* share

quotidiano(a) daily

R

R. street

rã *f* frog

rabanadas *fpl* French toast

rabanete *m* radish

rabino *m* rabbi

rabo *m* tail

raça *f* race (*people*)

radiador *m* radiator

rádio *m*: **a rádio** radio broadcasting; radio; **o rádio** radio set

radioactivo(a) radioactive

Radiodifusão *f*: **Radiodifusão Portuguesa (R.D.P.)** Portuguese Radio

radiografia *f* X-ray

rádio-telefone *m* radio-telephone

Radiotelevisão *f*: **Radiotelevisão Portuguesa (R.T.P.)** Portuguese Television

râguebi *m* rugby

raia *f* skate (*fish*)

rainha *f* queen

raio *m* beam; **raio X** X-ray

raiva *f* rabies

raiz *f* root

rali *m* rally(-driving)

ramo *m* branch (*of tree*)

rampa *f* ramp

rapariga *f* girl

rapaz *m* boy

rapidez *f* speed

rápido *m* express (*train*)

rápido(a) fast

raposa f fox

rapto m kidnapping

raqueta f racket; **raqueta de ténis** tennis racket

raro(a) rare

rasgado(a) torn

rasgão m tear (*rip*)

rasgar to tear

raspar to scrape

ratazana f rat

rato m mouse

razão f reason

R/C see **rés-do-chão**

R.D.P. see **Radiodifusão**

real real; royal

realizador m director (*cinema*)

realmente in fact

rebentar to blow (*fuse, light bulb*); to burst

rebocar to tow

reboques mpl towing service; breakdown service

rebuçado m sweet; **rebuçado de hortelã-pimenta** peppermint (*sweet*)

recado m message

recauchutado m retread

receber to receive

receita f recipe; **receita médica** prescription

receitar to prescribe

recepção f desk (*in hotel etc*); reception

recepcionista m/f receptionist

receptor m receiver

recheio m filling (*in cake etc*); stuffing

recibo m receipt

recinto: em recinto coberto indoors (*sports etc*)

reclamação f reclaim; complaint; **reclamações** complaints; **reclamação de bagagem** baggage reclaim

recolha f delivery; **recolha e entrega ao domicílio** collected and delivered to your home

recolher to collect

recomendar to recommend

recomendável advisable

recompensa f reward

recompor-se to recover

reconhecer to recognize

recordação f souvenir

recordar-se to remember

recostável reclining

recreio m recreation; pastime

rectangular oblong

recto(a) straight; honest

recuperar to recover (*from illness*)

recusar to refuse

rede f net; **rede de autocarros** bus network

redondo(a) round (*shape*)

redução f reduction; discount

reduza a velocidade reduce speed; slow

reembolsar to reimburse

reembolso m refund

refeição f meal; **refeição da casa** set menu; **refeições ligeiras** light meals; snacks

refogado fried in oil with garlic and vinegar

reformado(a)[1] retired

reformado(a)[2] m/f senior citizen; pensioner

refrescar to cool

refrescos mpl refreshments

regar to water

regatas fpl boat races

região f area (*region*); **região demarcada** official wine producing region (*on wine label*)

regional regional

registado(a) registered

registar to register

regra f rule

regressar to come back

regresso m return

régua f ruler

regulamentos mpl regulations

regular to adjust (*timing etc*)

rei m king

reina f queen

Reino Unido m United Kingdom

rejeitar to refuse

relâmpago m lightning

religião f religion

relógio m watch; clock (*small*); **relógio de calendário** calendar watch; **relógio de cozinha** kitchen clock; **relógio de mesa** table clock; **relógio de parede** wall clock; **relógio de pulso** wristwatch; **relógio de sala** living-room clock

relojoaria f watchmaker's shop

relva f grass; **não pisar a relva** keep off the grass

remar to row

rematar to kick; to shoot (*ball*)

remédio m medicine; remedy

remendar to mend

remetente m sender

remo m oar; rowing

renda[1] f lace; **rendas de bilros** handwoven lacework

renda[2] f rent

rendimento m income

reparação f repair; **reparações** repairs

reparar to fix; to repair

repartir to share

repelente m insect

repellent

repente: de repente suddenly

repetir to repeat

repolho *m* cabbage

reportagem *f* report

repousante relaxing

repousar to rest; to relax

representação *f* performance

reprovar to fail

réptil *m* reptile

república *f* republic

requeijão *m* curd cheese

rés-do-chão (R/C) *m* ground floor

reserva *f* reservation; booking; **reserva de hotéis e apartamentos** hotel reservations and apartments; **reserva de lugar** seat reservation; **reserva natural** nature reserve; **reservas e passagens** tickets and reservations

reservado(a) reserved

reservar to book (*room, sleeper*); to reserve

resfriamento *m* cold

residência *f* boarding house; residence

residir to live

respeito *m* respect; **no que diz respeito a** as regards

respirar to breathe

responder to answer; to reply; **responder a uma pergunta/a alguém** to answer a question/ someone

responsabilidade *f* responsibility

responsável responsible

resposta *f* answer

ressaca *f* hangover

ressonar to snore

restar to remain

restaurante *m*

restaurant; **restaurante chinês** Chinese restaurant; **restaurante disco** restaurant with disco floor; **restaurante grego** Greek restaurant; **restaurante panorâmico** restaurant with a view

resto *m*: **o resto** the rest (*those left*)

resultado *m* result

retalhista *m* retailer

retalho *m* oddment; **vender a retalho** to retail

retirar: retirar o auscultador do descanso lift the phone off the hook

retrato *m* portrait

retrete *f* lavatory

retrosaria *f* haberdashery

reumatismo *m* rheumatism

reunião *f* meeting

revelação *f* development (*of photos*)

revelar to develop (*photos*)

reverso *m* the other side

revestir to cover

revisão *f* revision; servicing

revisor *m* ticket collector

revista *f* magazine

ria *f* river mouth

ribeiro *m* stream

rico(a) rich

ridículo(a) ridiculous

rijo(a) hard; stiff

rímel ® *m* mascara

ringue de patinagem *m* skating rink

rins *mpl* kidneys; **rins ao Madeira** kidneys in Madeira wine sauce

rio *m* river

riqueza *f* wealth

rir to laugh

risca do cabelo *f* parting (*in hair*)

riscar to scratch (*paint*)

riscas: às riscas striped

risco *m* risk

riso *m* smile

rissol *m* rissole; **rissóis de camarão** shrimp rissoles

R.N. *see* **rodoviária**

robalo *m* rock bass

robe *m* dressing gown

rochas *fpl* rocks

roda *f* wheel

rodeado: rodeado de pinheiros surrounded by pine trees

rodovalho *m* turbot

rodoviária *f*: **Rodoviária Nacional (R.N.)** national bus company

rojões *mpl* cubes of pork; **rojões à minhota** fried pork loins in red pepper sauce

rolar to roll

roleta *f* roulette

rolha *f* cork

rolo *m* cartridge (*for camera*); roll; **rolos** roll of film; **rolo de carne** meat loaf; **rolo a cores** colour film

romance *m* novel; **romance policial** thriller (*novel*)

rosa *f* rose

rosé *m* light, dry or sweet wine

rosto *m* face

rota *f* course; route

roteiro *m* guide book; **roteiro de bolso** pocket guide

roto(a) torn

rótulo *m* label

roubado(a) stolen; **fui roubado** I've been robbed

roubar to steal; to rob

rouco(a) hoarse; **está rouco** he's lost his voice

roupa *f* clothes; **roupas**

clothes; **roupa interior** underwear; **a mola da roupa** clothespeg; **roupa suja** washing; laundry (*clothes*)
roxo(a) purple
R.T.P. see **radiotelevisão**
rua (R.) f street; **rua secundária** side street
rubéola f German measles
ruga f wrinkle
ruibarbo m rhubarb
ruído m noise
ruínas fpl ruins; **ruínas romanas** Roman remains
rum m rum
rumo m direction
ruptura f break

S

S. see **São**
sábado m Saturday; **sábados, domingos e feriados** Saturdays, Sundays and public holidays
sabão m soap; **sabão em flocos** soapflakes; **sabão em pó** soap powder
saber to know (*fact*)
sabonete m soap (*perfumed*)
saboneteira f soap dish
sabor m flavour; taste
saborear to taste
saboroso(a) savoury
saca f sack
sacarina f saccharin
saca-rolhas m corkscrew
saco m bag; handbag; **saco cama** sleeping bag; **saco das compras** shopping bag; **saco do lixo** bin bag; **saco de plástico** plastic bag; carrier bag; **saco de viagem** flight bag; travel

bag
sadio(a) healthy
safio m sea eel
safira f sapphire
saia f skirt
saída f exit; **saídas** departures; **saída de emergência** emergency exit; **saída de veículos – não estacionar** exit – keep clear
saiote m petticoat
sair to go out; to come out; **sair com** to take out (*person*); **ele saiu** he's out; **não sai** it won't come off (*mark*)
sal m salt
sala f room; **sala de aula** classroom; **sala de banho** bathroom; **sala de bingo** bingo hall; **sala de chá** tea room; **sala de conferências e banquetes** conference and banquet hall; **sala de convívio** lounge; **sala de divertimentos** amusement arcade; **sala de embarque** lounge (*at airport*); **sala de espera** waiting room; **sala de espera para partidas** departure lounge; **sala de estar** living room; lounge (*in hotel, house*); **sala de jantar** dining room; **sala de jogos** playroom; amusement hall; **sala de reunião** meeting hall; **sala de ténis de mesa** table tennis room; **sala de televisão** TV lounge; **com sala de conferências e de projecção** with conference hall and projection facilities
salada f salad; **salada de agrião** watercress salad;

salada de alface lettuce salad; **salada de atum** tuna and potato in egg sauce; **salada de chicória** chicory salad; **salada de frutas** fruit salad; **salada de gambas** prawn cocktail; **salada de lagosta** lobster salad; **salada mista** mixed salad; **salada de ovas** fish roe salad; **salada de pepino** cucumber salad; **salada de pimentos** green pepper salad; **salada à portuguesa** tomato, peppers, carrot, onion, beetroot, egg, cucumber and radish salad; **salada russa** Russian salad; **salada de tomate** tomato salad
salame m salami
salão m hall (*for concerts etc*); **salão de beleza** beauty salon; **salão de chá** tea room; **salão de convívio** lounge; **salão de festas** party lounge
salário m wages
saldo m sale (*of bargains*); **saldos** sales
salgado(a) salty
salmão m salmon; **salmão fumado** smoked salmon
salmonete m mullet; **salmonetes grelhados** grilled mullet
salpicão m salami sausage; spicy sausage
salsa f parsley
salsicha f sausage; **salsichas de cocktail** cocktail sausages; **salsicha de Frankfurt** frankfurter; **salsichas de peru** turkey sausages; **salsichas de porco** pork sausages
salsicharia f delicatessen

saltar to jump
salteado(a) sautéed
salto *m* jump
salvar to rescue; to save (*rescue*)
salva-vidas *m* lifeboat
salvo(a) safe
samba *m* samba
sandálias *fpl* sandals
sandes *f* sandwich; **sandes de fiambre** ham sandwich; **sandes de lombo** steak sandwich; **sandes mista** mixed sandwich; **sandes de paio** sausage sandwich; **sandes de presunto** ham sandwich; **sandes de queijo** cheese sandwich
sanduíche *f* sandwich
sangrar to bleed; **sangrar do nariz** to have a nosebleed
sangria *f* sangria
sangue *m* blood
sanitários *mpl* toilets
Santa (Sta.) *f* saint
Santo (Sto.) *m* saint
santo(a) holy
santola *f* spider crab; **santola gratinada** spider crab au gratin
São (S.) *m* Saint
são (sã) healthy; **são e salvo** safe and sound
são *see* **ser**
sapataria *f* shoe shop
sapateira *f* a kind of crab
sapateiro *m* shoemaker
sapatilhas *fpl* training shoes
sapato *m* shoe; **sapatos e malas** leather goods (*shoes and cases*)
saquinhos de chá *mpl* teabags
sarampo *m* measles
sarar to heal
sardinha *f* sardine; **sardinhas assadas** grilled

sardines; **sardinhas assadas na brasa** charcoal-grilled sardines
sardinhada *f* sardine party
sarja *f* serge (*cloth*)
S.A.R.L. *see* **sociedade**
satisfeito(a) happy; satisfied
saudação *f* greeting
saudades *fpl*: **ter saudades** to be homesick
saudar to greet
saudável healthy
saúde *f* health; **saúde!** cheers!; **bem de saúde** fit
sauna *f* sauna
se[1] if; **se bebeu não conduza** don't drink and drive; **se faz favor (S.F.F.)** please
se[2] himself; herself; yourself; themselves
sé *f* cathedral
seara *f* cornfield
sebe *f* hedge
sebo *m* suet
seca *f* drought
secador *m* drier; **secador de cabelo** hair drier; **secador de roupa** clothes drier
secar to dry; to drain (*tank*); **não secar à máquina** do not spin-dry
secção *f* department (*in store*); **secção de criança** children's department; **secção de perdidos e achados** lost property office; **secção de talho** meat section
seco(a) dry
secretária *f* secretary
secretaria *f* general office
secreto(a) secret
século *m* century; **no século vinte** in the

twentieth century
secundário(a) secondary
seda *f* silk
sedativo *m* sedative
sede *f* thirst; **ter sede** to be thirsty
segmento *m* piston ring
segredo *m* secret
seguinte following
seguir to follow; **seguir pela direita** keep to your right; **seguir pela esquerda** keep to your left
segunda-feira *f* Monday
segundo *m* second (*time*)
segundo(a) second; **segundo andar** second floor; **de segunda classe** second class (*seat etc*); **em segunda mão** second-hand
segurança *f* safety
segurar to hold
seguro *m* insurance; **seguros** insurance services; **a apólice de seguro** insurance policy; **a companhia de seguros** insurance company; **seguro de fronteira** green cards here; **seguro contra terceiros** third party insurance; **seguro contra todos os riscos** comprehensive insurance; **seguro de viagem** travel insurance
seguro(a) safe (*medicine, beach*); reliable (*method*); sure
seio *m* breast
seis six
seiscentos(as) six hundred
seixos *mpl* pebbles
sela *f* saddle
selecção *f* selection; **selecção de queijos** selection of cheeses;

selecção nacional national team
seleccionar to choose
self-service *m* self-service
selo *m* stamp; **selo de garantia** seal of guarantee; **selos fiscais** official stamps (*for deeds etc*)
selva *f* jungle
selvagem wild
sem without; **sem corantes** does not contain artificial colouring; **sem corantes nem conservantes** does not contain artificial colouring or preservatives; **sem entrada e sem juros em 12, 18 ou 24 meses** no deposit and interest free for 12, 18 or 24 months; **sem necessidade de marcação** no appointment necessary
semáforos *mpl* traffic lights
semana *f* week; **esta semana** this week; **para a semana/na semana passada** next/last week; **por semana** weekly (*rate etc*); **o fim de semana** weekend
semanal weekly
semanário *m* weekly newspaper
semelhante similar
sempre always
senha de saída *f* ticket (*at the cinema, disco etc*)
senhor *m* sir; **Senhor Mr; Exmo. Senhor** Dear Sir (*in letter*)
senhora *f* lady; madam; **Senhora** Mrs, Ms; **senhoras** Ladies'
senhoria *f* landlady (*of property*)

senhorio *m* landlord (*of property*)
sensação *f* feeling; sensation
sensacional terrific
sensato(a) sensible
sentado(a) sitting
sentar-se to sit (down)
sentido *m* sense; meaning; **sentido único** one-way street
sentimento *m* feeling
sentir to feel
separado(a) separate
separar to separate
sepultura *f* grave; tomb
sequer even
ser to be; **nós somos** we are; **vocês são** you are; **ele/ela é** he/she is; **eu não sou** I am not; **eles/elas são** they are; **a não ser que** unless
sereno(a) calm; quiet
série *f* serial; **série televisiva** TV series; serial
seringa *f* syringe
sério(a) serious
seronegativo(a) HIV negative
seropositivo(a) HIV positive
serpente *f* serpent; snake
serra[1] *f* saw
serra[2] *f* mountain range
serralheiro *m* locksmith
serrar to saw
servente *f* assistant
serviço *m* service; room service; service charge; cover charge; **vinte e quatro horas serviço de quartos** 24 hour room service; **com serviço à carta e ementa do dia** we serve both à la carte or menu of the day; **serviço de babysitter** babysitting service; **serviço expresso**

express service; **serviço (não) incluído** service (not) included; **serviços de informação** information service; **serviço de lavagem automática** laundromat service; **serviço de peças** spare parts service; **serviço permanente** 24 hour service; **serviço de pneus** tyre service; **serviço de pronto-socorro** breakdown service; **serviço rápido** speedy service; **serviço de reboque** breakdown service; **serviço de recepção e relações com o público** reception and public relations service; **serviço religioso** religious service; **serviço telegráfico** telegraph service; **serviço de telex** telex service
servir to serve; **serve-se das ... horas às ... horas** meals served from ... o'clock until ... o'clock
sessão *f* session; performance
sessenta sixty
sesta *f* siesta
seta *f* arrow; dart
sete seven
setecentos(as) seven hundred
Setembro *m* September
setenta seventy
sétimo(a) seventh; **sétimo andar** seventh floor
seu (sua) his; her; your; **o seu filho** his son; **os seus filhos** your sons; é **seu** it's yours; **a sua mãe** her mother; **as suas filhas** her daughters; **o seu é ...**

yours is ...; **os seus são** ... yours are ...
sexo m sex
sexta-feira f Friday; **a Sexta-feira Santa** Good Friday
sexto(a) sixth
S.F.F. see se¹
shampô m shampoo
si you; **para si** for you
SIDA f AIDS
sidra f cider
significado m meaning
significar to mean
silenciador m silencer
silêncio m silence
silencioso(a) silent
sim yes
símbolo m symbol
similar similar
simpatia f friendliness; kindness
simpático(a) nice
simpatizar to like; to get on with
simples simple; plain
sinagoga f synagogue
sinal m signal; deposit (part payment); **sinal de alarme** communication cord; **sinal de impedido** engaged tone; **sinal de marcação** dialling tone; **sinal de tocar** ringing tone; **sinal de trânsito** road sign
sinalização f system of traffic signs
sincero(a) honest
sindicato m trade union
sino m bell
sinónimo m meaning
sintoma m symptom
sinuoso(a) crooked
sirva-se: sirva-se à temperatura ambiente serve at room temperature; **sirva-se fresco** serve cool; **sirva-se gelado** serve chilled
sisa f property transfer

tax
sistema m system; **sistema de arrefecimento** cooling system
sítio m place; spot; **sítio tranquilo** quiet location
situação f situation
situado(a) situated
slide m slide (photo)
smoking m dinner jacket
snack-bar m snack bar
só only; **não só** not only; **só pode vender-se mediante receita médica** available only on prescription
soalheiro(a) sunny
soalho m floor
soar to sound
sob under
sobrancelha f eyebrow
sobre over; **sobre o mar** overlooking the sea
sobrecarga f excess load; surcharge
sobreiro m cork tree
sobremesa f dessert
sobressair to stand out
sobressalente: a peça sobressalente spare part; **a roda sobressalente** spare wheel
sobretudo¹ m overcoat
sobretudo² above all
sobrinha f niece
sobrinho m nephew
sobrolho m eyebrow
socialista socialist
sociedade f society; **Sociedade Anónima de Responsabilidade Limitada (S.A.R.L.)** Ltd.; limited company
sócio m member; partner
socorrer to help
socorro m: **socorro!** help!; **socorro 115** emergency service 999; **socorros e sinistrados**

accidents and emergencies
sofá m couch
sogra f mother-in-law
sogro m father-in-law
soirée f evening performance (cinema etc)
sol m sun
sola f sole (of shoe)
soldado m soldier
soldar to weld; to solder
soletrar to spell
solha f flounder; **solha assada no forno** baked flounder; **solha frita** fried flounder; **solha recheada** stuffed flounder
sólido(a) solid
solitário(a) lonely
solteiro(a) single (not married); **de solteiro** single (bed, room)
solto(a) loose
solúvel soluble
som m sound
soma f amount (sum)
somar to add
sombra f shadow (in sun); eye shadow
sonhar to dream
sonho m dream
sonhos mpl milk and egg fritter
sono m sleep; **estar com sono** to be sleepy; **ter sono** to be sleepy
sopa f soup; **sopa de agriões** cress soup; **sopa alentejana** egg, bread, garlic and coriander soup; **sopa de alho francês** leek soup; **sopa de amêijoas/conquilhas** clam/baby clam soup; **sopa de camarão** thick shrimp soup; **sopa de carne** bone soup with carrots, peas and turnip; **sopa de cebola gratinada** onion soup au gratin; **sopa de cozido**

meat soup; **sopa do dia** soup of the day; **sopa dourada** egg-based dessert; **sopa de espargos** asparagus soup; **sopa de espinafres** spinach and potato soup; **sopa de feijão-verde** green bean soup; **sopa de grão** chickpea soup; **sopa Juliana** vegetable soup; **sopa de lagosta** lobster soup; **sopa de legumes** fresh vegetable soup; **sopa de ostras** oyster soup; **sopa de ovo** boiled eggs in potato and onion purée; **sopa de pão e coentros** soup with bread and coriander; **sopa de pedra** tomato soup with spicy sausage, beans and potatoes; **sopa de peixe** fish soup; **sopa de pescada** fish head soup; **sopa de rabo de boi** oxtail soup; **sopa de sangue de porco** pig's blood and liver soup; **sopa de tartaruga** turtle soup; **sopa de tomate** cream of tomato soup; **sopa de tomate alentejana** tomato soup with bread, eggs, onion and garlic
soporífero m sleeping pill
soprar to blow
sorrir to smile
sorriso m smile
sorte f luck; fortune; **boa sorte** good luck
sorvete m ice cream
sossegado(a) quiet
sótão m attic
soufflé m soufflé; **soufflé de camarão** prawn soufflé; **soufflé de chocolate** chocolate soufflé; **soufflé de**

cogumelos mushroom soufflé; **soufflé de espinafres** spinach soufflé; **soufflé gelado** cream soufflé; **soufflé de peixe** fish soufflé; **soufflé de queijo** cheese soufflé
soutien m bra
sozinho(a) alone
squash m squash (sport)
Sta see **Santa**
stand m stand; **stand de vendas** car showroom
steak m steak; **steak com cogumelos** steak with mushrooms; **steak com molho de natas** steak in cream sauce
Sto see **Santo**
sua see **seu**
suave mild
subida f rise; ascent
subir to go up; **subir para o autocarro** to get on to the bus
súbito: de súbito suddenly
substância f substance
subterrâneo(a) underground
subúrbio m suburb
suceder to happen; to occur
sucesso m success
sudeste m south-east
sudoeste m south-west
suficiente enough; **pão suficiente** enough bread
sujar to dirty; to stain
sujo(a) dirty
sul m south
sumo m juice; **sumo de frutas** fruit juice; **sumo de laranja** orange juice; **sumo de lima** lime juice; **sumo de limão** lemon juice; **sumo de maçã** apple juice; **sumo de toranja** grapefruit juice; **sumo de tomate** tomato juice

suor m sweat
superfície f area; surface
supermercado m supermarket
superstição f superstition
supersticioso(a) superstitious
suplemento m supplement; **suplemento quarto individual** extra charge for single room
suplente m substitute
supor to suppose
suportar to bear; to tolerate
suporte m support; stand
supositório m suppository
surdo(a) deaf
surf m surfing
surfista m/f surfer
surgir to appear
surpreender to surprise
surpreendido(a) surprised
surpresa f surprise
suspeito(a) suspicious
suspender to stop; to hang
suspensão f suspension
suspensórios mpl braces
sustentar to support
susto m fright

T

ta = te + a; dou-ta ! give you it
tabacaria f tobacconist's; newsagent
tabaco m tobacco
tabela f list; table
taberna f wine bar
tablete de chocolate m bar of chocolate
tábua de engomar f ironing board
tabuleiro m tray
tabuleta f sign

taça *f* cup
tacão *m* heel
tacho *m* cooking pot
taco de golfe *m* golf club (*stick*)
tal such
tala *f* splint
talão *m* voucher
talco *m* talc
talheres *mpl* cutlery
talho *m* butcher's
talvez perhaps
tamanho *m* size
também also; too
tambor *m* drum
tamboril *m* frogfish
tampa *f* lid; cover; top; cap
tampão *m* tampon
tampões *mpl* tampons
tangerina *f* tangerine
tango *m* tango
tanque *m* tank; pool
tanto(a) so much
tão so; **tão bonito(a)** so pretty
tapeçaria *f* carpet weaving
tapete *m* carpet; rug; **tapete rolante** baggage reclaim; **tapetes e carpetes** rugs and carpets; **tapetes de Arraiolos** traditional rugs
tarde¹ *f* afternoon
tarde² late (*in the day*); **mais tarde** later
tarifa *f* charge; **tarifas na portagem** toll charges
tarte *f* tart; **tarte de amêndoa** almond tart; **tarte de cogumelos** mushroom quiche; **tarte de limão** lemon tart; **tarte de maçã** apple tart
tasca *f* tavern; wine bar
taxa *f* fee; **taxa de juro** interest rate; **taxa normal** peak-time rate; **taxa reduzida** off-peak rate; **taxa das**

comunicações telefónicas dialling rates
tax-free duty free
táxi *m* taxi; **a praça de táxis** taxi rank
te you
teatro *m* theatre; **teatro nacional** national theatre
tecelagem *f* weaving
tecer to weave
tecido *m* fabric; tissue; cloth; **tecido feito de pelo de cabra angorá** mohair; **tecido de xadrez** tartan
técnica *f* technique
técnico *m* technician
técnico(a) technical
tecnologia *f* technology
tecto *m* ceiling; **tecto duplo** fly sheet
teimoso(a) stubborn
tejadilho *m* roof-rack
telecomandado(a) remote-controlled
telecomando: com telecomando remote-controlled
teleférico *m* cablecar
telefonar to telephone
telefone *m* telephone; **telefone automático** self-dial phone; **telefone móvel** mobile telephone
telefonema *m* phone call
telefonia *f* radio
telefonista *f* operator
telegrafar to telegraph
telegrama *m* telegram
telejornal *m* newscast; bulletin
telenovela *f* soap opera; serial
telespectador(a) *m/f* viewer
televisão *f* television; **televisão o cores** colour television; **televisão portátil** portable television; **televisão a preto e branco** black

and white television
televisor *m* television set
telex *m* telex
telha *f* roof tile
telhado *m* roof
temperar to season
temperatura *f* temperature
tempero *m* dressing (*for salad*); spice; **tempero para a salada** salad dressing
tempestade *f* storm
templo *m* temple
tempo *m* weather; time (*duration*)
temporada *f* season
temporal *m* storm
temporário(a) temporary
tencionar to intend
tenda *f* tent; **o mastro da tenda** tent pole
ténis *m* tennis; **os ténis** gym shoes; **a bola de ténis** tennis ball; **o campo de ténis** tennis court; **a raqueta de ténis** tennis racket; **ténis de mesa** table tennis
tenista *m/f* tennis player
tenro(a) tender (*meat*)
tensão *f* tension; **tensão arterial alta/baixa** high/low blood pressure
tenso(a) tense
tentar to try
tentativa *f* attempt; effort
tépido(a) tepid; lukewarm
ter to have; **eu tenho** I have; **você tem** you have; **você teve** you had; **ele tem** he has; **tenho que** I must; **você tem que** you must; **não tenho dinheiro para ...** I can't afford ...; **ter êxito** to be successful; **ter febre** to have a

temperature; **tenho frio** I'm cold; **tenho medo** I'm afraid; **tenho náuseas** I feel sick; **tenho sede** I'm thirsty; **ter vontade de vomitar** to feel sick

terça-feira f Tuesday

terceiro(a) third; **terceiro andar** third floor; **para a terceira idade** for the elderly

terço m third

termas fpl spa

termo m (vacuum) flask

termómetro m thermometer

terno(a) tender(-hearted)

terra f earth; land; ground

terraço m veranda; balcony

terramoto m earthquake

terreno m ground; land

território m territory

terrível terrible

terylene m terylene

tesoura f scissors

tesouro m treasure

testa f forehead

testemunha f witness

tetina f teat

teu (tua) your; **o teu** yours

têxteis mpl textiles

ti you; **para ti** for you

tia f aunt

tigela f bowl

tigelada f cream cake

tigre m tiger

tijolo m brick

tímido(a) shy

tingir to dye

tinta f ink; paint

tinturaria f dry-cleaner and dyer's

tio m uncle

típico(a) typical

tipo m sort; kind

tira-nódoas m stain remover

tirar to remove; to take out (tooth)

tiro m shot; **tiro aos pratos e pombos** clay pigeon shooting

tive: eu tive I had

to = te + o; dou-to I give you it

toalha f towel; **toalha de mesa** tablecloth

toalhete m: **toalhetes refrescantes** baby wipes; **toalhete de rosto** face cloth; flannel (for washing)

tocar to touch; to play

todo(a) all; **todo o dia ou meio dia** all day or half a day; **toda a gente** everyone; **todo o leite** all the milk; **todo o vinagre** all the vinegar; **todas as coisas** everything; **todos os dias** every day; daily; **todas as raparigas** all (the) girls; **todos os rapazes** all (the) boys; **em toda a parte** everywhere; **para todos** for all ages

tom m shade (colour)

tomada f socket; power point; **tomada para a máquina de barbear** shaving point

tomar to take; **tomar banho** to bathe; to take a bath; **tomar banhos de sol** to sunbathe; **tomar consciência de** to realize; **tomar antes de se deitar** to be taken before going to bed; **tomar em jejum** take on an empty stomach; **tomar a seguir às refeições** to be taken after meals; **tomar ... vezes ao dia** to be taken ... times a day

tomate m tomato; **tomate pelado** peeled tomatoes; **tomates recheados** stuffed tomatoes

tombar to fall

tomilho m thyme

tonelada f ton

tonto(a) dizzy

tontura f dizziness

topo m top; summit

toque please ring

toranja f grapefruit

torcer to twist; to turn

tornar to turn; **tornar a si** to come round (after faint); **tornar-se sócio de** to join (club etc)

torneio m tournament; **torneio de golf** golf tournament

torneira f tap

tornozelo m ankle

torrada f toast

torradeira f toaster

torrão de açúcar m lump of sugar

torre f tower

torresmos mpl small rashers of bacon

torta f tart (cake); **torta de camarão** shrimps in egg fritter roll; **torta de laranja** orange roll

tortilha f Spanish omelette

torto(a) twisted

tosse f cough; **tosse convulsa** whooping cough; **o xarope para a tosse** cough medicine

tossir to cough

tosta f: **tosta mista** toasted ham and cheese sandwich; **tosta de queijo** toasted cheese sandwich; **tostas** French toast

tostões mpl: **25 tostões = 2.5 escudos**

total total

totalmente totally

totobola m football pools

totoloto m lottery
toucinho m bacon;
  toucinho do céu almond and egg roll
tourada f bullfight
toureiro m bullfighter
touro m bull
tours de autocarro mpl coach tours
tóxico(a) poisonous (*substance*); toxic
trabalhador(a) m/f worker
trabalhar to work (*person*)
trabalho m work;
  trabalhos na estrada roadworks
traça f moth
traçar to draw
tractor m tractor
tradição f tradition
tradicional traditional
tradução f translation
tradutor(a) m/f translator
traduzir to translate
tráfego m traffic
traje regional m regional dress
trajecto m journey; course
tranquilo(a) calm; quiet
transferência f transfer
transferir to transfer
transfusão f transfusion
transgressão f traffic offence
transistor m transistor radio
trânsito m traffic; **o polícia de trânsito** traffic warden; **trânsito condicionado** restricted traffic; **trânsito congestionado** heavy traffic; **trânsito fechado** road blocked; **trânsito proibido** no entry; **trânsito nos dois sentidos** two-way traffic

transparente transparent
transpiração f perspiration; sweat
transpirar to sweat
transportar to carry
transporte m transport
transtorno m upset; inconvenience
trapo m rag
trás: para trás backwards; **no banco de trás** in the back (*of car*); **a parte de trás** back
traseiro m bottom (*of person*)
tratamento m treatment
tratar to treat (*behave towards*)
travar to brake
travessa f lane (*in town*)
travessão m slide (*for hair*)
travesseiro m pillowcase
travessia f crossing (*voyage*)
travões mpl brakes
trazer to bring
treinador m coach (*instructor*)
treinar to train
treino m training
trela f lead (*dog's*)
trem de cozinha m set of kitchen equipment
tremer to shiver
trepar to climb
três three
trespassa-se business for sale
treze thirteen
trezentos(as) three hundred
triângulo m warning triangle
tribunal m court
tricotar to knit
trigo m wheat
trinta thirty
tripas fpl tripe; **tripas à moda do Porto** tripe Oporto style

tripé m tripod
triplo m triple
tripulação f crew
triste sad
triunfo m triumph; victory
troca f exchange; swap
trocar to exchange; to change
troco m change (*money*)
tronco m trunk
tropa f army; **estar na tropa** to be in the army
trovão m thunder
trovejar to thunder
trovoada f thunderstorm
trufas fpl truffles; **trufas de chocolate** chocolate truffles
truque m trick
truta f trout; **truta assada no forno** baked trout; **truta cozida** boiled trout; **truta frita** fried trout
T-shirt m t-shirt
tu you
tua see **teu**
tubo m exhaust pipe; tube; hose (*in car*)
tudo everything; **tudo para bebés** babywear
tulipa f tulip
túnel m tunnel
turismo m tourism; tourist information office; **turismos ligeiros** light vehicles this way
turista m/f tourist

U

úlcera f ulcer
ultimamente lately; recently
último(a) last
ultrapassagem f overtaking; **proibida a ultrapassagem** no

overtaking
ultrapassar to overtake;
to pass
um(a) a; an; one
unha f nail (on finger, toe)
união f union; junction
unicamente only;
unicamente para
adultos for adults only
único(a) single (not
double)
unidade f unit (hi-fi etc)
unido(a) united
uniforme m uniform
unir to join
universidade f university;
college
universo m universe
urbanização f estate
(housing)
urbano(a) urban
urgência f urgency;
urgências emergencies;
emergency hospital
urgente: é urgente it is
urgent
urgentemente urgently
urina f urine
urinol m public lavatory
(for men)
ursinho m teddy bear
urtiga f nettle
usado(a) used (car etc)
usar to use; **use sempre**
o cinto always wear a
seat belt
uso m use; **uso externo**
for external use
utensílio m tool
utentes mpl: **utentes**
com bilhete ticket
holders this way
útil useful
utilidade f usefulness;
utility
utilização f use
utilizar to use
uva f grape; **uvas brancas**
green grapes; **uvas**
moscatel muscatel
grapes; **uvas pretas** black

grapes

V

vaca f cow
vacina f vaccination
vagão m railway carriage;
coach
vagão-restaurante m
buffet car
vagar[1] m spare time
vagar[2] to be vacant; **a**
casa vaga em
Dezembro the house
will be vacant in
December
vagaroso(a) slow
vago(a) vague
vale[1] m valley
vale[2] m: **vale postal**
postal order
valente brave
valer to be worth
validação f: **validação de**
bilhetes punch your
ticket here
validade f validity
válido(a) valid; **válido**
até valid until
valioso(a) valuable
valor m value
valorizar to value
válvula f valve
vantagem f profit;
benefit
vantajoso(a)
advantageous
vapor m steam
varanda f veranda;
balcony; **varandas com**
vista para o mar e a
montanha balconies
overlooking the sea and
mountains
variado(a) varied
varicela f chickenpox
variedade f variety
vários(as) several
varrer to sweep

vaso m vase; **vasos e**
faianças tradicionais
traditional pottery
vassoura f broom
vasto(a) vast
vazar to empty
vazio(a) empty
veado m deer; **veado**
assado roast venison
vedar to stop up (hole,
leak etc); **vedado ao**
trânsito no thoroughfare
vedeta de cinema f star
(of cinema etc)
vegetação f vegetation
vegetal m vegetable;
vegetais congelados
frozen vegetables
vegetariano(a)
vegetarian
veia f vein
veículo m vehicle;
veículos longos long
vehicles; **veículos**
pesados heavy goods
vehicles
vela[1] f sail; sailing; **vela**
de bujarrona jib
vela[2] f spark plug; candle
velhice f old age
velho(a) old
velocidade f gear; speed;
a alavanca das
velocidades gear lever; **a**
caixa de velocidades
gearbox; **o limite de**
velocidade speed limit;
velocidade limitada
speed limit in force;
velocidade máxima ...
km/h maximum speed ...
km/h
velocímetro m
speedometer
veloz fast
veludo m velvet
vencedor(a) m/f winner
vencer to win
vencimento m wage
venda f sale (in general);
venda de cadernetas

prepaid tickets sold here; **venda por grosso e a retalho** wholesalers and retailers; **venda de passagens aéreas** plane ticket sales; **venda proibida** not for public sale; **vendas e reparações** sales and repairs; **venda através do correio** mail order; **venda através do telefone** telephone selling

vendedeira *f* seller; **vendedeira de flores** flower seller

vendedor *m* seller; **vendedor de jornais** newsagent

vender to sell; **vende-se** for sale

veneno *m* poison

venenoso(a) poisonous (*snake*)

ventilação *f* ventilation

ventilador *m* ventilator

vento *m* wind; **vento fraco ou moderado** winds light to moderate

ventoinha *f* fan (*electric*)

ventoso(a) windy

ver to see; to watch (*TV*)

verão *m* summer

verdade *f* truth; **na verdade** really; **é verdade** that's right; **não é verdade** it is not true; **não é verdade?** isn't it?

verdadeiro(a) true

verde green

vergas *fpl* wicker goods

verificar to check

vermelho(a) red; **vermelho vivo** ruby

vermute *m* vermouth

verniz *m* varnish; **verniz das unhas** nailpolish

verso *m* back (*of cheque, of page*)

verter to pour; to leak

vertical vertical

vertigem *f* dizziness

vespa *f* wasp

véspera *f* the day before; the eve

vestiário *m* cloakroom; changing room

vestíbulo *m* entrance hall

vestido *m* dress; **vestido de saia e casaco** suit (*woman's*)

vestígio *m* sign

vestir to dress; to wear

vestuário *m* clothes; **vestuário impermeável** waterproof clothing

veterinário(a) vet

véu *m* veil

vez *f* time; **às vezes** occasionally; sometimes; **uma vez** once; **duas vezes** twice; **cada vez mais** more and more; **outra vez** again; **em vez de** instead of; **em vez disso** instead; **de vez em quando** from time to time; **é a tua vez** it is your turn; **muitas vezes** often

via¹ *f* lane; **via rápida** dual carriageway

via²: **via aérea** by air mail; **via intravenosa** intravenously; **via Londres** via London; **via nasal** to be inhaled; **via oral** orally

viaduto *m* viaduct

viagem *f* trip; journey; **viagem de autocarro** coach trip; **viagem de barco** boat trip; **viagem organizada** package tour

viajante *m/f* traveller

viajar to travel

viatura *f* vehicle

vida *f* life

video *m* video (*machine*)

video-cassette *m* video cassette

videodisco *m* video disc

vidraria *f* glazier's

vidro *m*: **a fibra de vidro** fibreglass

vidros *mpl* glassware; **vidros e escapes** windscreens and exhausts; **vidros pára-brisas** replacement windscreens

vigarista *m/f* confidence trickster; swindler

vigia *f* porthole

vigiar to watch

vigilante *m* watchman

vila *f* town; **vila de pescadores** fishing village

vinagre *m* vinegar

vindima *f* harvest (*of grapes*); **o ano da vindima** vintage

vindimar to gather grapes

vinha *f* vineyard

vinho *m* wine; **vinho de aperitivo** aperitif; **vinho branco** white wine; **vinho da casa** house wine; **vinho clarete** light red wine; **vinho comum** ordinary wine; **vinho doce** sweet wine; **vinho espumante** sparkling wine; **vinho espumoso** sparkling wine; **vinho de Madeira** Madeira wine; **vinho de mesa** table wine; **vinho moscatel** muscatel wine; **vinho do Porto** port wine; **vinho da região** local wine; **vinho rosé** rosé wine; **vinho seco** dry wine; **vinho tinto** red wine; **vinho verde** semi-sparkling acid wine; **vinho de Xerez** sherry; **a lista de vinhos** wine list

vinte twenty; **vinte e quatro horas serviço de**

quartos 24 hour room service
viola f guitar
violino m violin
vir to come
virar to turn; **vire à direita** turn right; **vire à esquerda** turn left
vírus m virus
visita f visit; **visita a lugares de interesse** sightseeing
visitante m/f visitor
visitar to visit
vista f view
visto m visa
visto que since (*because*)
vistoso(a) gorgeous; attractive
vitamina f vitamin
vitela f veal; **vitela assada** stewed veal; **vitela com cogumelos** veal in mushroom sauce; **vitela estufada** roast veal
viúva f widow
viúvo m widower
vivenda f chalet; villa (*by the sea*)
viver to live; **ele vive em Londres** he lives in London

vivo(a) alive
vizinho(a) m/f neighbour
voar to fly
você you
vocês you (*plural*)
vodka m vodka
volante m steering wheel
voleibol m volleyball
volta f turn; **à volta de** about; **à volta da casa** round the house; **em volta de** around
voltagem f voltage
voltar to return (*go back*); to come back; **volto já** I will be back in a minute
vomitar to vomit
vontade f will; **à vontade** at ease
voo m flight; **voo fretado** charter flight; **voo normal** scheduled flight
vós you
vos you; to you
vosso(a) your
votar to vote
voto m vote
voz f voice
vulcão m volcano; **vulcão extinto** extinct volcano
vulgar ordinary; common

W

W.C. privativo m private toilet
whisky m whisky; **um whisky duplo** a double whisky; **whisky de malte** malt whisky
wind-surf m windsurfing

X Z

xadrez m chess
xiale m shawl
xarope m syrup; **xarope de groselha** blackcurrant syrup; **xarope de morango** strawberry liqueur
xerez m sherry
zangado(a) angry
zangar-se to get angry
zero zero
zombar de to laugh at
zona f zone; **zona azul** permitted parking zone; **zona de banhos** swimming area; **zona interdita** no thoroughfare
zoologia f zoology